PLATFORM 6

Platform 6 is structured around studio-based learning, as experienced through the sequence of core and option studios at the Harvard University Graduate School of Design. This environment supports a unique model of scholarship that encourages hands-on learning, strategic thinking, and incisive exchanges with faculty. The studio ritual signifies a deep faith in interpersonal engagement and constantly revised connections between research, knowledge, and disciplinary affiliation. The assessment given at the desk represents the most fundamental criticisms of the project or the proposal. This volume seeks to capture the vitality of this exchange, as sequences of student response—drawing, model, video, rendering, sketch, map, animation, photograph, installation—follow the initial brief.

Rosetta S. Elkin
Editor

Within the covers of this volume, as in the life of the School, key influences are threaded into the experience of studio—whether reinforcing or conflicting. These stimuli come in many forms: seminars and lectures, exhibitions, conferences, publications, symposia. Each circumstance reveals itself as a fluid theme that pulses and radiates against the studio format.

Harvard University
Graduate School of Design

Global Connections

The Harvard Graduate School of Design prides itself on the wide scope of its global aspirations, collaborations, and projects. Every semester a large portion of our programs engage in work that explores the interrelationship between themes and geographies. As a School, we are deeply interested in the conditions giving rise to new topics that benefit from the design imagination of our students and faculty across a range of fields and practices. This approach is not so much new as it is intentional, forming a deliberate cornerstone of our mission and pedagogy. We wish for our projects to be transformative in multiple locations and in richly varied geographies, societies, economies, cultures, and political circumstances.

In this context it is worth remembering that the founding of the GSD was inextricably linked to the internationalization of modern architecture. Walter Gropius, the first chair of the department of architecture (1937) within the newly established GSD, had years earlier referred to the concept of "Internationale Architektur," even before Henry-Russell Hitchcock and Philip Johnson's use of the term "International Style." Although the aims of this movement were fundamentally tied to specific conditions in Europe, its tenets were presented as a universal response to the necessities of building. And yet, the very attempt to see architecture as an endeavor that transcends locality ironically resulted in the unintended embrace of a diversity of people and cultures, though there remains an undeniable hegemonic dimension within the ethos of this architecture.

Such contradictions aside, from its early days the School attracted large numbers of faculty and students from various parts of the world, a manifestation of its influence and outreach. The appointment of Gropius, the first director of the Bauhaus, was followed by that of Spanish architect Josep Lluís Sert as Dean. The celebrated Japanese architect Fumihiko Maki, a student during Sert's tenure, later became one of the key members of the Metabolist movement that promoted a deviation from the universality of the International Style, marking a shift from architecture as a style to architecture as a condition.

We are cognizant of the value of the histories, traditions, and conventions of the disparate design disciplines and see our task today as one involving the continued advancement of landscape architecture, urban planning, and urban design, in addition to architecture. In light of interrelated and ever-changing global sites and situations, we need the expertise embedded in each of these disciplines as well as their interconnections to be able to respond in radical new ways to the host of challenges that face our planet today. The projects presented in this book all play their part in taking up this planetary imperative.

Mohsen Mostafavi
Dean of the Harvard Graduate School of Design and Alexander and Victoria Wiley Professor of Design

UT
UTOP
UTOPIO
UTOPIOIDS

What is the intellectual potential latent in extraordinarily large urban typologies, currently restricted by the typological tradition of urbanism and by the segregation of disciplinary domains? What is the reach of this potential to enable us to think aggressively about the contemporary metropolitan condition and to imagine future developmental models? Following on our three previous studios—Neonatures (2010), Overurbanism (2011), and Neokoolhisms (2012)— Utopioids / The Generic Sublime IV undertakes the project of radical integration in the ultimate post-urban megalomania: a complex building that organizes the territory via its assimilation in a synthetic field of competition and synergy.

Ciro Najle

Utopioids investigates how canonical utopian models from the twentieth century—from futurism to metabolism, from megastructures to megaforms, from the speculations of Soleri to the postulates of Team X, from the territorial imagery of Le Corbusier to that of Superstudio—can be reappointed and redescribed today to index the expansive logics of large-scale development now taking place around the globe, transcending the moral limitations of their own "authentic" idealistic mindsets toward the blatant generation of banal yet severe territorial-scale anti-urban models.

In the early 1970s, Henri Lefebvre anticipated a situation of "generalized urbanization" in which an "urban fabric" would be extended to encompass the entire planet. More recently, geographer Edward Soja declared that "every square inch of the world is urbanized to some degree." While the changing morphology and scale of urbanized regions has attracted considerable attention among urban scholars, the worldwide "urban fabric" postulated by Lefebvre and Soja remains under researched and poorly understood. The Urban Theory Research Lab Seminar (Neil Brenner) tests the Lefebvre-Soja hypothesis of complete urbanization with reference to "extreme territories" that are normally not considered to contain urban elements.

continued on page 13 >>

In re-elaborating Yona Friedman's utopian vision of the Ville Spatiale, this project designs a city to allow mankind to achieve the highest degree of personal freedom and self-expression. Through the emancipation from manual labor, human beings are finally freed from a geographically determined workplace. A liberated humanity is now free to move across the globe. Mass tourism acquires the proportions of a global migration from the inhospitable latitudes of industrial production to the warm cradle of the tropics; but instead of a job, future migrants will be seeking relaxation and recreation. The future city will transition seamlessly between artificial environment, in the form of an infrastructural grid that contains the elements to provide material comfort, and tropical natural landscape, thus creating a new third environment: *La Ville Tropicale*.

Alessandro Boccacci

Tectonic Visions Between Land & Sea
Works of Kiyonori Kikutake

excerpt from *Kenzō Tange: Architecture for the World*

Rereading Urban Space in Japan at the Crossroads of World Design

By Ken Tadashi Oshima

I would like to consider several orders according to which [the] super-human scale can be led into the human scale. I thought that it would be necessary to think in terms of a kind of space organization which would give a well-ordered order of space from the super-human scale which is expanded more and more by the new technology from the scale of nature itself, to what I call in my own words the mass human scale, and finally down to the level of the individual human scale where the individual life takes place.[1]
—Kenzō Tange

Kenzō Tange's discussion of dispersed "architectural elements (as) the basic structure of the city" beyond the megastructural "vertebrae" became the linear spine for the 1960 Tokyo Plan extending into Tokyo Bay, designed to address the burgeoning population problem.[2] As the Yale planner Christopher Tunnard noted at the World Design Conference, "American redevelopment architects could learn a great deal from some of the Asian and European postwar reconstruction schemes in which architects have tried hard and often successfully to fit their designs into the fabric and character of the older city."[3]

In addressing the specificities of Japan, the book *Nihon no toshi kūkan* (Urban Space in Japan) elucidated "principles of space order" rather than physical elements or emphasis on figure-ground urban plans. Drawing a contrast to historic cities in Europe, the book identifies fluid paradigms of spatial order in Japan as defined by "orientation," "hierarchical accessibility," "placement due to circumstances," and the "esthetic triangle."[4] This array highlighted dynamic principles based on asymmetry and development over time. Their qualities and characteristics are understood as formal-informal, process designing, imaginary space, and activity space.

The Tange research group's vision of the multiplicative and free-floating nature of urban signifying systems, depicting the kaleidoscopic reality of contemporary urban Japan, remains powerful today. These many readings of urban space in Japan came about within an international context through direct comparison and translation, both verbally and visually, highlighting the complexity of ways we see, perceive, and experience cities. In the twenty-first century, *Nihon no toshi kūkan* is not only situated in Japan but one can see Fumihiko Maki's vision of architecture and the city being realized within the World Trade Center development. Within an increasingly global-local world context, these connections and contradictions of a multidimensional "imageability" continue to map out trajectories of urbanism today.

---

1 World Design Conference Organization Editorial Committee/Kokusai Bunka Kaikan, *World Design Conference/Sekai Dezain Kaigi gijiroku* (Tokyo: Bijutsu shuppansha, 1961), 182.
2 Ibid., 222.
3 Ibid., 116.
4 Toshi dezain kenkyūtai, *Nihon no toshi kūkan*, 29.

Ken Tadashi Oshima is Associate Professor of Architecture at the University of Washington, Seattle.

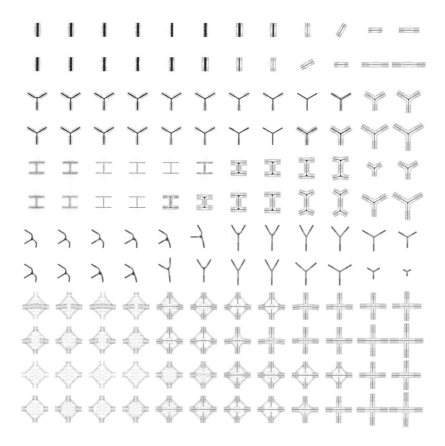

Through updating Le Corbusier's Obus Plan with the parameters of present-day highway design and suburban development, larger zones of excess are generated. This project occurs within these cloverleaf interchanges. Where sprawling infrastructure networks have historically produced vast territories of non-intersection, the project concentrates suburban development within introverted enclaves of retail and rest stops.

<< Max Wong

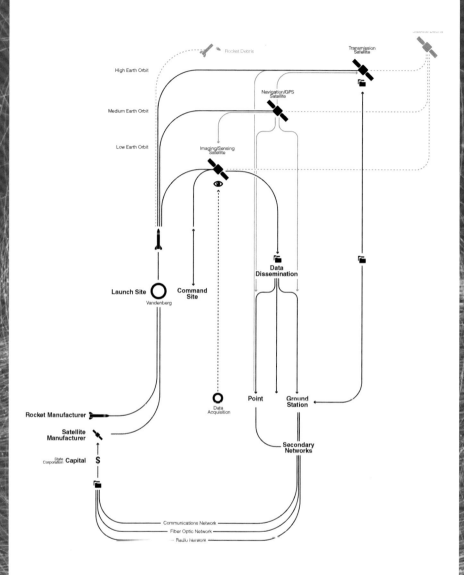

There is a direct transfer of fixed capital from Earth to orbit through satellite production and launches, illustrating the process of capital accumulation through the extended urbanization of Earth orbit. Satellites serve as a form of fixed capital, producing geospatial data—circulating capital that results from the transfer of the instrument's use—and value to the commodity. As more satellites are launched, the amount of space debris in the atmosphere increases, potentially causing satellite collisions, a reflexive cycle that could ultimately lead to the system's demise.

Robert Daurio & Melany Sun-Min Park

continued on page 351 >>

THE HIGH COAST
TOWARD AN ALTITUDINAL ECONOMY OF SNOW

Alexander Arroyo, MLA I

Advisor
Pierre Bélanger

As fragile interface between the geologic and meteorologic, the mountain is the avant-garde altitudinal threshold shaping downslope urban systems. Against fixation on deltas, coastlines, and other lowland landscapes as sites  of agglomeration, this thesis asserts the mountain to offer a distinct and decentralized view of urban systems, staged from the peaks. From this vantage point, montane and alpine zones mark a different kind of shore, mercurial and manifold, delimiting an often unrecognized altitudinal, latitudinal, and ultimately thermodynamic threshold between the cryosphere––places of frozen water—and other climatic geographies. This "high coast" demarcates a massive, diffuse, yet largely unseen reservoir, a freshwater ocean floating 1,000 meters above sea level: the snowpack. That up to 80 percent of the western United States depends on the snowpack of the Rockies, Sierra Nevadas, and other ranges has, more than any other force, shaped the geo-technical systems of regional urbanization, from Colorado to California. >>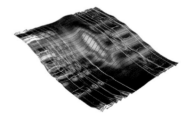

The infrastructural components of such systems express the vernacular geographies of ecology and economy unique to each altitudinal and orographic range. Distinguished from the charismatic megaforma typical of engineered 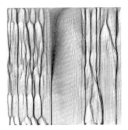 lowland waterways and coastal armoring, these components are most often dispersed, fragmented, and banal: snow-plows, bridges, and sheds, road cutting and slope grading, switchbacking and salting, patch-cut forests and living snow fences, avalanche protection "dams" and high-altitude reservoirs, ski lifts and snow-mobiles, and snow-making, -melting, -sensing, and -shaping machines operating on, under, and above ground.

Through the cacophonous coupling of such components, the seasonal management of snow emerges as an underthought agent in the general economy of urbanization. The resultant management regimes are inherently heterogeneous and often internally contradictory, mediated through diverse "cryotechnical" infrastructures across altitudinal and jurisdictional borders. Operating through overlaid organizational frameworks and spatial scales, snow proves not simply a hydrologic, ecologic, and climatic medium, but a political

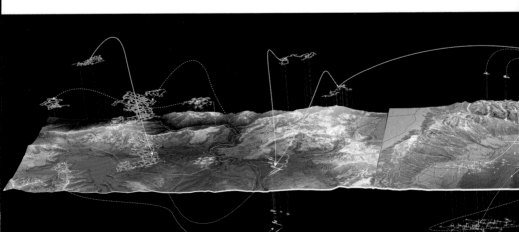

one as well. This thesis aims, therefore, to explore the political cryology of snow across multiple scales, from the crystallographic (ice particles) to the topographic (slope), and from the orographic (massif) to the mesographic (climatic system). Using these four scales this investigation develops a spatial, technical, and conceptual vocabulary for the agency of snow in "remote" urban processes beyond the city, strategically inflecting its thermodynamic states to work as seasonal reservoir, bioclimatic modulator, ephemeral landform, and geopolitical catalyst.

Rather than select a single site of experimentation, the diverse phase states of snow are used to propose a cryotechnical index of performative profiles, long-term potentials, and spatial techniques for organizing highly politicized, high-altitude land use, management, and occupational systems. Ranging in scale and scope from fungal snow-seeding to avalanche herding, and from switchback-based residential subdivisions to evapotranspiration feedback loops between forestry and grazing patterns, this index proposes a "cryologic turn" for landscape architectural thought, using snow to reimagine the logics and scales of territory as inextricably embedded in a thermodynamic landscape.

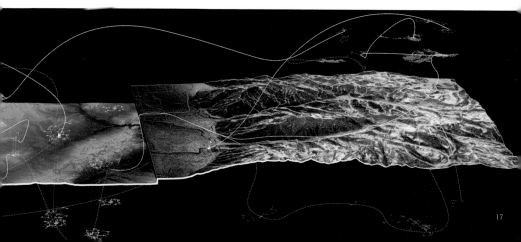

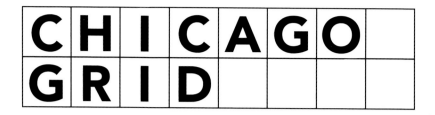

CHICAGO GRID

Chicago can be seen as a paradigm city for its rapid growth and transformation, its economic importance, and its innovative contributions to the techniques of urban design and planning. Many cities have studied its seminal episodes as a source of inspiration and reference. The potential of its strategic geographical position, with its system of lakes and the canal, allowed it to build a strong port and growth based partly on the urban grid and partly on the territorial grid designed by Thomas Jefferson. This provided an efficient, versatile base for formation and transformation for different uses, creating a very dense central space with the use of infrastructures on exciting multilevels.

Joan Busquets

Chicago Grid: In Search for New Paradigms aims to present an experimental approach to the reality of Chicago, taking as a hypothesis the value of city design at the intermediate scale. This is one way of responding to the needs of the emerging urbanistic culture, where judicious use of energy and the correct formulation of the urban metabolism guarantee a more sustainable, harmonious city. In this respect, strategies of reclassification and densification will be models to experiment with. Chicago offers a compelling case study capable of suggesting new paradigms of city design.

Maps do not represent reality—they create it. As a fundamental part of the design process, the act of mapping results in highly authored views of a site. By choosing what features, forces, and flows to highlight—and implicitly, which to exclude—the designer first creates the reality into which their intervention will be situated and discussed. Furthermore, the usage and materiality of space is increasingly measured, categorized, and circulated by all manners of institutions; these competing data representations often become the primary way of understanding and responding to a site. It is not enough to represent complicated networks of site forces and interactions as a neutral backdrop to one's design; we are tasked with actively shaping them. It is within the framework of a highly authored design process that Mapping: Geographic Representation and Speculation (Robert Pietrusko) presents the fundamentals of geographic analysis and visualization.

continued on page 23 >>

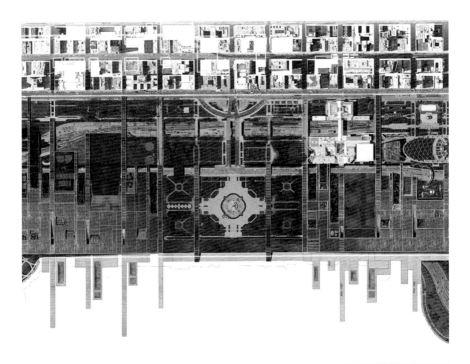

By addressing an extensive fragmented park area, this project re-introduces the grid as a system defined by lines and borders, aiming at activating a continuous flow throughout a unified space.

Santiago Orbea & Aphrodite Stathopoulos

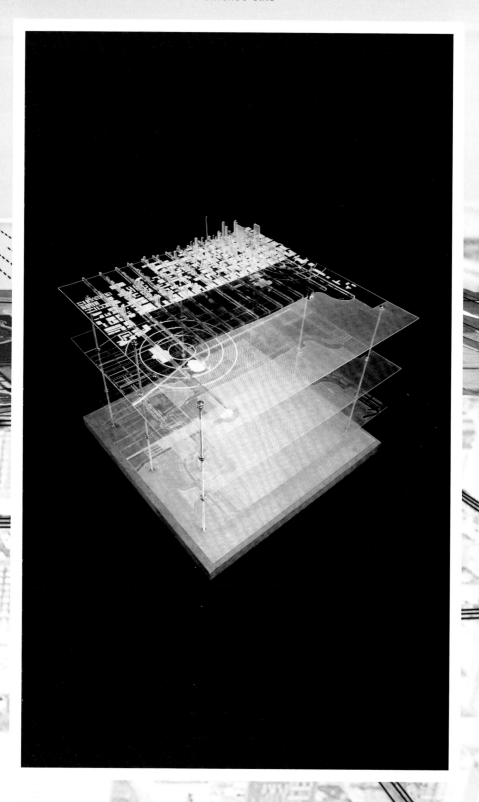

"It is abundantly clear that the street, the road, the highway—while often treated as a kind of object form or 'thing'—is almost always an act of form, controlling a stream of spatial consequences."

- Keller Easterling

Cambridge Talks VII: Architecture and the Street

March 29, 2013

continued on page 67 >>

Through studying the notated movements of GSD students, it became evident that a high concentration of their lives, even of professed "ideal" days, was directly related to Gund Hall as a space. To portray this complexity, we designed models intended to be devices of condensed representation, objects that would allow an exploration of many types of representation simultaneously.

Juan Cristaldo & Karl Landsteiner

<< Miguel Lopez Melendez

AIR OPS
A RETROACTIVE PLATFORM
FOR ENERGY EXCHANGE

James Leng, MArch I

Advisor
Eric Höweler

Re-envisioning zoning and energy use in a post-Hurricane Sandy Manhattan, the project hinges on the notion that zoning has always been one of the most potent elements in shaping the city. For architecture to tackle the problem of energy at the urban scale—especially as a response to the increasing volatility of climate—it must bring topics of sourcing and using energy into active dialogue with zoning, real estate, and the public realm.

As a point of departure, the project delves into a careful investigation of New York City zoning codes. Ultimately, a reimagination and an unconventional implementation of air-rights zoning regulations enable the creation of a new urban typology. This new paradigm volumetrically inverts the convention of the set back: the top surface is maximized for sustainable energy collection, and the setback is then cut from the underside of the volume to ensure access to light and air for buildings below.

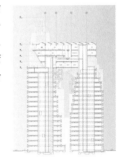

THERMO ΔYNAMIC MAΔRIΔ

Thermodynamic Madrid: A New Good Life explores new methods, tools, scales, and materials to address the renovation of historic centers outside of both the radical preservationism of protectionist theories and the destructive practices and social expulsion of *sventramento*. The studio aims to test parametric techniques applied simultaneously to urban space and building space (essentially analyzing radiation torque/ventilation), and to identify improvement strategies applied to both the public and the private realms without modifying either the existing density or the configuration of public spaces (and maintaining an untouched historic patrimony). In practice, the studio identifies critical "stripes" in downtown areas both public and private and evaluates thermodynamic imbalances in indoor and outdoor spaces by applying strategies based on changes in size in the residential fabric through subtractions and additions as well as material and constructive strategies (referring to both natural and artificial systems). The goal is to make a positive impact simultaneously on the thermodynamic balance of both domains without affecting the amount of final built mass.

Iñaki Ábalos
Matthias Schuler

What is atmosphere? Is it air and weather? Or is it the in-between—effect, matter, the immaterial, space, and ephemera? How is atmosphere designed when it seems to start where design stops? Within these questions lay implicit issues of time and material presence, scientific inquiry and description, space, phenomena, and the body. On Atmospheres and Design (Silvia Benedito) examines definitions and investigations of atmosphere in the context of history, philosophy, art, film and photography, science, design, and the cultural imagination. It investigates built works that inform conditions of atmosphere. Our experiences are shaped in spaces that are not only of a visible and measurable reality, but also of the immaterial and ephemeral conditions that affect what we see, register, and experience.

continued on next page >>

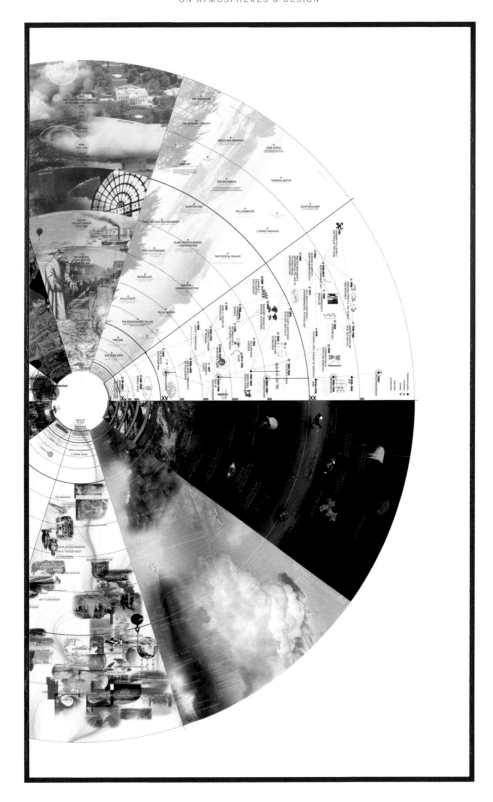

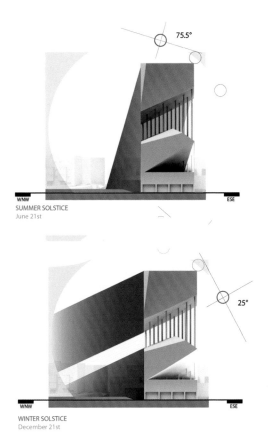

75.5°

WNW   ESE
SUMMER SOLSTICE
June 21st

25°

WNW   ESE
WINTER SOLSTICE
December 21st

Located in the neighborhood of Tetuán, Madrid, the project creates an index and catalog of outdoor comfort for the site. By cross referencing these references and using them as design tools, the needs of the neighborhood are improved through the optimization of outdoor spaces, accounting for different seasons. Aside from outdoor interventions, such as the creation of green space and natural shading, a tower on top of the existing community pool is created to passively address the resource consumption of outdoor mediations.

Felipe Silva & Ziyin Zhou

The Monster of Energy

Q&A with Kiel Moe

Your pedagogy almost begs us to be more precise about defining systems and energy. Why so urgent, and why now?

In the last decades we developed some amazing solutions and answers to what are actually the wrong problems and questions. As Gregory Bateson observed, "[t]here is an ecology of bad ideas, just as there is an ecology of weeds and it is characteristic of the system that basic error propagates itself."[1] Without a more precise vocabulary for energy in design, we will continue to propagate the same basic errors. A necessary component of design pedagogy and research today, then, must be a lexicon of energetics that is at once much more broad and totalizing yet simultaneously more precise and deep. Anything less seems like platitude from a compelling but unreliable narrator.

It seems that a more accurate definition will ultimately generate a noticeable impact on practice, most acutely in the physical building system. This expression stands in stark contrast to other, more common technological advancements. How do you think the next generation of designers will articulate these lofty ambitions?

The laws and implications of thermodynamics have yet to fully enter the discipline of architecture and urbanization. The articulation of these implications will appear in novel ways, but only once designers begin to peer into the inherent thermodynamic depth of buildings and cities. I see this depth as the most sublime and delirious aspect of contemporary design—especially because it remains so untapped, so latent.

In terms of articulation, I do know that many contemporary compositional preoccupations—accumulation, intricacy, and differentiated repetition, for instance—are uncannily astute aims and means for designing the optimal velocity and thermodynamic depth of energy in the formation of a building. I think it will take years, if not decades, for a statement like that to be highly legible in design discourse, but it is one indication of where and how these implications will be articulated and directed in design. In short, design might yet see a profound influx of thermodynamic vitality, but in the most worthy of examples it will only amplify our enthusiasm for the salient task of design: formation. Another aspect of future articulation is more methodological. Today I think there is great efficacy in deeply studying the processes and outcomes of self-organized "design": the pre-academy, multi-millennial paradigms of buildings and cities that, in my view, manifest some of the most ecologically and architecturally powerful modalities of design that humans ever encountered. These precedents do not really point to any particular articulation of thermodynamic depth that might be designed in the future, but they do point to certain habits of mind that are conducive to novel instantiations of future buildings and cities. I see this quick look back as the core of some real forward progress. Such a mode stands in stark contrast with the more common stairmaster of tawdry technological escalation. In these self-organized precedents, I am most struck by buildings without infrastructure.

You make things with your hands—practice is for you is an act of physical exertion. There are few architects now who actually build their buildings and fewer still that would even know how. Please elaborate.

Architects do not build buildings. They design and develop instructions for future construction. I have a deep aversion to the "master-builder" rhetoric that some architects deploy today. It is true that I build almost everything that I design, but only as a necessary means of inquiry. That is the modality of my experimental practice—every construction is an experiment. Each project reflects a very necessary cycle of inquiry: research and writing feeds directly into the composition and specification of the ambitiously modest building. In turn, observation during construction inevitably triggers questions and surprising answers about buildings, pushing my research in a new direction.

Why? I think the dominant modes of construction, especially in North America, routinely reflect flawed pathologies. The determinisms of air-conditioning and insulation, for instance, have deeply distorted the many of the prime obligations and opportunities of buildings in respect of our physiologies and ecologies. Yet they unreflectively determine so much of how and why buildings get built the way that they do. It is very disturbing for me to look back and realize how acquiescent and complicit architects and academics have been in this regard. The absurd separation of energy and construction content in architectural curricula, for instance, severs what is actually a deeply connected thermodynamic continuum. So I have to merge them in practice.

What motivates me about architecture has little to do with the capitulations architects habitually made to various master modernization processes in the twentieth century. So I am compelled to pursue what I see as more sane and powerful alternatives to normative practices. Those alternatives will not emerge in either practice or the academy alone.

Most of what I design and build would not get built in a normal model of practice and building delivery. There is great resistance to any deviation in the building industry from normative construction practices. For instance, my most comfortable buildings paradoxically do not even meet energy code. The resistance to architecturally and ecologically more powerful buildings, while strongly expressed, has little factual grounding. So an experimental practice that questions basic assumptions and pushes alternative paradigms is absolutely necessary today.

Since you work across scales and fields, do you also believe that the idea of multi-disciplinary design is outdated? Shall we trash it along with other overused semantics, such as sustainability and green infrastructure?

In the name of knowledge, disciplines segregate what is not in fact segregated in reality. In the twenty-first century, I do not think knowledge or design can sustain the conceits of this divided knowledge. Experts tend to professionalize these partitions. As Ivan Illich observed, the first task of an expert is to establish need—the second is to mandate and regulate that need.[2]

Whether administratively convenient or epistemologically necessary, disciplines and sub-disciplines tend to chop up the world into the most peculiar of partitions, typically for the purposes of short- and long-term market differentiation. In their own way, multi-/trans-/inter-disciplinary design nonetheless place emphasis on distinct disciplines even as they aim for some productive form of convergence. Worse, the design disciplines today (and their professional counterparts) are largely based on the culture of expertise that emerged in the twentieth century. This disabling culture of expertise—the basis of much collaborative theory—is by now known to be a phantom culture of experts buoyed by hubristically and hilariously isolated forms of knowledge. But no systems, no disciplines, no ecologies, no cities, and no people are laughing.

With that in mind, it must be noted that no one is an expert within the most important horizon of design activity today: the complexity of the large-scale systems that currently lie latent, untapped by the design disciplines. I was trained as an architect, but my ultimate discipline is actually more akin to what Nietzche called "[t]his world: a monster of energy, without beginning or end."[3] I can think about what that means as an architect, through buildings. But I am simultaneously aware that the idea of disciplines, and their institutional realities, tend to strain against cogent observation about the difficult whole of this monster of energy.

I find more traction with fellow non-expert travelers who have enough irony to constantly doubt their certitude about the system boundaries that were imparted through their professional training. Instead, we peer deep into the vital thermodynamic complexity and depth of this world. Who cares if a material scientist, kayaker, and archaeologist are the team that day? I am totally agnostic about their disciplinary background. I am far more concerned what they can contribute—and how they contribute—to completely fresh and thoroughly invigorating perspectives on the operative dynamics of the twenty-first century world and how to intervene in the most powerful and elegant, if not magnificent, ways possible.

I think the primary task of design research today is one of, as Sloterdijk described, explication: "the revealing inclusion of latencies and background data in manifest operations."[4] We first need to begin to see around our own disciplinary corners to even see the mess our twentieth century externalities have made in the world. We have such misplaced virtuosity when it comes to design but I am confident that design in this century will increasingly swerve from matters of form to the far more consequential and systemic matter of formation. Formation belongs to no single discipline.

Under the paving stones of the disciplines, the beach!

There is no template for design. Everyone is a designer, and given the new speed of information, the common assumption is that special training is unnecessary, if not superfluous. This indifference is becoming more and more apparent in our built environment. With the increasing complexity of human knowledge and the escalating difficulty of the present conditions—how can architecture be taught and how can our models of teaching be reformed?

Information is but captured energy. While it is true that information circulates with greater velocity and in greater quantities today, as with energy it is extremely consequential to distinguish between various qualities of information and not just focus on astonishing quantities. Yes, information fluxes in impressive quantities and great velocities but so much of it is but the detritus of entropic dissipation. As I mentioned earlier, information is a sport of quantities and qualities. As such, there are legitimate claims that we actually know less about the world today for two reasons. First, the few bits of life-shaping, trajectory-shifting information are ever more buried in the undifferentiated flood. Second, individually we know less and less about the difficult whole of the world.

It is easy to get bad information. What schools offer today, in this regard, is essentially filtered, high-quality knowledge. So I think schools have little to with the docility training mandated by professional accreditation (don't get taught architecture that way!) and far more to do with knowledge that can trigger relevant research about the future trajectories of buildings, landscapes, and urbanization. Thusly, I think it is key to adopt a post-professional ethos.

At the same time, we must recognize that what you call the escalating difficulty of present conditions is the direct outcome of hubristic applications of knowledge. As Ulrich Beck explains, if science and engineering trigger a set of risks and calamities, for instance, it is bit mindless to assume that more science and engineering hold any solution.[5] So research and projections today deserve a degree of minor thought and healthy dose of irony to be most relevant in this century.

1 Gregory Bateson, *Steps to an Ecology of Mind* (Chicago, IL: University of Chicago Press, 1972).
2 Ivan Illich et al., *Disabling Professions: Ideas in Progress* (London, UK: Marion Boyars, 1977).
3 Freidrich Wilhelm Nietzsche, *The Will to Power: An Attempted Transvaluation of All Values* (New York, NY: Russell & Russell, 1964).
4 Peter Sloterdijk, "Airquakes." *Environment and Planning D: Society and Space* 27.1 (2009).
5 Ulrich Beck, *Risk Society: The Interaction of Science, Technology, and Public Policy* (Dordrecht: Kluwer Academic Publishers, 1992).

140°
angle to maximize year-round solar exposure

75.5°
angle to maximize solar exposure during the
winter months for outdoor program

North
orientation of air intake to capture and
distribute wind at night and the morning

50 meters
above urban context into undisturbed wind
flow areas, where air temperatures are less
influenced by the urban heat island effect

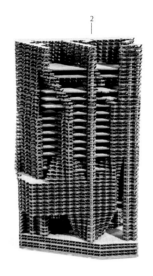

1 Ingrid Bengston
2 Jim Peraino
3 Natsuma Imai
4 Lauren Bordes

CORE III
ARCHITECTURE

Core III Architecture focuses on the primary forces that shape an architectural project—site, situation, and systems—to develop the project as a comprehensive design, from concept to constructability. The studio pedagogy treats the building as a material and cultural artifact, with an emphasis on tectonics, materiality, structure, envelopes, and urban and site-specific concerns.

Eric Höweler
Iñaki Ábalos
Vincent Bandy
Danielle Etzler
Jonathan Levi
Maryann Thompson

The notion of site is expanded to include the physical urban context, the environmental context of the design, as well as the cultural and institutional context. The studio site is the intersection of Massachusetts Avenue and the Massachusetts Turnpike. Historically a site of disruption within the urban fabric, the trajectory of "the pike" produces a zone of discontinuity and incompleteness that requires both urban and architectonic solutions. The situation of the studio may define the project more temporally as part of the larger cultural or political context. This also includes the type of program or intended use of a building— for our purposes, a 300,000-square-foot mixed-use institutional building, housing a large auditorium, university dorms, retail spaces, and gallery. The combination of programs on a small-footprint site create a new building type: a vertical urban campus. Building systems, including structural, environmental, circulatory, and envelope systems, are developed as part of an integrated design.

The air has been treated in architecture as an element whose existence is recognized, but about which one only could speak metaphorically, poetically, or phenomenologically. The focus of Air in Motion/Thermodynamic Materialism (Iñaki Ábalos, Matthias Schuler) is to study the movement of air in its different manifestations, to reveal its power through meticulous analysis and mappings, and to conceptualize a new idea of thermodynamic beauty, which completes the tectonic tradition and points to new directions for the architect's work.

continued on page 42 >>

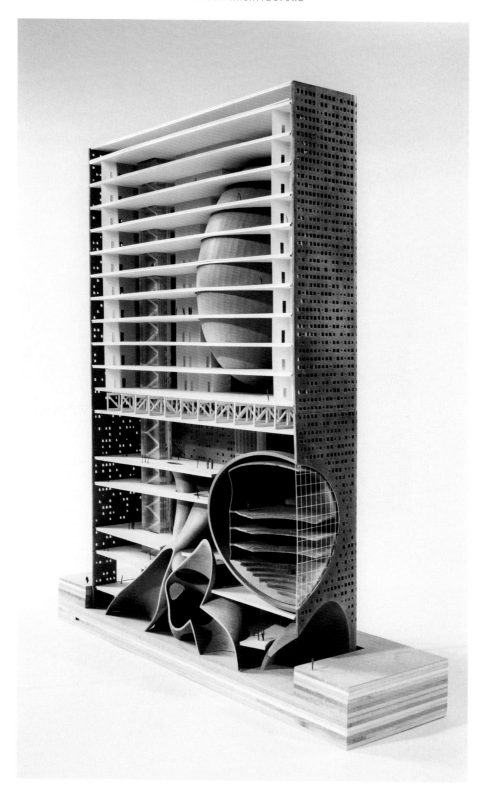

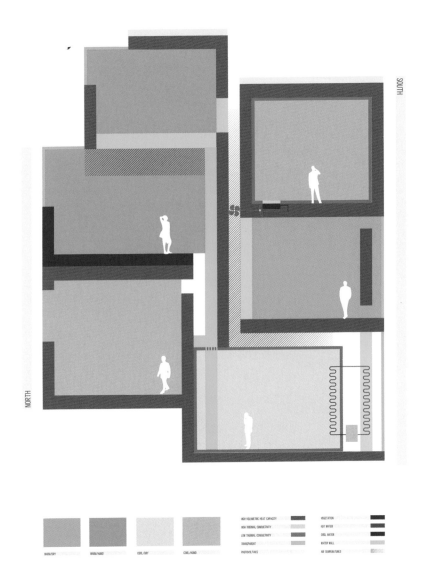

What Is an Envelope? A Thermodynamic Prototype
Collin Gardner, Ryu Matsuzaki & Elizabeth Roloff

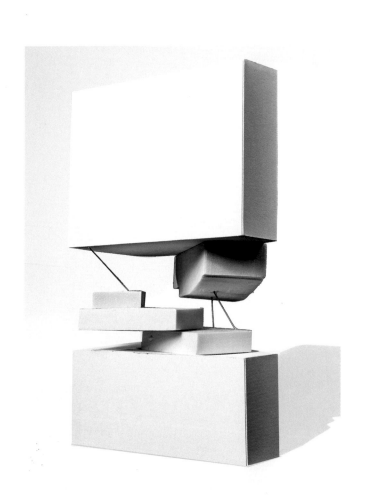

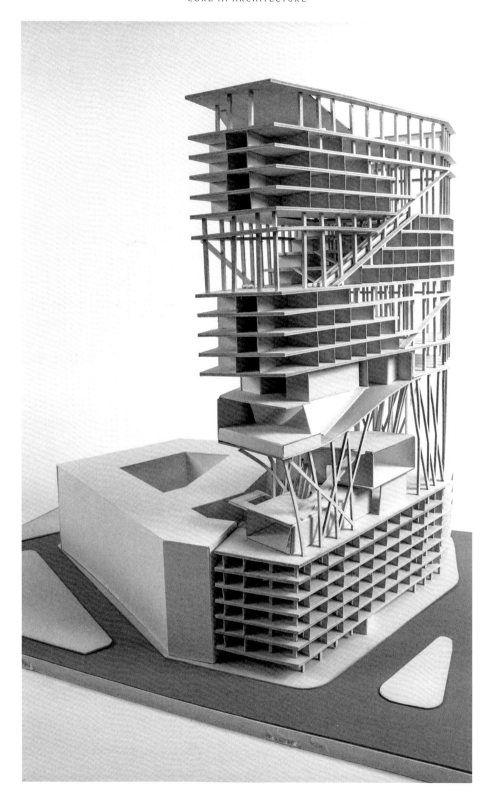

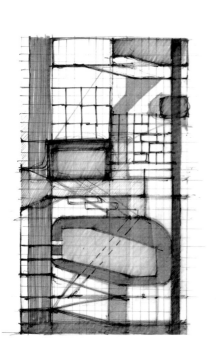
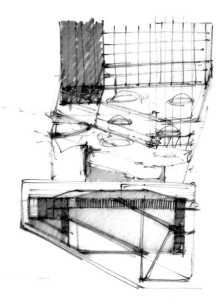

Advisors
Kiel Moe
Mark Mulligan

Students
Matthew Conway
Robert Daurio
Cerezo Davila
Ana García Puyol
Mariano Gomez Luque
Natsuma Imai
Takuya Iwamura
Thomas Sherman

The contemporary dwelling must expand its thermodynamic and ecological boundaries. This requires the engagement of both the local economy and the inhabitant in the sourcing and manufacture of its tectonic components, to better understand the energetic process.

Horizon House was the winning competition entry for LIXIL's Third International Architectural Competition and will be built by November 2013. Located on Japan's rural northern island of Hokkaido near the town of Taiki-cho, Horizon House was conceived not as an object but as a process for embracing both local and seasonal qualities of place. The project addresses the concept of "retreat in nature" by framing a seasonal dialogue between inhabitant and environment. Horizon House incorporates locally harvested and salvaged wood, replacing high embodied-energy materials, such as concrete. Within the house a continuous band of windows provides a 360-degree view to the landscape. The activities of the user shape the indoor thermal comfort envelope through radiant and ground-storage systems, powered only by the combustion of local forest by-products.

Toyo Ito

What Was Metabolism?
Reflections on the Life of Kiyonori Kikutake

Toyo Ito: The three key phrases that emerge when I start to synthesize the lessons from Kikutake are "agricultural landscape," "primitiveness," and "symbolism." I see perhaps his particular sensitivities going counter to modernism in many ways, in the pursuit of urban form and in the anti-symbolic notions of modernism in this force going to these roots.

I would like to reconsider the symbolic nature of agriculture in terms of Kikutake's work. In Kikutake's later years, he spoke about how Japanese culture was formed through agrarian culture. So I perceive the importance of re-examining these landscapes that might have disappeared for various practical reasons, but especially in this period after the 3/11 disaster, as incredibly high. For myself, I feel the need to rethink the fundamental question: What is the village? What is the future paradigm?

I see Kikutake's metabolism not as an industrial future but rather in this natural context that is shaped by natural forces, and is organic and metabolically changing.

Toyo Ito is the founder of Toyo Ito & Associates, and the recipient of the 2013 Pritzker Prize.

Interpreted by Ken Tadashi Oshima.

SOMETIMES ALONE.
MOSTLY WITH OTHERS.

John Todd, MArch I

Advisor
Toshiko Mori

The city is a political entity. It is a place for escape into worlds of our own identities, but it is also the place of negotiation between individuals and ideologies. The density of our capsular domesticities in the city provokes stimulation of the mutually shared cell wall. If our domestic space is our capsule of individuality, how we aggregate these co-isolated capsules into larger structures of foams becomes a place for critical examination. The Metropolis of Tokyo becomes a test case, provoking the nodal and nested depth of its network structure, the capsular history of the Metabolist Project, and the corporatized *Plan Voisin* of contemporary development to propose an alternative urbanism—engaging new ways to live within the density of the city.

This architectural investigation is the form of form, it is the curation of physical and affectual conditions into a dense structural mesh of latent relations, affording possible narratives activated through acts of inhabitation. This curated group functions simultaneously as one building and many buildings. It fluctuates between autonomy and connectivity, between singularity and the multitude. It is the creation of worlds—of many simultaneous worlds within worlds—apart from, and within, the city. A city in which we live sometimes alone. Mostly with others.

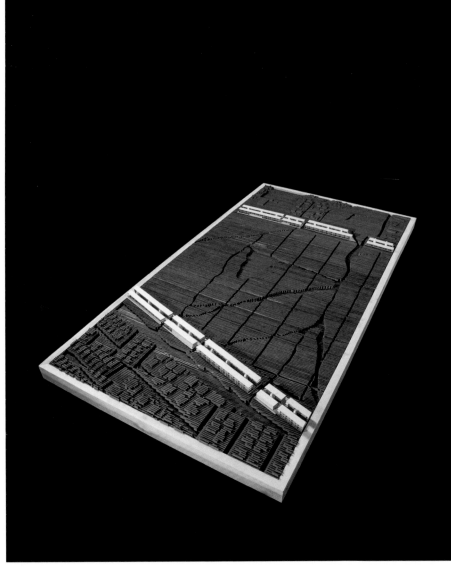

OUAGADOUGOU

With more than 1 million inhabitants, Ouagadougou is the largest city in Burkina Faso and the country's administrative, economic, and cultural center. The city experiences a population growth of approximately 100,000 migrants each year from the surrounding rural areas, creating new neighborhoods, many without electricity or running water. Moreover, the majority of Ouagadougou's buildings are one-story clay constructions. The aim of this design studio is to generate new affordable living spaces for the low- and middle-income groups within the city. The project involves the creation of a 45-square-meter modular housing unit for a family of five. This standard module is used in a new urban development of 10,000 units. The intervention is integrated in the city center to avoid creating a socially segregated society. Throughout the process it is important to take into consideration the layout of existing neighborhoods, the city's economic situation, and the local climate. Students are required to consider economic, cultural, environmental, and social factors to design a suitable house with available resources. The project gives students an insight into some of the important challenges facing the developing world.

Francis Kéré

The world today is interrelated and complex, and the built environment at any scale cannot ignore its role as the critical hub of emergent issues. The increased frequency of crisis is exacerbated by the interdependence of a multitude of issues, and we as the custodians of the environment cannot ignore the need to understand this relationship. The Global Redesign Project (Toshiko Mori) extends our skillset as designers of the built environment to outside our immediate expertise. It has become fashionable to use the word "architecture" to give certain credibility to the stability of complex systems within policy, economics, and finance. The true capacity of architecture enables the embrace of complexity within its inclusive system of integration, its cross-disciplinary structure, its communication of feedback, and its collaborative work model dependent on the coexistence of multiple stakeholders.

continued on next page >>

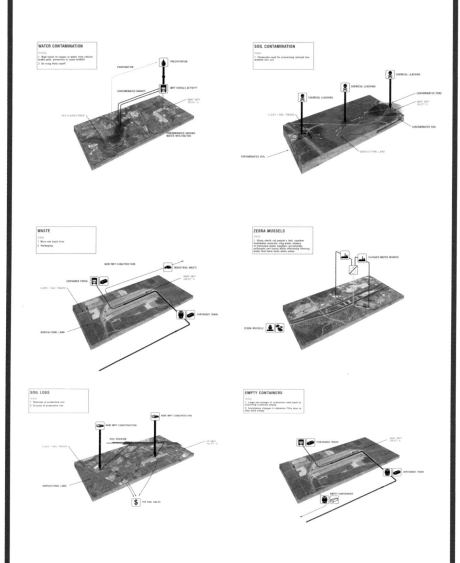

Through proposing a metabolic prototype for harnessing externalities produced by networks of containerized transport, this rescale project situates logistical networks historically and spatially within specific material and environmental contexts in the United States. These opportunistic metabolic strategies aim to alleviate some of the hidden costs associated with the movement of containers by ship, train, and truck. The Chicago Metropolitan Area, where six of North America's Class I railroads intersect, is used as a case study.

Conor O'Shea

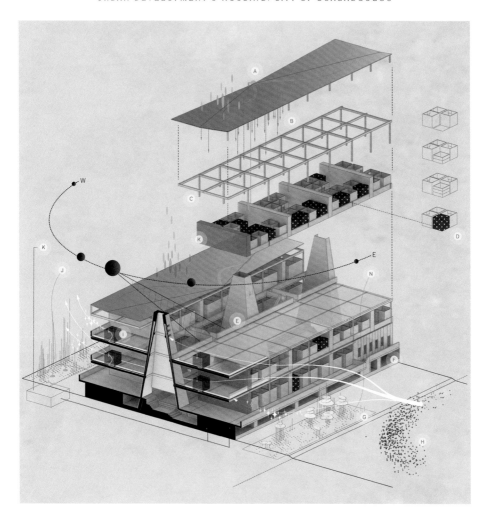

As affordable housing demand increases, a system of agricultural "silos" shift function and begin operating as "collectives —intrastructural chimneys—around which housing is constructed. While the "collectives" act as an infrastructural seed, the housing they support rings preserved agricultural land within Ouagadougou's greenbelt. This insertion of a new housing typology, where human agency can assist with the protection and maintenance of public infrastructure, addresses Ouagadougou's growth at an urban level. While the local government would initially fund construction of the "collectives," standard methods of taxation on informal economic activity would replace government assistance. Collaborative construction, locally sourced materials, and sweat equity, all familiar to rural-to-urban migrants, supports housing construction. Existing housing settlements are connected to and through the site by preserving and intensifying the well-worn paths in place, becoming evidence of the human agency of the place.

Kwabena Abrah-Asiedu, Edward Becker, Osaruyi Igiehon & Kayla Lim

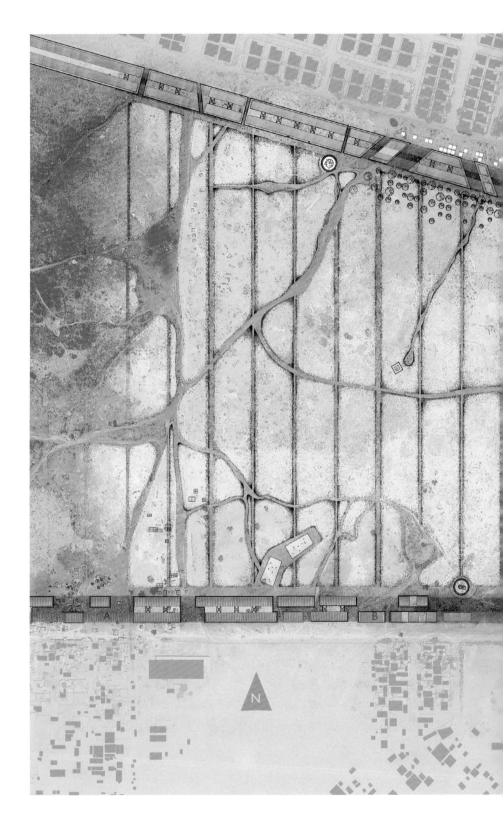

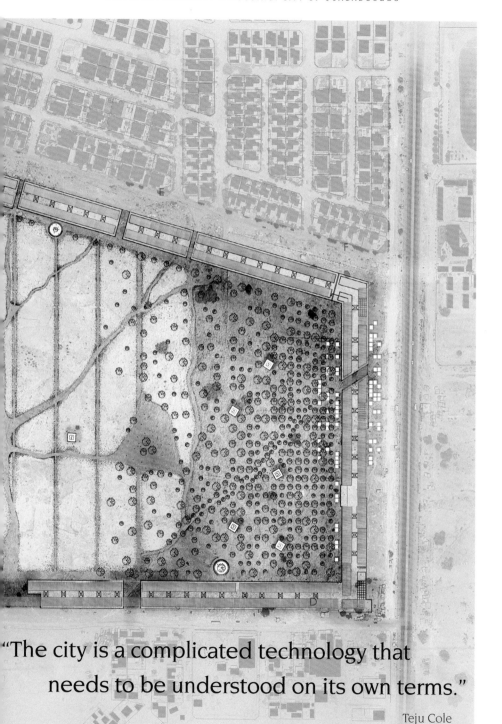

"The city is a complicated technology that
    needs to be understood on its own terms."

Teju Cole
The City as Palimpsest, November 7, 2012

continued on page 279 >>

LEVIATHAN

Mexico City is one of the most dynamic and complex metropolitan areas in the world today. With over 20.1 million inhabitants, remarkable urban growth, an active yet dual economy, and a palimpsest of material histories centuries old, it presents a compelling case study for architecture and urban planning today. Iztapalapa, located in the southeast part of the metropolitan area, is the most populated *delegación* (borough) in Mexico City with over 1.8 million inhabitants. Within Iztapalapa, the *Centro Oriente* site is close to 40 hectares in size and one of the largest open territories within the urban area of Mexico City. As a terrain surrounded by large-scale infrastructures, formal and informal housing, squatter settlements, complex geological and hydrological issues, as well as massive housing estates, *Centro Oriente* offers a possibility to reimagine urban planning as a tool of socio-spatial transformation. The Flexible Leviathan seeks to produce a vision for *Centro Oriente*, both in the local context of Iztapalapa and in metropolitan terms, thus theorizing the meaning of sustainable urbanism in large cities while also engaging the real world—the local context of urban policy-making through urban planning and design intervention. The guiding hypothesis is that by reframing the issues of scale and temporality, we can create a different urbanity, one that is better able to address the social, economic, ecological, and programmatic imperatives of the contemporary metropolis.

José Castillo
Diane Davis

One of the highlights of my year in residence as the first Loeb Fellow from the field of public health was my semester long engagement with the two studios for which Mexico City served as the site. Through the semester, I gained a new appreciation for this type of learning process, helping me to better support studios based in my home of New Orleans and the neighborhood groups that often serve as partners. I arrived at the GSD looking to examine how designers can collaborate with public health and development professionals to anticipate global trends and support people as they respond to these challenges. I leave inspired and recommitted to shifting the boundaries of what is considered possible.

Ann Yoachim, Loeb Fellow

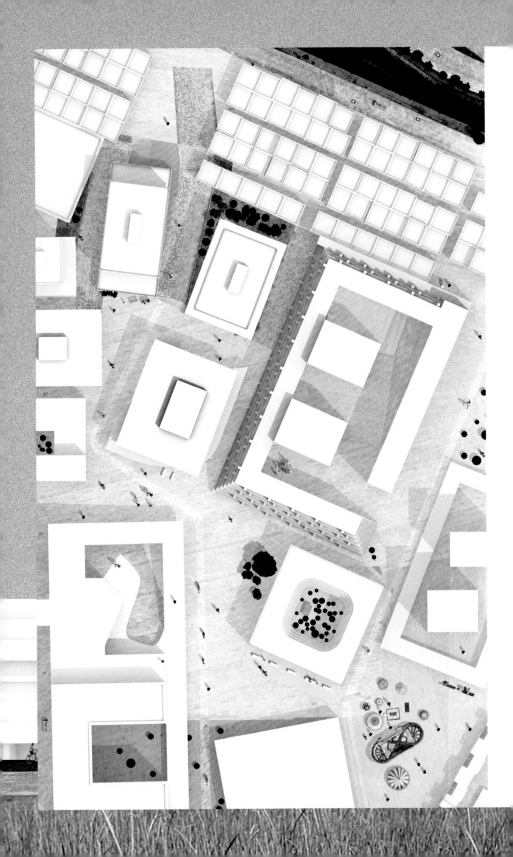

The novel urban experience of this project is defined by two innovations. First, a *Fideicomiso* composed of federal housing agencies and represented stakeholders is established to strategically distribute ownership and tenancy rights to select entities—public institutions of health and education, and private developers. By strategizing tenants ahead of time, the proposal sets up a scenario of mutual dependency between the market and socially oriented enterprises. Second, the *Fideicomiso* collectively oversees a rigid land rights scenario that restricts ownership of the ground entirely, instead establishing an air rights category at or above 10 meters high. Within the unique mixture of uses and residents at the site, a novel set of civic responsibilities and reciprocities for the urban environment emerge. This new form of city-making contests neoliberal tendencies of land use; no longer a calculus between efficiency in transport and land value, the street grid disappears. In its place comes slowness, encounter, friction, and the deliberate construction of interactions as the ultimate new priority for urban life.

Simon Battisti

The commons offers an age-old, yet underutilized lens through with which to understand the relationship between infrastructure and wellness within urban ventures in Mexico City. Within a megalopolis with high rates of preventable diseases, a socio-economic disparity that plays itself out through the distribution of water across the east-west axis of the Valley of Mexico, with the eastern section relying on trucked-in water despite high development pressures. Communal land tenure and usage (*ejido*) provides a precedent for laying the groundwork for a new type of urbanism within Iztapalapa—an otherwise sidelined area of the city. Richard Sennett in *Together: The Rituals, Pleasures, and Politics of Co-Operation* speaks of co-operation in communities through the creation of porosity and barrier removal. Employing this logic through the communal building and ownership of local infrastructure systems, this project stretches the gradient between traditionally held public and private spaces on a site that is currently divided by multiple political and physical obstructions. Beyond this, the potential then is created for a community to embrace new opportunities in the health sector for citizen science, small-scale clinics, and environmental monitoring that could change the relationship that Iztapalapa has with the city and territory as a whole.

Lauren Elachi & Beth Lundell Garver

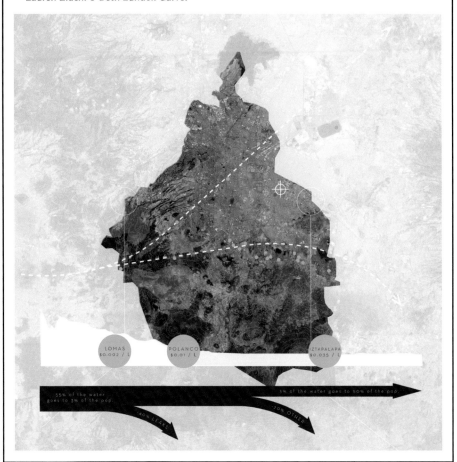

CORE
URBAN PLANNING

Core Urban Planning I introduces students to the fundamental knowledge and technical skills used by urban planners to create, research, analyze, and implement plans and projects for the built environment. The studio uses the city of Boston as the students' planning laboratory, and students are expected to understand the city through the lenses of planning elements such as demographics, economic attributes, market forces, and public and private stakeholder interests, all of which shape the city and inform decisions about land use, development, and infrastructure.

Core Urban Planning II focuses on a real-world planning project in the context of diverse community needs. The studio collaborates with the city of Malden and the Metropolitan Area Planning Council to create a draft district plan for Malden's downtown, an immigrant hub where two-thirds of the district's residents were born outside of the United States. The site's redevelopment contributes to regional sustainability goals. In the studio students investigate issues related to district-scale planning in the context of city and regional goals; approaches for involving diverse groups of the public in planning; methods for generating alternative options across a variety of planning topics; ways to represent plan ideas to multiple constituencies; strategies for plan implementation; and how the physical and master-planning process can reflect, mediate, and highlight community values, public goals, and private markets.

UP 1
Judith Grant Long
Peter Park
Kathy Spiegelman

UP 2
Ann Forsyth
Daniel D'Oca
Kathryn Madden
with
Robert Pietrusko

"The street is a very specific way of ordering the city. Even as we probe in depth and in detail the forms of the street, we must also somehow simultaneously think beyond the centrality of the street as the arbiter of social and urban order. Mapped out but not socially recognized... As we go through our study of the street, we have to keep in mind the street's other."

K. Michael Hays
Cambridge Talks VII: Architecture and the Street
March 29, 2013

continued on page 70 >>

Proposal for Longwood's Institutions

The Longwood Medical and Academic Area, an economically important agglomeration of twenty-four institutions on a 213-acre site in west Boston, anticipates strong growth. Although it attracts a large number of commuters, it is infrequently visited by, and offers little to, the sizable residential population encircling it. However, this urban centrality, and indeed the many similarities to downtown Boston, come with a responsibility. To address existing tensions and pre-empt their exacerbation, the public character of the medical and educational institutions should be increased. Thus, new developments need to advance accessibility to some of the existing, rich institutional assets. This proposal is two-fold: first, ground floors should be rethought as circulation and semi-public space within institutional buildings. Second, if slightly modified, the abutting Fens offers the open space requirements of a denser built form as well as presents itself as a connective tissue to the adjacent residential areas.

Benjamin Scheerbarth

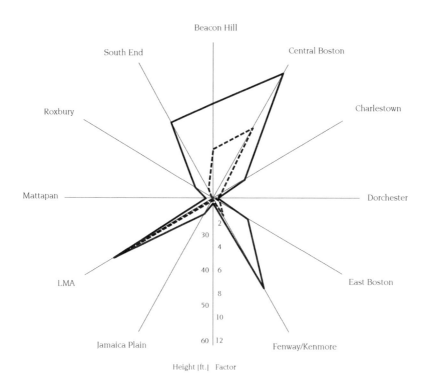

Height [ft.] Factor

——— Mean building height

- - - - Employment to population ratio

Housing: Malden, Massachusetts

Downtown Malden is home to a diverse community of residents who represent a wide spectrum of cultural backgrounds, professions, age groups, and interests. The proposed plan to address the housing needs of this transforming community envisions a substantial increase in the local housing supply that will meet the growing demand of Greater Boston, improve downtown business conditions, and ensure that affordable housing options remain available for current and future residents. By empowering the community, increasing the housing supply, zoning for smart growth, and maintaining existing affordable units, Malden can achieve this vision and will attract a diverse set of residents and serve as home for a thriving community for generations to come.

Mariana Barrera, Theodore Conrad, Bill Hewitt & Tom Skwierawski

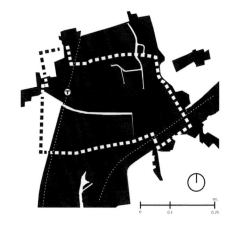

Proposals

1. Create Community Development Corporation (CDC) to ensure that the many constituencies in Malden are represented in housing policy and development.
2. Create "Smart Growth" Zone to encourage transit-oriented, affordable housing development near the train station.
3. Use subsidies and tax incentives to build, renovate and/or preserve affordable housing units.
4. Establish an Inclusionary Zoning Ordinance, incentivizing the growth of affordable units.
5. Promote development and residential occupancy on upper levels of existing, redeveloped, and future properties along Pleasant and Exchange streets.

Benefits of "Smart Growth" Zoning (40R): Setting standards for affordable housing requirements; development efficiency and profitability; access to public transit.

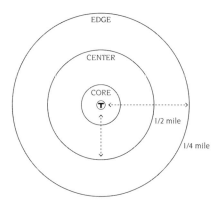

Proposed "Smart Growth Zoning": Development is most dense in the core, achieving enough of a support base for ground floor retail.

Cambridge Talks VII: Architecture and the Street
excerpt from "Street Paint: Research as Public Works India c. 1960"
Ateya Khorakiwala, PhD Candidate

"Delhi is giving the finishing touches to a welcome fit for royalty, with three days to go for Queen Elizabeth's arrival. A dust free Connaught Place will greet the Queen with flags, bunting, banners, a black carpet of bitumen underfoot and a net of paper flowers overhead."

- Times of India News Service, 1961[1]

Please try to imagine Queen Elizabeth II with "a black carpet of bitumen underfoot" in New Delhi. It is not often that the materiality and iconography of bitumen— black, sticky, resinous bitumen, the petro-product that makes up 5 percent of asphalt—come together in the news to welcome a queen. My paper investigates bitumen and the street paint that coated it as they emerged in the 1960s at the intersection of the Indian state's road-building project and petro economy.

Street paint (or "road-marking material," as it is officially called in the industry) is usually applied to the surface of bitumen (asphalt), to indicate the correct ways to use the street. The language of street markings and road signs emerged in the postwar period as roads and highways began to cover the world. Most standards were set by the United Nations, but in the case of India, the Economic Commission for Asia and the Far East created the country's codified system. In considering the representational history of this system that offers instructions on how to navigate roadways, it is crucial to remember that it was also embedded in the political economy of the time.

Here I distill a small portion of technical material from the larger body of road research that occurred in the 1960s. This research in the production of durable surface markings on bitumen roads, I argue, metonymically represented the state's imagined extensive paved territories, and their failure to manifest condemned its modernity to remaining inside the laboratory.

In 1947, at the point of independence, India had only 0.75 miles of road for every 1,000 people, compared to the United Kingdom's 3.5 and the United State's 21 miles per 1,000 people. Any expansion of the network demanded research and development of road engineering to provide a successful model. In 1952, cognizant of its shortcomings in this area, the planning commission budgeted a small amount (1 percent of the total transport and communications budget) for construction and the purchase of equipment for a Central Road Research

Institute (CRRI) because "adequate facilities for road research were practically non existent."

A central research facility, it is not surprising that the CRRI defined the problem of establishing an extensive system of roads—a territorial network—as a severe deficiency of knowledge, which required a large volume of technical data. In calling for specific responses to geographic conditions, soil studies, and material development, they also outlined the problem as specifically Indian. The question they were trying to answer was: How do we "Indianize" road engineering and still produce a modern network of transport?

Undergirding the research into new materials and methods was the economy of scarcity, within which resources will either be too divided to be useful or unjustly distributed. Planning was, after all, a system to unevenly distribute resources, so that the multiple problems of development could be tackled one at a time. By researching locally available materials and techniques, the organization hoped to expand the available pool of resources, thus responding to India's inability to import raw materials, expertise, and equipment, given the lack of access to foreign exchange and a focus on an import substitution model of growth. The combination of the economy of scarcity and the systems of national planning are embodied in the research of the CRRI. Their framework of a technologically modern state is undercut by the fact that regardless of research, the state remained without the resources to deploy its knowledge outside the space of the laboratory. These dilemmas were represented both materially and semantically in their research to create standards for road-marking paint.

1 Capital Gets Ready: Welcome Fit for Royalty, The Times of India News Service, The Times of India (1861-current); Jan 18, 1961; ProQuest Historical Newspapers: The Times of India (1838-2003) 7.

Post-Planning in Mumbai

By Rahul Mehrotra

In Mumbai today, planning is about incremental moves, without any coherent strategy for the orchestration of the city's structure. Mumbai has clearly entered an era where laissez-faire growth as well as large-scale infrastructure development is combining to create a peculiar urban landscape—a landscape that is not the result of a discernible vision for the city but rather one that has evolved out of a series of tactics played out independently by various constituent groups. This makes for complex and shifting sets of relationships between the physical artifacts and the people who occupy this urban system.

Today Mumbai is comprised of two components occupying the same physical space. One, which could be called the Static City, is built of more permanent material—concrete, steel, and brick. It is the two-dimensional conception that appears on conventional city maps and is monumental in its presence. The other is a Kinetic City. Incomprehensible as a two-dimensional entity, it is perceived as a city in motion—a three-dimensional construct of incremental development. The Kinetic City is temporary and often built with recycled material—plastic sheets, scrap metal, canvas, and waste wood. It constantly modifies and reinvents itself. The Kinetic City is not perceived in architectural terms but rather in terms of spaces and patterns of occupation. It is an indigenous urbanism with its own local logic. The Kinetic City is not necessarily the city of the poor, as most images might suggest; rather it is a temporal articulation and occupation of space that not only creates a richer character of spatial occupation but also suggests how spatial limits are expanded to include formally unimagined uses in dense urban conditions.

In fact the Kinetic City has the potential to foster a better understanding of the blurred lines of contemporary urbanism and the changing roles of people and spaces in urban society. Increasing concentrations of global flows have exacerbated the inequalities and spatial divisions of social classes. In this context, an architecture or urbanism of equality in an increasingly inequitable economic condition requires looking deeper to find a wide range of places to acknowledge and commemorate the cultures and environments of those excluded from the spaces of global flows. These realities don't necessarily lie in the formal production of architecture but often challenge it. Here the idea of a city is an elastic urban condition—not a grand vision, but a grand adjustment. These adjustments are often made through localized tactics and negotiations that involve the complex nexus between authorities and citizens.

Post-Planning in Mumbai

How does the city position itself to grapple with this explosive urbanization during a period of economic liberalization, in which commercial gains are not only taking precedence over everything else but are also negating traditional planning processes? The term "post-planning," coined by Chinese art critic Hou Hanru, seems appropriate in describing the condition of Mumbai. This is a situation in which any planning is systematically "posterior"—a recuperative and securing action. Economics and profits are the central players, replacing traditional ideological, social, environmental, historical, and aesthetic elements as the driving forces behind the creation and expansion of cities. Citizens have to confront urgent questions of instability, indecision, changeability, and survival as established social and urban fabrics are deconstructed and reorganized at an alarming rate. Major urban interventions undertaken in this manner often result in dramatic, chaotic, and unexpected visual arrangements—a new emergent landscape.

What then are the challenges facing Mumbai today? Perhaps the effects of globalization and the urgency of integrating with a broader economic system have completely changed the priorities of the authorities responsible for making the city. Singapore architect William Lim describes this phenomenon, which has swept Asia, as cities being "Shanghaied." The experience of Shanghai as a city that has effectively and with great speed transformed its urban landscape to embrace a global identity is one that politicians in Mumbai use as their benchmark for progress (the formerly favored model was Singapore). Ironically, the use of this model ignores the crucial fact that such growth arises out of a political system far removed from democracy.

The most fundamental shift that has occurred in the planning process is the privatization of city development by the government. While with this shift the government has rid itself of the responsibility of delivering urban amenities within a strategic framework, it has not defined its new role. Should it still be the custodian of the public realm? Should it put into place the checks and balances required when private enterprise is unleashed for city development? Aside from the imbalance that this creates in allocations of funding and city resources, these infrastructure interventions wreck havoc on the city fabric and the numerous neighborhoods they traverse. In fact, today there is an incredible disjuncture between existing and allocated land uses and the positioning of new infrastructure—a symptom of the "post-planning" condition where land use, transportation planning, and urban form are unrelated in the emergent landscape. How then does one orchestrate growth and planning, and create visions for the city in the future?

continued on next page >>

Participatory Planning

In the post-planning scenario in Mumbai, the most crucial issue is that of the participation of citizens in the policy-making process. At the city level, the policy-making body should largely consist of professionals, because a focus on relevant technicalities cannot be achieved without depoliticizing the planning authority. Ideally, the city should then have an elected executive who is responsible directly to the people for the state of the city. This cannot be achieved as a top-down approach, however, but rather one initiated at the grassroots, with the formation and strengthening of local citizens groups as the first step. It is here that activists, environmentalists, planners, engineers, and architects have a contribution to make—an integral role in creating an appropriate process with a system of checks and balances, so critical for a decentralized mode of planning, to ensure that the public good is not edged out in the guise of privatization.

The most needed shift for this system to work will be a substantial body of people within the profession of urban planning and architecture working with the concept of "advocacy planning." This concept has its origins in the perception that interested citizens groups need planners to formulate and present their case and express their aspirations. This has become particularly crucial in the post-planning scenario where agencies engaged with city governance do not attract planners and other professionals, while they continue to articulate policy for the city that is cast in technicalities too abstract for ordinary citizens to comprehend.

Ambiguity regarding the urban form of Mumbai and the dominant image of the city prompts the question, "Whose city is it anyway?" This question goes beyond the politics of occupation and challenges the processes by which the city is made—perhaps most critical when negotiating between the Static and Kinetic Cities, for here is an effective point of intervention. Through the city-making process, globalization and its particular transgressions in the urban landscape are realized, but it is also how the Kinetic City can simultaneously resist and participate in globalization as well as reconfigure itself socially, culturally, and spatially. This particular urban condition represents a fascinating intersection of a landscape of dystopia and a symbol of optimism; it challenges the power of architecture and urban design to reposition and remake the city as a whole. The Kinetic City forces the Static City to reengage itself in its present conditions by dissolving its utopian project to fabricate multiple dialogues with its context. Could this become the basis for a rational discussion about coexistence? Or is the emergent urbanism of Mumbai inherently paradoxical, with the coexistence of the Static and Kinetic Cities and their particular states of utopia and dystopia inevitable? Can the spatial configuration for how this simultaneity occurs actually be formally imagined? Or perhaps within this urbanism, the Static and Kinetic Cities will necessarily coexist and blur into an integral entity, even if only momentarily, to create the margins for adjustment that their simultaneous existences demand.

Rahul Mehrotra is Professor of Urban Design and Planning and Chair of the Department of Urban Planning and Design at the Harvard University Graduate School of Design, and the founder and principal of RMA Architects.

This essay was excerpted from *In the Life of Cities*, ed. Mohsen Mostafavi (Zürich and Cambridge, MA: Lars Müller Publishers and Harvard Graduate School of Design, 2012): 334-344.

April 15, 2013, 2:49 pm EDT

671–673 and 755 Boylston Street

Putting Public Space in Its Place

From Tahrir Square to Zuccotti Park, physical public space reminded us of its multiple ambitions and capabilities for accommodating consequential political activities as well as everyday leisurely pursuits. The production of public space simultaneously implicates and transcends technical decisions with regard to design, financing, and management considerations.

"To me, it is not unimaginable to embed a 'right to public space' in our thinking, aspirations, and ethical stance, if not in our laws."

- Jerold Kayden

"It's that mix, that serendipity, that sense of surprise that Jane Jacobs and others have written about so powerfully, that I think makes the difficulty of democracy its genius. The barriers about securing the ideals of freedom, participation, and equality can be overcome if you have the hope that it can be overcome with the serendipity of human exchange."

- Martha Minow

"What makes public space distinctively public? And how is it distinct from other types of space? In a nation polarized by politics and fragmented by race and class, does public space still retain its own steadying capacity to act as a social mixing chamber that simultaneously expresses and facilitates the highest aspirations of democracy?"

- Blair Kamin

"How do we make a project with empathy?"

- Adriaan Geuze

"In a world in which coastal and river cities are increasingly susceptible to floods attributed to the effects of climate change, cities are positioning parks and plazas as places where water can come and go without permanent damage to the urban infrastructure. Is this a fad or a meaningful part of the solution?"

"I think that all these issues—being ecological, economic, social, or cultural—have a spatial impact. And this spatial impact makes planning and design so important. It gives us the opportunity to engage and influence the effects, but moreover it also influences the origins of the issues at stake. If we design, organize, and plan in a meaningful, resilient way, we can not only make better places, cities, and urban and rural landscapes, but we can actually influence the roots of the issues."

Henk Ovink

"I think the tension and moments of high anxiety around a space like Zuccotti Park in the end make for a much richer public space, and bring a renewed visibility for privately owned public space. What are they supposed to be, and how should they be regulated? Who gets to use them? Stewardship is one of the biggest things that comes out of those moments of tension."

- Holly Leicht

"In this digital age, physical public space still matters. It turns out that revolutions still derive some of their juice from people gathering together in one space proximate to each other, and proximate to structures of power."

- Jerold Kayden

"The predicates of a constitutional democracy are free people who are equal, and who can participate. And you can't have a democracy if you don't have those things. But it's also the case that the democracy is supposed to produce those things. So, the question is how do you make that possible? Well, I think that space is a big part of that. Space in which people can be free, in which people can both be equal and express their equality, and can participate."

- Martha Minow

A FRANCHISE OF DIFFERENCE

Dasha Ortenberg, MArch I

Advisor
Mack Scogin

Today we understand a franchise as an instance in a repetitive series, a symbol of globalization and a catalyst of homogeneity. Is it possible to create an architecture of overt hypocrisy, which seeks consistency but accepts the futility of this pursuit; simultaneously embraces and undermines stereotypes and stereotypical behaviors; and teeters on the brink of imposition, exhibition, and liberation? If it is possible, can architecture

Greetings

reference this kind of abstraction or generality through a close engagement with and integration of the very specific? In other words, can an a priori, utopian society be approximated by a flawed and thoroughly dystopian one, and is it possible to find an ultimate underlying (common) set of values through relativism? These moments already exist in the United States. What is lacking, however, is a space that continuously fosters and generates these encounters. Wittgenstein would say, "[t]he word is on the tip of [their tongues]." The encounters have not been activated; the link—the magic, the architecture—is missing.

This thesis is about the practice and process of design, not about a particular aesthetic, formal, or structural approach. It is about using a designer's set of tools, which includes technique, precedent, and context, to communicate with those who experience a building; it is about realizing the potential of architecture to stimulate critical thought and conversation in a country whose greatest asset is its under-represented diversity.

CURVED TERRAIN	STEPPED TERRAIN	SKATE RAMP	FACETED TERRAIN	HILLED TERRAIN

CURVED PATHWAY	PATHWAY CONNECTORS	QUAD PLATFORMS	CIRCULAR PLATFORMS	POLYGONAL PLATFORMS

SHREDDED TIRES	SAND	WOOD DECKING	WOOD CHIPS	BLACKTOP

RUBBER MATS	ARTIFICIAL TURF	BERM	CHAIR-FENCE	WHEEL WALL

INDOOR PLAY SPACE	OVERHANG	HANDBALL WALL	CLIMBING WALL	PLANTER BARRIER

CYLINDER	SWING SET	ICE SKATING RINK	RUNNING TRACK	SWIMMING POOL

BATTING CAGES	AMPHITHEATRE	MINI-GOLF	BOCCE BALL	JACUZZI

BENCH O' PEDDLIN'	BENCH O' STRETCHIN'	GAME CUBE	OUTDOOR LIBRARY	TRAMPOLINE

THE GOOD OLD DAYS

Thanks to longer lifespans, lower fertility rates, and the aging of the baby boomer population, the United States is getting older. Already there are more Americans age sixty-five years and older than at any other time in United States history; between now and 2020, the population of persons sixty-five and older will increase by 50 percent. How will our cities and suburbs manage this massive demographic shift? The Good Old Days: Design for the Age-Friendly Environment, considers a model that the American Association of Retired Persons recently called "the most dormant and overlooked form of senior housing": Naturally Occurring Retirement Community (NORC). A NORC is a place—a building, development, or neighborhood—with a large senior population that wasn't purpose-built to be a senior community.

Daniel D'Oca
Jana Cephas

This interdisciplinary studio challenges students of all departments to come up with creative ways to help seniors in NORCs in New York City and Long Island age in place. After visiting a sampling of NORCs, students meet with seniors, NORC directors, healthcare professionals, medical researchers, and representatives from New York City's Department for the Aging, Housing Authority, Department of Transportation, and others involved in the city's pioneering "Age-Friendly New York City" initiative to better understand the challenges and opportunities that come with aging in place in New York. Students then draw on this research to creatively identify opportunities for architectural, planning, or landscape-based interventions.

Architects and urbanists are good at responding to briefs. Traditional design briefs are conceived as abstractions of perceived needs, specifications, or market opportunities. The resulting solutions work for contexts where economy or the designer's vision rules, but often fall short in responding to the real needs of people. Considerations of human factors, worldview, social implications, and product life cycles call on the designer to combine intuition and technical skill with a more ambiguous ability to empathize with users and make their latent needs tangible. Designing Things for Humans (Ari Adler, Bradley Crane) provides an opportunity to answer this call by working with subject matter experts from IDEO.

continued on page 83 >>

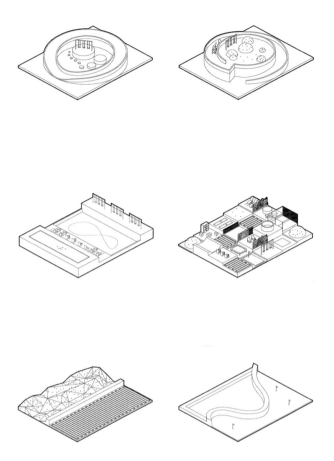

Aiming to design a fun, interactive, and safe environment in which people of all ages can physically, mentally, and visually engage with one another, this project explores ways to enhance the recreational lives of children as well as adults and senior citizens. The typologies of the multi-generational playgrounds are based on the potential (as well as law-restricted) interactions of user-groups. Accompanying the typologies, the multi-generational playground kit-of-parts consists of various components from child-safe surface materials like shredded, recycled tires to exercise equipment that allow adults and seniors to engage in physical activity while nonetheless keeping an eye out for their children and grandchildren. These components can be implemented within the three typologies to create numerous, unique variations of multi-generational playgrounds for the twenty-first century.

Jenny Jiae Lee

Based on interviews with a user group of parents with young children, the design addresses the challenge of wanting stay connected in a creative and collaborative way with your children while away from home. This hybrid physical-digital product is a quilted mat that lights up with colored LEDs as each pillow is clicked, creating glowing images that can be sent to the parent's mobile app.

Beth Eckels, Wenting Guo & Chuhan Zhang

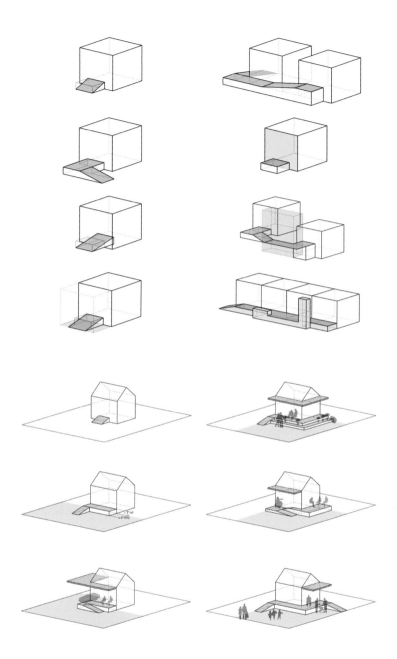

In each location, this project asks what else the typology of the ramp can do beyond solving problems of accessibility. Whether it is generating new forms of interaction or providing public spaces, ramps move beyond issues of mobility to reactivate the built environment.

Katherine Chu

ARCHITECTURE
FOR THE AGING

Jeongyong Mimi Kim, MArch I

Advisor
Mack Scogin

Through exploring the potential of architecture to change preconceived societal notions, this thesis takes as its departure point the pressing issue of the global aging population. In reframing this issue it also questions standard architectural response to it and ultimately, accepted notions of design within the discipline of architecture itself.

In the field of architecture, the geriatric topic centers around senior housing typologies, urban reconfigurations, universal accessibility, and the creation of new programs for the increasing elderly population. However, a deep examination of the issue of aging and an attempt to extract a specific topic results in

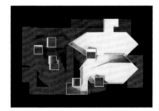

the discovery of the negative associations with the elderly in society. This thesis asks: How can architecture create a new perception toward the elderly? Implicit in this question is another: How can architecture change preconceived societal notions? The initial architectural move is to take a multigenerational family dwelling underground, the home being the beginning of all societies and architecture. The elimination (or the control) of light and, subsequently, the different spatial experience and the changed relationship between the exterior and interior are reinterpreted to generate the new underground spaces.

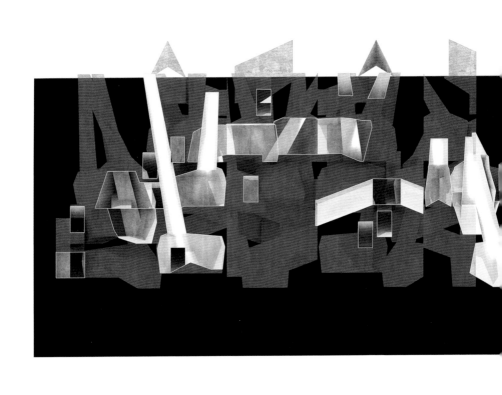

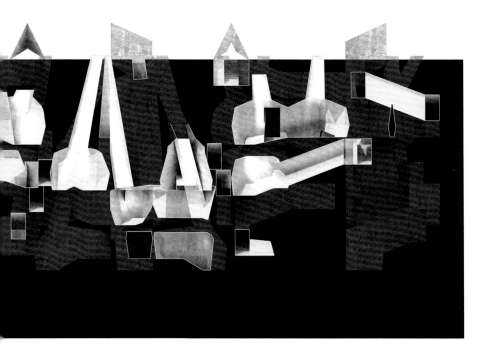

John Portman

A Conversation with John Portman

Mohsen Mostafavi: How did the atrium hotel idea begin?

John Portman: We were fortunate enough to get an opportunity to do housing for older people. I could speak to that maybe even better now [*laughs*]. I'm a sidewalk philosopher; I became interested in philosophy way back then, and in understanding how people dealt with their times. It really made me begin to focus more and more on people, and realize that architecture is about people—and that means it's about life. So if that's true, then I wanted to see how we could take architecture and add to the enhancement of life.

We started thinking about how people live, and the housing in the past. I wanted to create a community, and give it a life—how I would like to live if I was in their place, and how it would be meaningful to me. I approach every project that way, from the human side. I'm much more interested in the spiritual side than I am in the "things" side. Architecture is imposing. It sits out on the sidewalk—I'm interested in the little guy that's walking around down there among it.

When people get older, they want to have a situation where they can expect privacy, where they can be alone, have intimate space—and at the same time they want a community and to be able to meet with their friends and so forth. That is what created the first atrium idea: something that was just the opposite of what you would expect from arrival, so that you come in out of this cacophony of noise and clutter and walk into this huge spatial relief.

John Portman is an architect and real estate developer based in Atlanta, Georgia, and is the founder of John Portman & Associates.

Photo: Embarcadero Hyatt, San Francisco. 1973

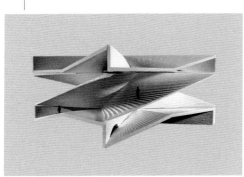

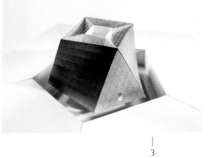

1 Patrick Baudin
2 Jonathan Rieke
3 Fred Kim
4 Nancy Nichols

CORE I
ARCHITECTURE

Architectural conventions and typologies are taught by means of anomalies: extreme or exceptional conditions of space and form that elicit a heightened awareness of the norms that are customarily taken for granted. The aim is to bring architecture to heightened consciousness and to confront it at a deeply conceptual level while learning the fundamental tools of the architect's craft.

Preston Scott Cohen
Katy Barkan
Jeffry Burchard
Mariana Ibañez
Kiel Moe
Ingeborg Rocker
Cameron Wu

The Hidden Room project within Core Architecture I involves designing a group of five rooms, one of which seems to be hidden from the other four. The program requires providing a means of access to the hidden room while controlling the degree to which the room becomes vulnerable to disclosure, involving the art of camouflage and surreptitious passage. In order to effectively conceal a room, knowledge of the entire building is likely to be deferred for both the inhabitants of the building and for the audiences of its representations— the architectural critics. In other words, it is unlikely that there will be a single plan or section that is capable of describing the entirety of the proposal. The dualities of the project (open and closed; public and private; exposed and hidden; transparent and opaque) will be played out as a result of the hybrid nature of the project and its programmatic coupling. Duality and tension can be subtly manifest or negated— able to be masked not only through modes of spatial communication but also, by the understanding of the exterior massing and fenestration from within. The project requires the exploration of the techniques by which spatial and organizational paradigms become formalized.

Billie Tsien and Tod Williams barely stopped to sleep during their week as Senior Loeb Scholars at the GSD in March. In addition to lectures, reviews, and class visits, they generously spent many informal hours in lively conversations with students and Loeb Fellows and affiliates over meals. Tsien was a guest in the Issues in Architectural Practice and Ethics class taught by Maryann Thompson and Jay Wickersham. Her discussions with students about the roles of women in architecture effectively served to relaunch the Women in Design group at the GSD. Tsien and Williams spent an afternoon with the Core I Architecture students to explore their distinctive approach to materials, and they participated in the midterm review for the Core II Architecture students. The highlight of their residency was a public lecture for a full house in Piper Auditorium.

continued on page 98 >>

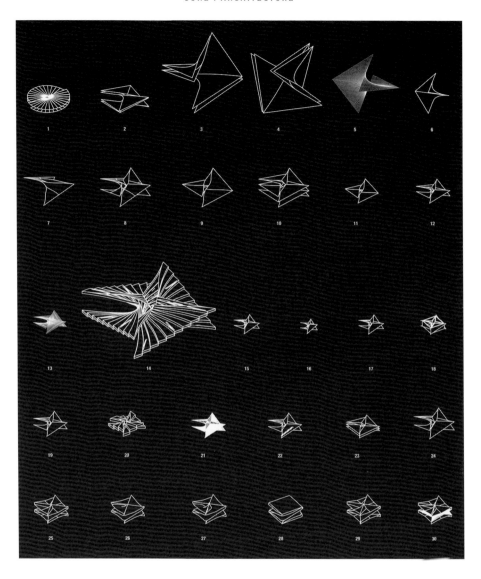

Inspired by the Hitchcockian cinematic narrative, where the viewer experiences a series of conflicts and plot twists that culminate in full disclosure of the story, the project explores the relationship between narrative structures in film and spatial sequencing in architecture. The user is led over and under the building through each of the first four rooms, confronting thicknesses along the way. These thicknesses suggest the presence of another room and establish a conflict that is resolved only at the end of the sequence.

Patrick Baudin

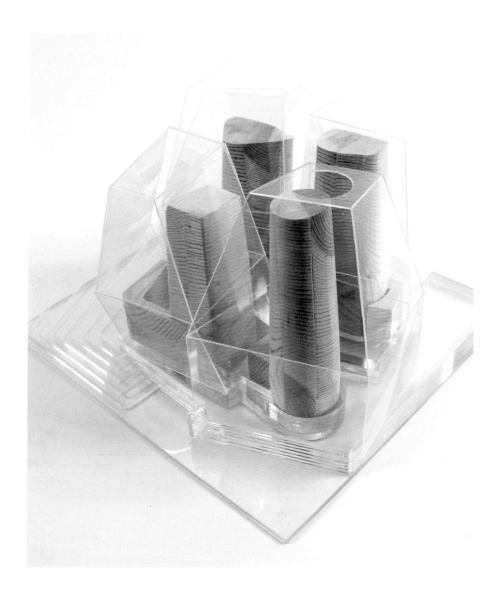

"Architecture is mostly about the hands
that make it and the hands that live in it."

Billie Tsien & Tod Williams

continued on page 98 >>

Billie Tsien & Tod Williams

Senior Loeb Scholar Lecture

James Stockard: A couple of years ago I asked Tod what part of the design process he specialized in and what parts Billie was best at. He said, "We design together. By the time a building is finished we can't even remember whose ideas were whose." What a statement, about two strong designers, immersing themselves in the process so passionately that the concepts overwhelm any desire for personal credit.

Tod Williams: I think that we as architects believe the work is about the work, but in a way I think that as we've come to live life, we believe that it's just as much, or ever more, about the way we work and not just the work itself. Our life invades everything that we do. The way we lived and live is actually a part of our work. And that's why our first apartment remains the precedent of precedents.

Billie Tsien: I think I'm the kind of person who wants to think about being still and Tod always thinks about wanting to move. People think that we're sitting around, inventing materials, and pulling ideas out from the sky but what we really do is to go to places where people make things and understand what people are doing, take their knowledge, and see what we can do with what they know. That's much easier than trying to invent something from scratch.

T.W.: We wanted to really talk about the issue of the work that we're interested in making—which is collaborative work—and which is taking architecture and knowing that it's as much about abstraction as it is about the beauty of the object. But it's mostly about the hands that make it and the hands that live in it, and what we give and what we leave behind that really counts.

B.T.: We live our lives in architecture, with this desire to make these things that will last. And if for one reason or another they don't, that's very difficult, but it doesn't stop us from wanting to make these places on the earth that will last.

Tod Williams and Billie Tsien are co-founders of Tod Williams Billie Tsien Architects.
James Stockard is the Curator of the Loeb Fellowship in Advanced Environment and a Lecturer in Housing Studies at the Harvard University Graduate School of Design.

"We design together."

Preston Scott Cohen

Walter Gropius Lecture
Successive Architecture

It would seem today that as far as architecture is concerned, digital instruments are capable of effectively displacing authorship in several important regards. They can be employed to displace authorial will, composition, and artistry. Computation is attractive to us because it reaches beyond architecture to the sciences, communication, and other technological spheres. It lends architecture greater relevance.

But more attractive still is the way in which the displacement of authorship aligns architecture with avant-garde art. The renunciation or disavowal of authorship was among the most important projects of twentieth-century art. Take two of the most salient examples, Dada and Pop Art, both of which aestheticized the products of the processes of commodification. The Dada readymade called attention to the power of the museum to designate what deserves to be art. Just putting it there with the signature, it becomes art. And in this case, of course, it becomes a canonic work.

Yet for all of this, computational modeling of form has generated mostly cladding and facades—which, like past modes of cladding, are destined to be the most supplementary parts of buildings, and more often than not have little impact on the structural frame and the functional spaces of buildings. That is, they have little profound impact on the social institutional agency of architecture.

continued on next page>>

Actually the cladding-versus-structure divide is but one manifestation of a far more profound earlier form of authorship displacement, which was wrought by urbanization—what I will call vertical succession. Vertical succession, unartistically considered, is the nonhierarchical piling of discrete horizontal slabs of space, a pervasive organizational constituent of architecture that began in the late nineteenth century, with the arrival of the elevator, steel, and reinforced concrete construction. "The Frame," as Colin Rowe aptly called it.

Whereas horizontally, buildings are arranged in discrete units strung together, block after block, building after building, spaces piled vertically almost always produce an individual building. Thus while the horizontal series is one of the most pervasive forms of urbanization, the vertical series is decidedly architectural. True, cities are often layered, but they rarely exhibit the characteristics of vertical succession, as defined by spatial stacking. Cities, more often than not, do not pile up.

Vertical succession makes another major schism, the separation of interior and exterior architectural composition. It makes this become more emphatic than it ever was before. Thus for all the spatial and social ambitions of modern architecture, the schisms of succession end up relegating the architect's role to that of designing surfaces or spaces of shallow relief more than anything else.

Ultimately succession, of both the horizontal urban and the vertical architectural kind, are fundamentally discordant with architecture. For a building is, finally, a discrete object. They aggregate, they can be composite programs, but almost always a building is a building. The problem of succession is the irreconcilability of the oneness with the many. The one is form, bound and delimited, at least in aspiration at some point. The many is formlessness, unbound, unauthored as a totality, the sprawl, the field of one stories. Or it can be authored, but only in fragments, the accumulation of which is eventually unauthored.

The argument that I would like to make is that architecture must re-author the disintegration rather than accept the given terms of succession. It must re-author the one-thing-after-another-ness of vertical succession, and the way that disintegrates architecture. It must contend with the way the discrete building comes to terms with unauthored horizontal succession.

Preston Scott Cohen is the Gerald M. McCue Professor of Architecture and the former Chair of the Department of Architecture at the Harvard Graduate School of Design. He is the founder and principal of Preston Scott Cohen, Inc.

Successive Chairs:
Gerald M. McCue, Harry Cobb, Rafael Moneo, Mack Scogin, Jorge Silvetti, Toshiko Mori & Preston Scott Cohen

STUDIO
STUDIO

The architectural treatise and manifesto have disappeared. Today, we have architectural theory and criticism of architecture. But is it possible to call any contemporary building theoretical?

Preston Scott Cohen

The goal of this studio is to write studio briefs that elicit the production and interpretation of theoretically cogent exemplars of architecture. The Studio Studio is conducted as a pedagogical experiment, the results of which are the invention of studio pedagogy and buildings that demonstrate the motivating hypotheses. The pedagogy to be created addresses several theoretical conundrums of contemporary architecture. These are established along the contours of broad themes—spatial, programmatic, material, structural, technological—defined in dialectical terms, such as transparency versus concealment, discretion versus licentiousness, composed versus unauthored, and so on.

Preselected projects and buildings that embody these concepts are used as the basis to conceive of studio project briefs. What could make these buildings come about in the way that we are interpreting them to embody productive paradoxes? How can we define the preconditions that would lead to the design of these buildings? The briefs are defined by specific devices and rules, written and drawn in diagrams, plans, sections, and in models and scripts. These cause the students to give form to extraordinary mental and physical spatial constructs. During the first two-thirds of the semester, each student writes a brief and completes a project based on a brief written by another student. The writers of briefs serve as critics. In the final weeks of the semester, each student produces a conceptual design of an exemplar, a building that embodies the thesis of one or more of the briefs, which could very well have served as an illustration for introducing the pedagogy.

"There is a possibility that architecture can curate, can call attention, can turn things on and off. It calls into question—what is mediation, and what is technology? There are many themes that run through our work, but the most important one is that we are tired of inheriting program."

Elizabeth Diller
Discussions in Architecture
January 31, 2013

The Multimedia Language of Models

Pierre Bélanger

We shape our tools, and thereafter, our tools shape us.
—Marshall McLuhan, Understanding Media

When Marshall McLuhan observed that technology and its environment are "extensions of ourselves," the twentieth-century communications theorist recognized the emergence of an information age whose growing electronic aspect was already shaping contemporary society. In considering the passage from mechanization to automation, McLuhan presaged the digital era by noting processes of change that rethought technology as both carrier and content of information—as media and model that operated simultaneously as interface and influence on contemporary society.

Today the models of thought that underlie the tools and technologies we use remain fundamentally overlooked. From the measures and materials to the techniques and technologies upon which we conceive ideas, there is a growing imperative to reconsider the models that precondition our motivations in design.

While we spend much of our time making models and scaling realities in the worlds of design and engineering at large, little attention is given to the genesis of modeling—the process of generating abstract, conceptual, graphic, mathematic, or material representations.[1] What are models used for? Why do we make them? What are they based on? How are they conditioned? Who else builds models? As measures of our own methodologies, the model is a heuristic medium, an analogous measure, and a collaborative, cognitive medium of communication.

Model as Media, Model as Medium

We often consider models as graphic artifacts and visual displays, expressed through materials (static, live, temporal), their fabrication methods (manual, mechanical, digital), and their physical environments (from site-specific exhibitions to virtual environments). As media, they also act as two-way mirrors. As projections, models reflect current conditions. Like maps, models not only construct realities but also operate as lenses through which we see: they image existing conditions, and in turn, condition our image of them.[2] As screens, they process and filter perception, as much as they provide views and open horizons that shape alternative futures.

Beyond the postmodern, object-oriented discourse associated with architectural representation and the hegemony of drawings (such as Farshid Moussavi's *The Function of Ornament* and Peter Eisenman's "Post-Functionalism"), a methodological discourse on models is remarkably absent from discussion and debate in design schools today, yet holds remarkable potential (see Sanford Kwinter's "The Genealogy of Models" or Klaus Herdeg *The Decorated Diagram*) to bring together digital pedagogies, material practices, fabrication labs, field work, and work environments as the design diagrams we inhabit, and the immersive research that envelops us.

Analogical, figural, and literal, models are the elemental media (means of communication) and visceral, material medium (agents of action) that precondition and most often preload processes of visual representation, and are intrinsically charged with meaning and measure. Yet at their irreducible core, the most integrative aspect of models is their capacity to transcend and conflate the languages, notions, concepts, challenges, and complexities of diverse disciplines and schools of thought from a vast array of knowledge.

As measures of our own methodologies, the model is a heuristic medium, an analogous measure, and a collaborative, cognitive medium of communication.

Models to Maps

As imaging instruments, models are tools of representation as much as they are techniques of communication that express different intentions. Yet for the most part, we use them for their literal and more simulative character, as if the message is more important than the medium. Instead the performative, interpretive, and even subliminal potential of models implies a reflection of process or pattern—an effect or force, which is commonly implied in the sciences, with modeling as the bridge between measuring and testing. In design, this reflexive methodology requires consistent leaping between the quantitative, the qualitative, and the temporal performed through mapping. As systematic and nonsystematic descriptions of spatial patterns, the mediated process of mapping shares important characteristics with the process of scientific modeling, which is inherently material, visual, mathematical, and computational. If maps are models, then they can also be conceived as theories.

In the context of positivistic overtones of quantitative modeling from the sciences, the discourse on models—the bones of design and research—also present fundamental challenges. Beyond the visualization of known or idealized conditions, models also present the possibility, in the Popperian sense, for representing failure: tests, trials, experiments, imperfections, biases, reverse scenarios, reverse engineering, reverse-innovations, deformations, degeneration, degradations, downgrades, counter-construction, and counter-systems—where risks and vulnerabilities are exposed, and creative accidents become a co-purpose and reoccurring practice.[3]

Time as Model and Measure

If the noise of reverse innovation is the new sound, then the design of time is the new movement. While scale models often present the complexities of representing physical environments through physical scale and strata, diagrammatic models can respond to different dimensions of time. In the well-established tradition of timelines and pattern sequences, one of the most important challenges in time models is the perception of digital processes and workflows as analogous time machines. The techniques that we use to conceptualize, fabricate, and test models are capable of advancing, accelerating, interrupting, or arresting time. Different machines are synonymous with soft applications and live processes, capable of exploring temporary morphologies and provisional configurations through subtractive and additive parameters. Time-scale modeling establishes a new base, a new platform for rediscovering media associated with change and movement.

More than a mere presentation or quantification of existing conditions, the models of maps represent a flatbed of potential scenarios and spatial possibilities.

They are "operational graphics" that, in lieu of forecasts and predictions, explore simultaneous futures and call into question the past models that we are constantly repackaging with new media, instead of generating new content.[4]

Form and Fluidity

Ironically, in the production of models, we speak of form but very little of flow. We speak of formative mechanisms but very rarely about deformative processes or agents of acceleration.[5] We speak of the future but fail to survey present conditions or current catastrophe in great detail. Ecologies of risk—environmental, fiscal, societal— are often unrepresented or unmodeled, and therefore unseen and marginalized.

In the same way that function determined form in the engineering ideology that guided most architecture and planning schools of the twentieth century, fluid ideology yields an entirely new mandate for the deployment of different models and alternative design agency.[6] If form follows flow, then the representation of relations, exchanges, interactions, engagements, contacts, transitions, temporalities, synergies, and reciprocities are the new soluble agents. Fluid as form becomes both a spatial and a social imperative for any pedagogical practice and live material endeavor.[7] In this interactive environment, fluidities take precedence and new questions are revealed: in an age confronted by the failures of Fordist models of accumulation, do we design for fluid models of exchange? How do we accommodate the vast fluctuations across models of production and formats of consumption? How do we adopt models of indeterminacy? How do we simulate live biotic processes and metabolic flows? How is urban life, a conflation of multiple flows, supported?

Tools, Toys, Techniques

Designers, by and large, fail to place these occupational hazards and real risks into the contexts of their work, or into the models of their practices. How can we speak of performative representation and evaluative language that invites other disciplines across the sciences and the humanities? Instead, designers offer levels of representational specificity and polished imaging often so complex and so specialized that it lies beyond easy comprehension.

Heuristically, the use of toy models in science lends a practical understanding of engaging the use of models beyond mere simulation with more strategic, simplified, interpretive devices. Toy models offer open-ended language to communicate and build interaction, an interface for rapid research, interactive innovation, and expedient decision making in complex conditions—conditions that are often emergent and indeterminate. Using these "base models" for core learning is a promising method to borrow as we move across a paradoxical age with disintegrating precision and pervasive forecasting, whose need for increased flexibility ironically grows greater and greater.

Design and Designation

If design is about persuasion, then modeling is about subliminal influence. The strategic process of designation (characterizing the complexities, identifying the programmatic questions, proposing research methodologies, identifying relevant precedents) is therefore a methodological process—a model of augmented understanding, as important as the technical work of design. Helping other fields to determine parameters and approaches toward the realization of their ambitions is as important, if not more so, as generating them themselves.

It is in the making of these prime models and indivisible concepts that designers will find relevance of their creative potential, through their ongoing outreach with the public and the public engagement of institutions. This fluid, urban interactivity acknowledges design as continuous planning and interactive engineering.

> We speak of the future but fail to survey present conditions or current catastrophe in great detail. Ecologies of risk—environmental, fiscal, societal—are often unrepresented or unmodeled, and therefore unseen and marginalized.

From Language to Landscape

If McLuhan's "the medium is the message" was the motto of the second half of the twentieth century, then models are our new means and landscape is our language. As extensions of our minds and means, the inventory of diagrams, drawings, profiles, prototypes, bedforms, and platforms of pre-design processes are the forces and effects in shaping perception and understanding.[8] Therefore if models are our language, then the environments in which they are produced are intrinsically the new learning landscape.[9]

Whether they come in the form in learning models (interactive or hierarchical), quantitative models (measures, performances, or tests), or representational models (flow-based or scale-based), the pedagogical space of these models in which we absorb and process information is as important as the content of the information itself.[10] How, then, can pedagogical space contribute to this new potential, rather than hinder it?

The greatest promise lies within relational spatial models, as we witness an intensifying imperative for interactive learning and collaborative projection. It is perhaps in this light that the current undergraduate and postgraduate schools of design—the open-space plans for project research, iterative spaces for failures and experiments, and interactive immersion through open visual access—presents itself less as a vanguard model of learning and much more as an experimental-scale model for integrating the disciplines across multiple institutions, through the transparency of open and continuous communication as well as through the visible engagement of the public.

These models open a greater discussion on the spaces and sites of learning where greater pedagogical explorations and reciprocities can take place—between studio and classroom, theories and applications, student and instructor, papers and models, screens and maps, evaluation and exchanges, individuals and institutions, and so on—and where internal pedagogies and internal space planning can be combined with external engagements with urban economies, regional explorations, and transnational travel.[11]

If learning is a landscape and education is about exchange, then studios are the new laboratories.

Pedagogical Proving Grounds

Since "environments are invisible" and "their ground rules, pervasive structure, and overall patterns elude easy perception," the formation of new models goes hand-in-hand with new pedagogical spaces and exploratory environments.[12] By flattening the taxonomy of learning that has structured the humanities and the sciences since the formalization of learning in 1956 by Bloom's Taxonomy, the age of studios themselves—open, interactive, iterative environments where design-based research and research-based design not only occurs but is incubated. If learning is a landscape and education is about exchange, then studios are the new laboratories.

One can argue that the future distribution of programs, gradual deprofessionalization of disciplines, and the deinstitutionalization of administration will yield an unprecedented open space—*un plan libre académique*—to ask the small and big questions and to develop micro-projects and macro-initiatives through inferences, educated guesses, operative generalizations, and precise approximations in order to actualize the abductive logic that design offers.[13]

The battleground—that is, the intellectual battleground between institutional structures—will take place in the studio, the design incubator, the counter laboratory, for the next generation of the School of Design to be seen as the new school of urbanism.[14]

As it becomes popularized and emulated, the greatest influence for this transdisciplinary model to accrue lies in its ability to respond to important shifts in allied disciplines and fields: from the spatialization of the social sciences to the urbanization of the natural sciences, to the socialization of the applied sciences. As the interactive studio becomes the new classroom and an incubator of innovation, the battleground of new collaborations will continue to attract large bodies of students who come from varied backgrounds and are often self-taught from their own experiences.[15] It is in this digital environment and age of live information and process automation that the multimedia landscape of large institutions will express urban engagement and sociopolitical strategy.[16]

To bring this future into focus, tools that are currently marginalized from this learning environment by bureaucratic centralization or technocratic isolation will have to weaken to the force of distributed digital knowledge, where new interactive pedagogies and learning diversities can be created. If we have allowed the individual constitutions and professional disciplines to influence the space of the School in the past century, perhaps we should let the tools, techniques, and technologies—the multimedia landscape—shape us. Perhaps by weakening administrative superstructures and letting go of the institutional verticalities that centralize and homogenize learning spaces, we can make room for collaborations and cultivate a new learning landscape across emerging and alternative pedagogical latitudes for the next urban century.

This disruption of the floor plan of institutions will necessarily create workshops out of offices, kitchens out of classrooms, laboratories out of libraries, clubs out of cafeterias, and think tanks out of schools, where the workshopping of ideas will rely on a generation of new models and the unlearning of old ones, where the field becomes a proving ground for concepts and applications, in the open-learning system that is the new school of urbanism of the future.[17]

1 The Harvard Initiative for Learning and Teaching conference convened in the spring of 2013 to address the convergence of pedagogical practice, technological media, and learning environments. "In the name of progress," Marshall McLuhan would characterize, "our official culture is striving to force the new media to do the world of the old." See McLuhan and Quentin Fiore, *The Medium Is the Message: An Inventory of Effects* (New York: Bantam Books, 1967), 81.

2 James Corner, "The Agency of Mapping: Speculation, Critique and Invention," in Denis Cosgrove, ed., *Mappings* (London: Reaktion, 1999), 213–252.

3 See Karl Popper, *The Logic of Scientific Discovery* (New York: Routledge, 2002). Also see Henry Petroski, *To Engineer Is Human: The Role of Failure in Successful Design* (New York: Vintage, 1992).

4 See Jacques Bertin, *Sémiologie Graphique: Les Diagrammes, Les Réseaux, Les Cartes* (Paris: Gauthier-Villars, 1967).

5 See René Thom, *Towards A General Theory of Form and Morphogenesis*. Also see E.C. Zeeman, *Catastrophe Theory-Selected Papers 1972–77* (Reading, MA: Addison-Wesley, 1977), and D'Arcy Wentworth Thompson, *On Growth and Form* (Cambridge, UK: Cambridge University Press, 1917).

6 See Siegfried Giedion, *Space, Time and Architecture: The Growth of a New Tradition* (Cambridge, MA: Harvard University Press, 1967).

7 "One misunderstands the diagram when one conceives of it as a template rather than as a flow." See Sanford Kwinter, "The Genealogy of Models," *ANY* 23 (Fall 1998), 59.

8 "This is merely to say that the personal and social consequences of any medium—that is, of any extension of ourselves—result from the new scale that is introduced into our affairs by each extension of ourselves, or by any new technology." See Marshall McLuhan, *Understanding Media: The Extensions of Man* (New York: Signet, 1964), 23.

9 See Anne Whiston Spirn, *Language of Landscape* (New Haven, CT: Yale University Press, 1998).

10 See Benjamin Bloom, *Taxonomy of Educational Objectives: The Classification of Educational Goals* (New York: Longmans, Green, 1956).

11 See Burolandschaft, "Office Landscape" (1969).

12 See Marshall McLuhan and Quentin Fiore, *The Medium is the Massage: An Inventory of Effects* (Singapore: Hardwired, 1967), 84–85.

13 Unlike those in other disciplines or practices, designers are especially skilled and talented at jumping to conclusions, at formulating strategies, and at synthesizing complex working situations with partial and often incomplete information to communicate possibilities, directions, and outcomes.

14 See Bruno Latour, "Building Up Counter Laboratories," in *Science in Action: How to Follow Scientists and Engineers through Society* (Cambridge, MA: Harvard University Press, 1987), 79. Also see Peter Galison, "Three Laboratories" and (with Caroline A. Jones) "Factory, Laboratory, Studio: Dispersing Sites of Production," in *The Architecture of Science*, eds. Peter Galison and Emily Thompson (Cambridge, MA: MIT Press, 1999), 497.

15 Ivan Illich radically advocated for open-learning processes and experiential learning environments in lieu of administrative bureaucracies and quantitative procedures that the industrialization of knowledge by large institutions often privilege. Illich says, "Then the members of that [education] society, by making schooling compulsory, are schooled to believe that the self-taught individual is to be discriminated against; that learning and the growth of cognitive capacity, require a process of consumption of services presented in an industrial, a planned, a professional form; [...] that learning is a thing rather than an activity. A thing that can be amassed and measured, the possession of which is a measure of the productivity of the individual within the society." See "Ivan Illich,"trans. Marcelo Gajardo, *Prospects: The Quarterly Review of Comparative Education*, vol. XXIII, no. 3–4 (1993): 711–720.

16 This long-standing tradition of research and design is also expressed in the involvement of landscape architect Carl Steinitz at Harvard's Laboratory for Computer Spatial Graphics and his leadership in the formation of the Advanced Studies Program (Masters in Design Studies) at the Graduate School of Design in the 1980s.

17 Galison and Jones, "Factory, Laboratory, Studio" in *The Architecture of Science*.

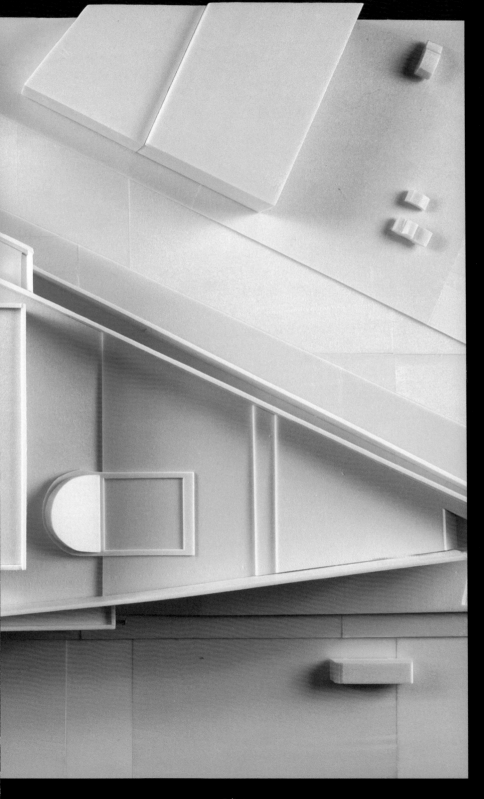

Structure
'What is architecture?' is answered by distinguishing architecture from non-architecture. This distinction requires that the historian define the relationship between the two, as well as give an internal structure to the aspects of architecture that explains how they hold together.

independent
Architecture and non-architecture are ontologically independent. This does not mean they are not related, but rather that architecture's existence as architecture is a fundamentally autonomous, organic whole.

dependent
Architecture and non-architecture are ontologically dependent. The relationship is dialectical in that architecture only exists as something tangled up with life.

Genesis
'Where does architecture come from?' is answered by distinguishing architecture from pre-architecture. This distinction requires the historian to conceptualize how architecture is created and what precedes this creation.

representational
Architecture emerges in the formation of signifiers. The pre-architectural is that which has not yet been given architectural significance, a base that architecture comes to represent (the relationship need not be understood as only a vulgar uni-directional flow of influence from pre-architectural to superstructural signifiers).

productive
Architecture produces the form of its own medium. It does not simply give visible form to pregiven structures, but further generates the territory within which it realizes itself. Pre-architecture is understood as first-nature or the not yet territorialized. Architecture generates ways of distinguishing inside and outside.

Form-image	**Contingency-image**
Architecture is a system of visible *styles or symbols that represent culture* (often a state or a people) but have independently substantial value. One of the earliest images of architectural history, architecture is treated as a fine art representative of a Zeitgeist.	Architecture is *a set of cultural relations and institutions that represent a particular base*, or that further act as both signifier and signified in a multiplicity of representational relations. The definition and interpretation of architecture and its history are always contextually dependent.
Hegel's account of architecture as symbolic; Wölfflin's classical-baroque binary; Wittkower's Renaissance forms	Banham's technological determinism; Tafuri's dialectic of architecture and the city; contemporary accounts of power
Space-image	**Experience-image**
Architecture is *the production of spatial typologies that define inside and outside*, and architecture's history is the movement from primitive to more developed modes of containment. This image establishes a continuity to architecture's history through the unified domain of space.	Architecture is *the production of the embodied relationship of life to its world*. Architecture's history cannot be recounted in terms of abstract, objective space or institutions but rather only in embodied, relational space. Architecture's history is a history of the production of place.
Schmarsow's spatial essentialism; Giedion's three-fold history of spatial types; Zevi's dialectic of spatial types	Worringer's psychological empathy; Riegl's Kunstwollen; Norberg-Schulz's phenomenological account of place

The Images of Architectural History
Brian Norwood, PhD candidate

Architectural history has, since the early stages of the architecture school, played an indispensible pedagogical role in the education of the architect. But historiographical reflection on architectural history remains underdeveloped—architectural history is still not sure of its position and purpose. Is architectural history a slice of the larger body of cultural history, or is it a field defined by a practice that needs it? What is the body of knowledge, objects, and practices that fall in architectural history's domain? Key in answering these questions is the image of history that architectural history uses to understand what falls within the limits of the story or stories of architecture's past. This image defines the body of architectural history with (a) a structure that answers "What is architecture?" and (b) an account of genesis that answers "Where does architecture come from?"

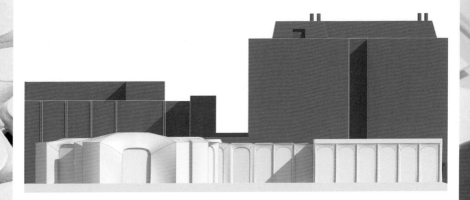

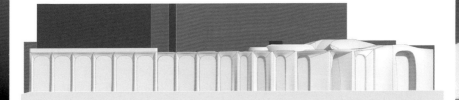

Unlike an ideal that is symmetrical, unified, and objective, the new model becomes irregular and particular. The logic and language of an original state is contained within the DNA of the new model, yet it distinguishes itself to become a new architectural typology. The binding and oneness that is usually characteristic of an ideal model begins to come apart, as it transforms itself into multiplicitous and cellularized parts.

<< Rachel Dao

UNFINISHED WORK

In our previous studio, students addressed the question of knowledge space and how such spaces facilitate the generation and dissemination of information. The interest of the studio was in the approach to design, and how surprise, repetition, proliferation, and systems thinking can open up new opportunities and generate new design outcomes.

Ben van Berkel
Imola Berczi

Our current research agenda broadens this as we look at the relationship between architecture and emerging modes of production. Drawing from experiences in technology companies, professional service firms, communications agencies, and other practice-based organizations, Unfinished Work explores how changing ideas about work alter the demands and performance of space. Students select a new method of production (such as iterative development, rapid prototyping, co-creation, agile approaches, or design thinking) that is reshaping the work environment. Case studies look at how these models alter the ways in which people work, communicate, and solve problems. Tandem research explores the impact of emerged and emerging work models, and their concentration in "knowledge cities" such as Barcelona, Bangalore, and San Francisco. The end product is the visual representation of the production process as it applies to a singular building program and the design of a working environment that encompasses the principles, values, and attributes of the new method studied.

Since the arrival of a connected digital information age and with it, a plethora of productivity technology and mobile devices, the nature of work has been rapidly changing. In how and when we work and in what we produce, our jobs are different from those of the quintessential postindustrial office. The new productivity technologies pose special problems for architects and interior designers, whose designs often amount to outer shells whose insides must be dealt with in the future. This discussion brings together experts from architecture, psychology, technology, furniture, and industrial design to debate the future of workspace.

The Future of Workspace Conference
April 4, 2013

continued on next page >>

Innovation doesn't want a building, innovation demands infrastructure. The machines within the factory work continually, both day and night. Collectively they serve the factory; some producing, some upgrading, some maintaining the various aspects that the factory requires to continue to innovate. Individually they service the users, whom migrated in and out of the factory, and supply the thoughts. The interior spaces vary in scale and volume, though all specific to the scale of a particular mechanized unit production of innovation. Some spaces privilege the user, some the machines, some struggle to accommodate both, some simply do not care.

Jason Hoeft & Mark Rukamathu

"If we are witnessing a paradigmatic shift in how the workplace is viewed as an architectural space, we also need to think about the relationships within the content of work, the technologies that facilitate it, and the social landscape in which it is handled."

Nashid Nabian

Visual effects companies have been destabilized, moving from country to country as 'subsidy nomads'. This project proposes a stable infrastructure for the industry, providing flexibility for different sized companies and operation modes, in order to reduce the financial risk for visual effects companies to enter the European market, and relocate in Amsterdam.

Yaohua Wang

"The workspace should no longer be considered a fixed and closed container, but a node in a more complex network of places."

-Antoine Picon

121

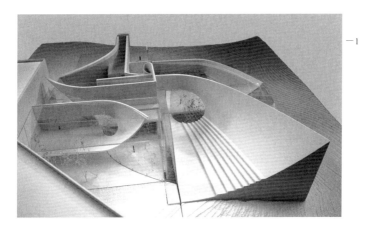

—1

|
3

2—

1 Iman Fayyad
2 Bennett Gale
3 Daniel Carlson

CORE II
ARCHITECTURE

The pedagogical agenda for Core II Architecture is to expand on the methodologies presented in the first semester such that students develop an increased understanding of the complex relationship between program, form, structure, context, and materiality. Core I Architecture employs specific constructs and instruments, which motivates the production of architectural form, while this studio seeks to expand on these techniques—making them more complex and demanding, yet paradoxically more open-ended. The preceding devices of motivation related to geometry, dimension, and transformation might be understood as heuristic placeholders, which now give way to criteria more commonly understood within the discipline: materiality, structure, site, and program.

Cameron Wu
Katy Barkan
Jeffry Burchard
John Hong
Mariana Ibañez
Elizabeth Whittaker

While continuing to develop techniques to define form and organization, students must now address the visceral effects of architecture—its qualitative attributes. If the most rigorous production of form produces undesirable qualities, then it is a failure. While the added consideration of variables such as materiality, structure, tactility, light, and acoustics allow for richer embodiments of space, it can also frustrate and make elusive its successful production

Disciplinary themes and dialectics recur in related exercises, and students work iteratively—potentially recycling methodologies, which reinforce or challenge tendencies of preceding solutions.

The organizational logic of the project addresses programmatic and climatic concerns specific to the building type in question. The ambition of the project is to maintain visual and formal continuity between adjacent spaces that are hermetically sealed from one another, in an effort to promote an integrated and mediated programmatic progression through varying climatic zones. The formal vocabulary of the right circular cones allows for the stitching of "normalized" vertical and horizontal planes while maintaining surface continuity. The intersection of the cones, along with their rotationally symmetric arrangement, allows for different greenhouses and laboratories to weave and interlock in section, resulting in the nesting of volumes.

Iman Fayyad

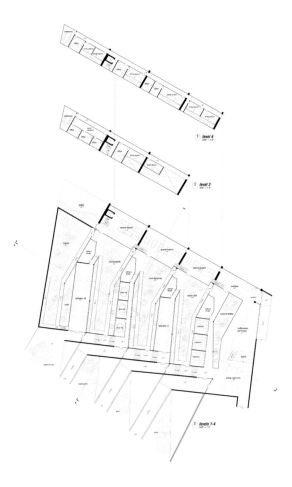

Bennett Gale

This project seeks to create an institutional landmark that is stitched into Wellesley College's historic campus—providing spaces for learning, gathering, and research, as well as a public display of the school's expansive collection of plant species. This proposal for a Botanical Research Center motivated by the competing circulation of the building's public and private areas; laboratory and classroom spaces are intertwined with meandering interior paths that traverse the building's terraced climate zones. Greenhouse design accounts for various climate zones' demands for variable heights, different amounts of solar exposure, as well as their relative accessibility to both research and service areas. Structural and programmatic organizations are inherently responsive to the project's overall site, whose extreme topography provides unique opportunities for subdividing interior spaces.

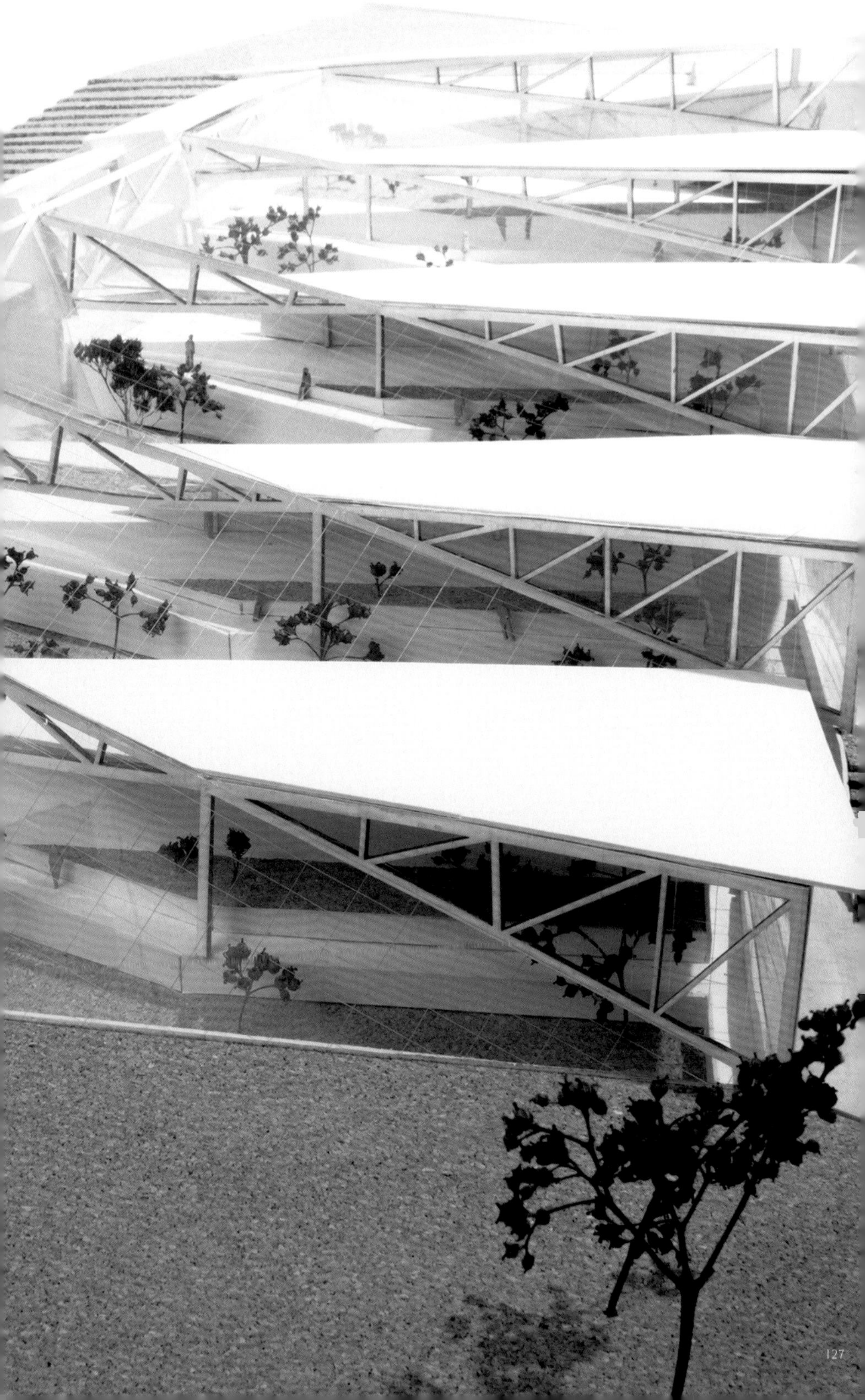

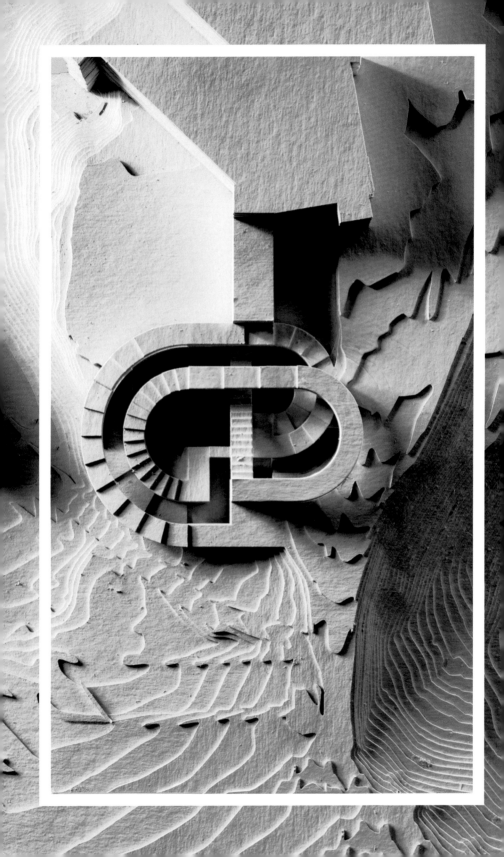

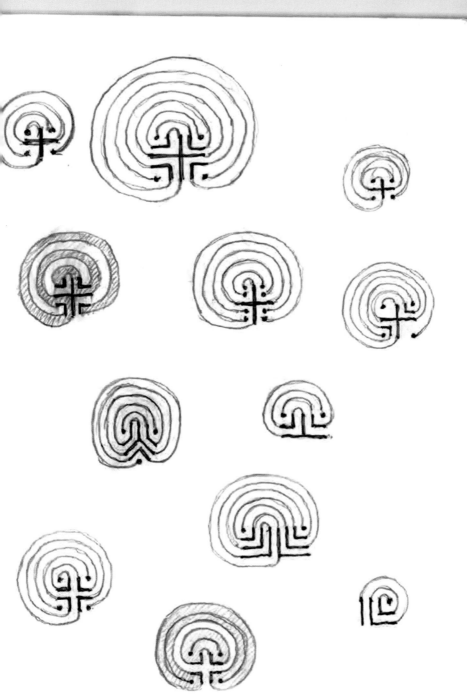

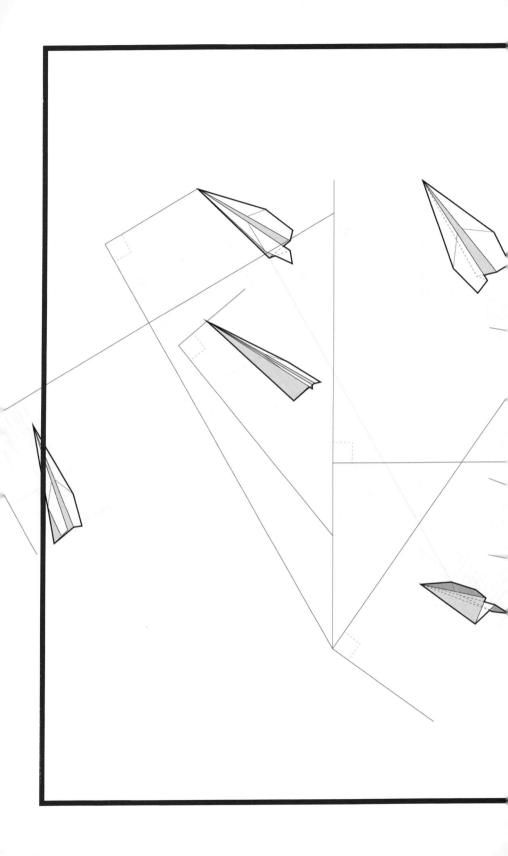

Projective Representation in Architecture (Cameron Wu) examines the history, theory and practice of parallel/orthographic and central/perspective projection. The objective is to provide the tools to imagine and represent with precision, dexterity, and virtuosity an expanding repertoire of three-dimensional architectural form. The representation of objects as we see them and their measured description, two tasks that are conventionally distinguished in architectural drawing, are shown to have been unwittingly, in many respects, mutually determined and transformed.

Nancy Nichols

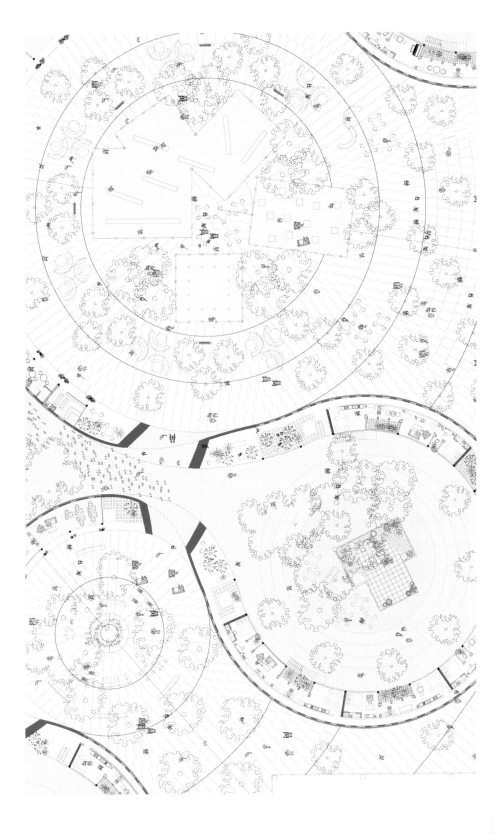

FRAMEWORKS
COMMON

Common Frameworks: Rethinking the Developmental City works typologically. It approaches the problem of the city through the investigation and redefinition of its persistent architectures—its dominant types. Any attempt to define type is an attempt to define what is typical; and what is most typical is common to all. As such, type lends itself as an effective heuristic device to locate commonalities. This search for what is common in architecture is not to locate formal or tectonic similitude, but to identify an idea that can be commonly held to invest architecture with a social and political

Christopher Lee
Simon Whittle

role. As the first studio of a three-year sponsored research program on China, the course begins with the city of Xiamen, followed by Macao and Shenyang. The premise of this investigation rests on rethinking the developmental city, defined as the city conceived and constructed through mega-plots and used primarily as a developmental tool, instigated primarily by speculative capital. The urbanization of these mega-plots results in the dissolution of the city as a legible artifact— bereft of a civic dimension and public sphere.

The conjecture of this studio is that the ability of these cities to be accommodative can be found in the very nature of the city as a common framework. Thus these cities offer the possibility to reconceive the developmental city as a space of cooperation and partnership—the idea of the city as a common space par excellence.

Urban Form: History & Theory (Eve Blau) is concerned with the economic, social, and political factors that shape urban processes and environments, and the efforts of individual actors, interventions, conceptual models, and practices to comprehend, gain control over, regulate, and reshape those processes and environments. The time span is from the end of the nineteenth to the beginning of the twenty-first century, focusing the dialogic relationship between urban planning and urban design and the technological, institutional, political, and cultural contexts in which they operate. The emphasis of this critical history is on strategy, agency, and actors; on formal aspiration, authored intervention, and the production, instrumentation, and transfer of a form of knowledge and set of practices that are urban and architectural. This knowledge also includes ways in which the city has been perceived, imagined, represented and projected into the future; the aspirations built and unbuilt of a range of urban actors, and the multiplicity of logics that underlie the forms themselves.

continued on page 135 >>

Aanya Chugh & Lik Hang Gu

excerpt from Groundwork: The Roots of the Radical
Art Terry

Long before the October Revolution swept the Bolsheviks into power, Russian culture had developed a notion of the *byt*, or "way of life" whose complexities and intricacies are lost in translation and do not exist in western thought as a single idea. According to Catherine Cooke, "The *byt* is the totality of inter-personal relationships, collective consciousness, spiritual values, and their forms of material expression or manifestation ."[1] This all-encompassing, self-contained, and self-consistent conception of "a way of life" served to codify the experience of the multitude into a unit open for modification and exchange. The image of a shared way of life contributed greatly to a collective identity that consisted of a multi-ethnic, religiously diverse, and socially stratified group of people without resorting to the overt nationalism so prevalent in Western European countries during the eighteenth and nineteenth centuries. This allowed for continual revision of the *byt* as well as the expectation for remaking the *byt* in the image of the times.

The idea of a linear strategy for organizing urban development became a central de-urbanist theme because of its affinity with the *byt* of the first five-year plan. Central to this early Soviet thought is the linear efficiency of mass production, of rail and highway transportation, and of electrical and communicative transmission. Thus the linear city is seen as the device with which it would be most directly possible to achieve one of Lenin's dictums regarding the overthrow of the bourgeoisie: the "new distribution of mankind" according to the ideals of communism. This redistribution of mankind ties the production line to the dissolution of both the urban-rural transect and the distinction between manufacturing and agriculture. It is also important to note the similarity between linear city proposals and the *mir*, or commune, prototype. The typical village consisted of "an agglomeration of log cabins lining both sides of a road running through it."[2]

The rich urban projects of the first five-year plan represent an interesting contradiction of terms from our contemporary perspective, but are rooted absolutely in the deep cultural traditions of the Russian vernacular. The urban projects, proposed by urban professionals, looked and felt like the product of the urban culture that gave rise to the technology around which they were centered, yet they were anti-urban in theme. Their goal was to slowly dissolve the city into nothing. New communist utopias had to reject the city not only as crowded and unhealthy, but as the product and space of bourgeoisie capitalism in order to fully realize the potential of communist workers. Dmitry Miliutin stated the position clearly: "The modern city is a product of a mercantile society and will die together with it."[3] The dissolution of the city into the country, the merging of industry and agriculture, and the liberation of the masses for intellectual pursuits can been seen as the logical, idealized conclusion of rural romanticism in the age of industrial production carried out by an intellectual class idealizing the communal vernacular of the peasant.

[1] Catherine Cooke, *Russian Avant-Garde Theories of Art, Architecture and the City* (London: Academy Editions, 1995).
[2] Richard Pipes, A *Concise History of the Russian Revolution* (New York: Knopf, 1995).
[3] N. A. Miliutin, *Sotsgorod; The Problem of Building Socialist Cities.* (Cambridge, MA: MIT Press, 1974).

Landscape is often subjugated to flows of capital and condemned to the interstitial space between buildings within the Chinese mega-plot. This leads to a perception of Xiamen as a "city in a park"—the implication of which is that landscape is a continuous field condition that proliferates endlessly. Through a framework of limits and juxtaposition, this project runs counter to predominating notions of capitalist development and seeks to reorient landscape in Xiamen toward the experience of the event.

Matt Scarlett & Jisoo Yang

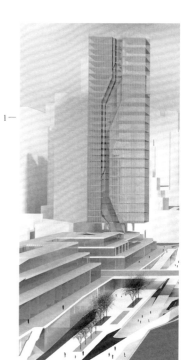

1 Mitch Crowder & Alessandro Boccacci
2 Victor Perez-Amado & Emmanuel Torres-Reyes
3 Noam Dvir & Christina Geros

CORE
URBAN DESIGN

While the "traditional" city at the turn of the twenty-first century has witnessed a period of reinvention, coalescing a plethora of strategies and scales to restructure its long-established quarters, the vast majority of the urbanized terrain continues to operate under the influence of watered-down postwar functionalist schemas. Given this framework, the moment is ripe to redefine the role of the urban project. How are we to approach this task? What should guide the designer conceiving new relationships among existing urban parts?

Felipe Correa
Gines Garrido
Robert Lane
Linda Pollak

with

Carlos Garciavelez
Robert Pietrusko
Renata Sentkiewicz

How can the designer act as a critical agent, in regard to the spatial particularities of these parts themselves and within the larger expanded field?

Core Urban Design introduces critical concepts, strategies, and technical skills associated with current thinking on urbanism, and speculates on the designer's role in analyzing and shaping complex metropolitan systems. Applied research and lectures will inform a series of interrelated exercises that construct diverse hypotheses about new formal and experiential urbanities, across multiple scales of intervention and development.

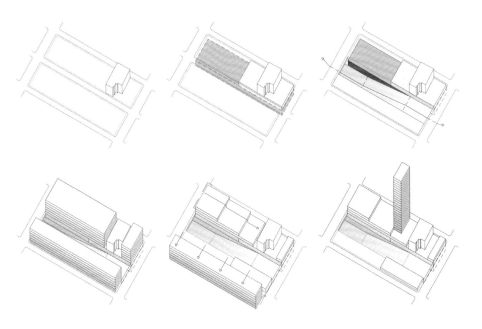

Using the campus as a programmatic device, the project investigates the modern-day role of large-scale singular interventions within an urban context and their relation and adaptability to the metropolitan grid of New York City. Through the rescaling of bus infrastructure, the campus design redefines the role of the urban block as a woven spine of integrated public and private function, both as built form and as open space, thus originating a new metropolitan entrance into Manhattan.

Mitch Crowder & Alessandro Boccacci

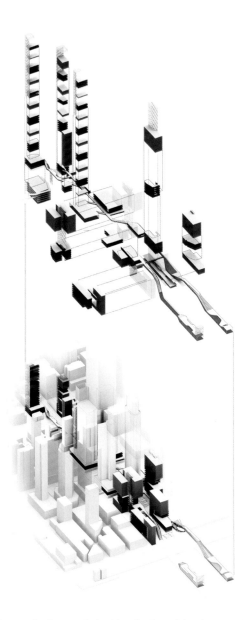

The geography that evolved around the Lincoln Tunnel in the seventy-five years since its opening reflects major economic shifts and radical transformations in transportation patterns in the New York metropolitan region. Our project aims to reimagine the role of manufacturing and distribution in the post-industrial city and to integrate public space in these infrastructural systems.

Noam Dvir & Christina Geros

PLATFORMS OF VISIBILITY
EXPLORING LEGIBILITY THROUGH THE CONTEMPORARY LATIN AMERICAN CITY

Emmet Truxes, MArch I

Advisor
Felipe Correa

Global networks and processes transcend immediate notions of site and adjacency, forcing the restructuring of relationships around new definitions of scale, boundary, and spatio-temporality. Current networked and mobile infrastructures have radically redefined not only communication, but also how we interrogate and see our surroundings. For users of these networks, the whole idea of urban

legibility and navigation has become immediate and much easier. But for those who study the contemporary city, these networks and processes only make the study of urban legibility that much more complex. By examining how architecture, as a primary participant in this stage, can serve as a legibility platform for the modern urban condition, this thesis re-establishes and advances the necessary toolkit for radical urban transformation in twenty-first century Latin America. The interrogation of the research data at multiple scales and mediums in Quito, Ecuador, serves as primary driver for an architectural proposal sited in that city.

The ambition for this thesis is to present a platform within the context of urban Latin America through which the dynamic contemporary urban condition, and by extension the dynamic architectural condition, can be put into focus.

Responding to contemporary urban patterns, ecological pressures, and decaying infrastructures, Theories of Landscape as Urbanism, Landscape as Infrastructure: Paradigms, Practices, Prospects (Pierre Bélanger) brings together a series of influential thinkers and researchers to discuss different methods, models, and measures of large-scale, long-range design for the twenty-first century. Foreshadowing the preeminence of ecology in cities and infrastructures, the motive of the course is to construct a clear, multivalent discourse on the field of landscape as it becomes the locus of intellectual, ecological, and economic change of significance globally.

continued on page 149 >>

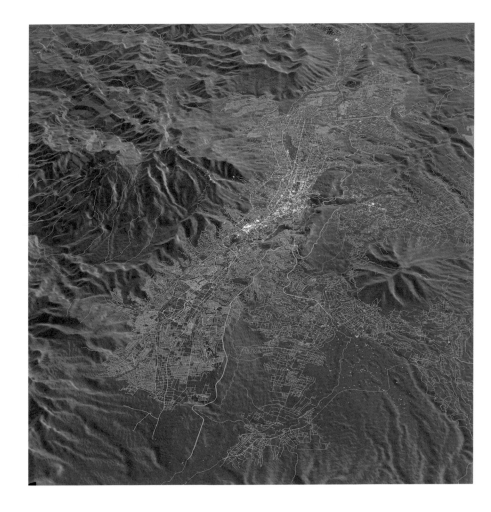

Mapping Imageability: Quito, Ecuador

The 'Least Mapped Place in the World': Urban Present & Projection in an Arctic Watershed
Anya Domlesky & Martin Pavlinić

MISSION 032154678A //
PETERS POND

DETECTING NITROGEN INFLUENCE
IN LIMINAL BODIES
STREAMING TO EMBAYMENTS
OF CAPE COD BAY

1

2

3

1 Manuel Colon, Wendy Wang & Phoebe White
2 Jing Guo, Kyle Trulen & Cara Walsh
3 Carolyn Deuschle, Gabriella Rodriguez & Ziyi Zhang

CORE III
LANDSCAPE ARCHITECTURE

As ecology becomes the new engineering, the synthetic and contemporary alignment of the disciplines of landscape architecture, civil engineering, and urban planning is producing new opportunities in design at new scales of influence and intervention. Predominant challenges facing urban regions today—including shifting climates, changing resource economies, and population movements—are redrawing the contours of conventional practices and the boundaries of sites as they form a more complex terrain of engagement with competing socio-economic and hydro-climatic forces. With a focus on multilayered ecological processes, Core III Landscape Architecture engages the process of design through a series of collaborative exercises leading to a large-scale design project with an outlay of prospective scenarios. Drawing from canonical case studies and strategic projects in landscape architecture, the studio is further enhanced by a robust, representational program that addresses a gamut of ecological flows at a range of scales through the multimedia language of maps and models. Contributing to the telescopic profiling of site as "system'" and the reformulation of program as "process," the studio establishes a platform for responding to a web of varied dynamics related to site contamination, biophysical systems, risks and vulnerabilities, military and rescue operations, urban infrastructures, economic geographies, and regional ecologies. Advancing the agency of ecology as dominant driver in design, the studio thus involves the formulation of "infrastructural ecologies" as a synthetic landscape of living systems that operate as urban infrastructures where the flexibility of biophysical processes can help shape, direct, and prepare for imminent, urban complexities of the twenty-first century.

Pierre Bélanger
Luis Callejas
Kelly Doran
Rosetta S. Elkin
Niall Kirkwood
Juan Manuel Rois

with
Philippe Coignet
Robert Pietrusko

Urban and Suburban Ecology (Richard T.T. Forman), begun in 1992, may be the first course of its title anywhere. In the early years, the class explored the scientific concepts based on a limited literature and attempted to delineate patterns and principles for an intellectual core of the subject. Over time the core of urban ecology coalesced, with students exploring urban areas—from a tiny spot to a megalopolis—focusing on soil, air (microclimate and pollutants), water systems and water bodies, plants and vegetation, and wildlife and biodiversity. These basic dimensions are considered from two major perspectives: the landscape ecology framework of spatial patterns, flows and movements, and changes over time; and types of urban areas. Applications to planning, conservation, design, management, and policy are mentioned; the course highlights concepts and principles usable worldwide.

continued on page 155 >>

151

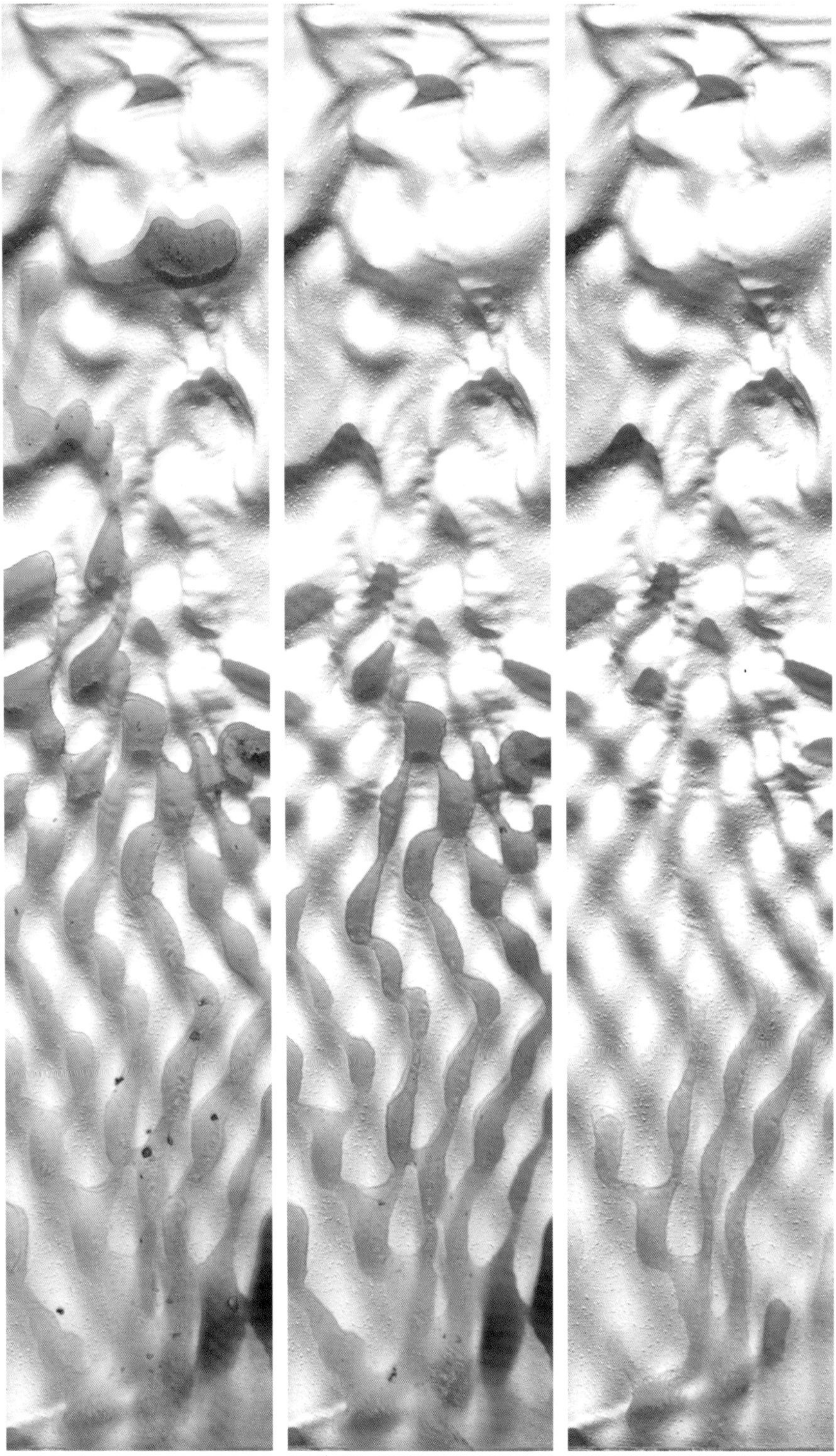

MISSION NP1240XA //
WELLFLEET NATIONAL SEASHORE

SANDPLAIN HABITAT MONITORING +
BOBOLINK MIGRATORY PATTERN REGISTER

MISSION 88B3564A //
PINQUICKSET COVE

EXAMINING SPONTANEOUS WETLAND
PLANT SPECIES + THE CREATION OF
NEW HABITAT TYPOLOGIES IN
ABANDONED CRANBERRY BOGS

MISSION 035670A //
COTUIT INLET

CRUSTACEAN HABITAT MONITORING +
ALGAL BLOOM RATE DETECTION
IN TIDAL DEAD ZONES

MISSION 032154678A //
PETERS POND

DETECTING NITROGEN INFLUENCE
IN LIMINAL BODIES
STREAMING TO EMBAYMENTS
OF CAPE COD BAY

MISSION 03567D
SIPPEWISSETT M

MONITORING SAL
BETWEEN HARBOR
THE BLACK BEACH

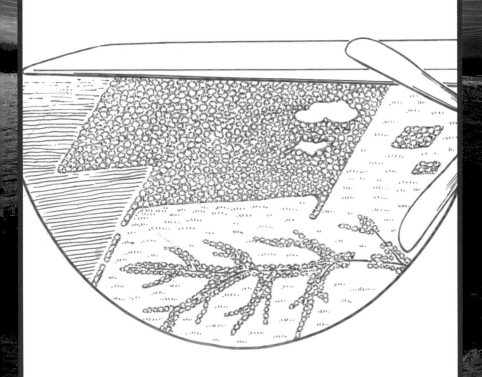

" indicating mosaics and the patch-corridor-matrix model.
Looking only at pattern, "landscape detectives" gain extensive
information about the ecology of a landscape. Wind is from the
left in this cool Russian area, which shows patterns typical of
landscapes worldwide. "

excerpt from <u>Land Mosaics</u> (1995)
reprinted with permission from Cambridge University Press

The geographic complexity of the Massachusetts Military Reservation insists upon a careful examination of various types of nutrient flows, from the atmospheric to the hydrogeologic. Necessitated by the broader idiosyncrasies of Cape Cod itself—registered through various ecological, economic, and civil flows—this project strives to investigate these dynamics through the horizontal axis, while exploring cross-relationships from the altitudinal to the bathymetric. The unique condition of the cape as a place defined by its economic viability and ecological vulnerability registers the pressures of its vital resources.

- Jing Guo, Kyle Trulen & Cara Walsh

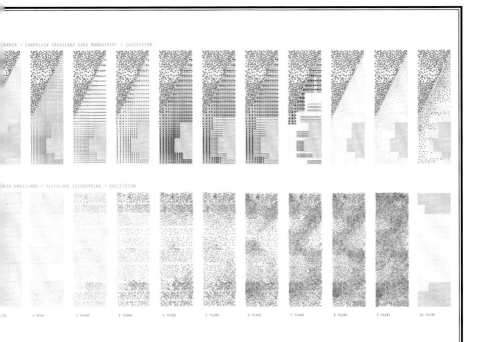

ARREN + SANDPLAIN GRASSLAND EDGE MANAGEMENT + SUCCESSION

IN GRASSLAND + HEATHLAND SEEDBOMBING + SUCCESSION

| 0 | 1 YEAR | 2 YEARS | 3 YEARS | 4 YEARS | 5 YEARS | 6 YEARS | 7 YEARS | 8 YEARS | 9 YEARS | 10 YEARS |

Anticipating the decommissioning of the Massachusetts Military Reservation and a growing need to understand and embrace the role of conservation within military perimeters, this project sets up an operative platform for the U.S. Army National Guard and the Massachusetts Department of Environmental Protection to ecologically service the region. A mosaic within a large-scale patch, the project seeks to transform the Massachusetts Military Reservation through cycles of selective arrested succession and the promotion of seed dispersal to create a network of diverse and evolving habitats as an innovative mode of conservation: conservation through adaptation. Fieldcraft, a military term referring to the codified reading of the landscape for survival, is adopted as a framework for encoding and deciphering micro- and macro-ecological processes within the designed landscape, as a means to extract the most ecological value by promoting biodiversity from large, open spaces. Instead of approaching conservation with the aim of preserving a static definition of the landscape, the project aims to exploit on-site unexploded ordinance detonation and circulatory flows, wind, hydrology, bird migration, transportation networks, and human movement, to make conservation an active agent in changing the land, by recovering and progressing past and present conditions. Working primarily with flows and processes that are active agents in seed dispersal, the understanding of vegetation—native and non-native—is used as a means to nurture flexible and resilient landscapes, both locally and regionally.

Carolyn Deuschle, Gabriella Rodriguez & Ziyi Zhang >>

Exploring contemporary methods and emerging techniques, Indexing Topographies (Pierre Bélanger, Phillippe Coignet) introduces basic methods of topographic representation through terrain modeling and surface manipulation while advancing the overall discourse on the agency of topography in design. As a subtractive process, CNC technology is thus analogous to the processes and practice inherent to landscape architecture.

continued on next page >>

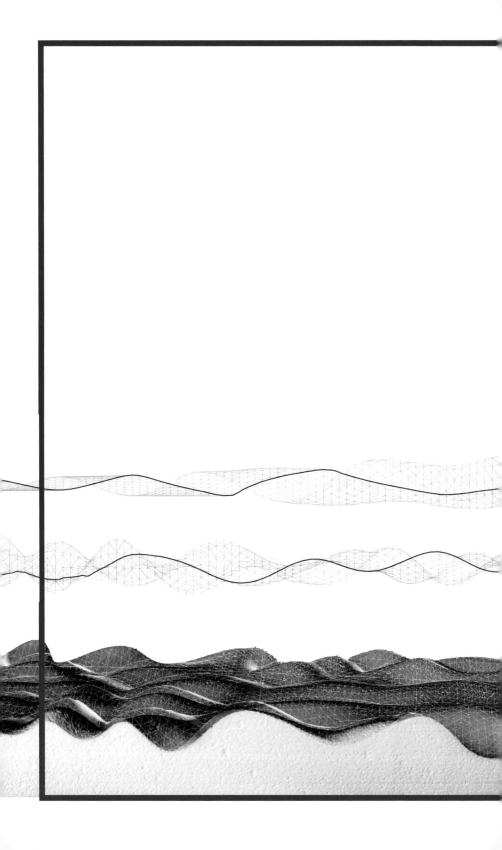

<< Milling equipment works like a time-machine: accelerating the processes of removal, deposition, and erosion, where material is removed from an existing, uniform block as prototypical samples of larger systems and larger scales. This process is similar to the way that the ground is modified and shaped: earth is subtracted, added, or displaced. Surface topography underlies the design and performance of urban land-scapes. If we consider topography as a membrane that responds to various parameters, then we can imagine and deploy a new set of relationships and effects between indexes, gradients, and tools that inform several parameters. As a registration of ecological processes and urban functions, topographic design is thus a method to encode surfaces with parameters and processes that underlie landscape architecture: elevations, water levels, fluctuations, material porosities, hydrological flows, properties, constituencies, mobilities, utilities, and economies. Each of them act on the ground, and in turn, they react upon it. Ranging from the manipulation of the ground and the modeling of large earthworks to the management of hydrological flow and conditioning of micro-climates, topographic design is an extensive and wide ranging practice, integral to the infrastruc-ture of urban sites. Both as factor and force-generator of hydrological and geological systems, topography is often a subtle dimension of urban environments due to its large scale, extensive horizontality, and multi-varied performance. Consequently, its design is best expressed through the patterns, materials, levels, transitions of different materials and the degrees of ground occupations, over time.

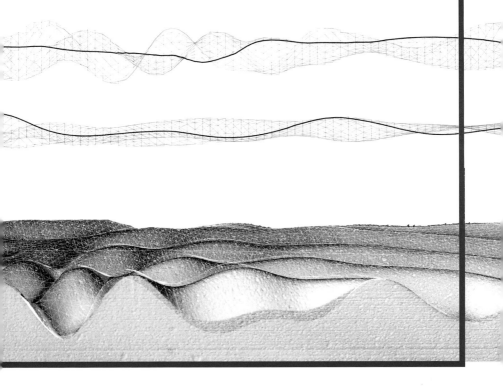

THE RURAL DESIGN ALMANAC

Michael Luegering, MLA I

Advisor
Rosetta S. Elkin

Grasses, legumes, and forbs stitch together in formation of pastureland; a cross-stitch of ideas manifesting themselves through a mixture of devotion and ecology. The history of these grasslands extends beyond the categories of rangeland and pastureland into grazing land and grazing park. Their formation is chronicled by the dialogue between rural devotion and federal policy. These measures of conservation and struggle come home to roost most strongly in the eastern and southern pastureland, underlain with rich soils fed by karst formations and "improved" by a pastoral tradition of husbandry, where 200 years of devotion have resulted in a naturalized landscape.

From the global speculation of their value as vacation destinations and second home sites to the playgrounds for the next class of barons to the impending drought cycles that will register their karst hilltops grass-less—the scale of operations is changing in a way that has not changed before. It is no longer the simple scaling up of grass farming but rather the phasing out of a rural pasture-based lifestyle.

Offering an alternative relationship to the land, this thesis employs the basic elements of pasture creation, albeit in alternative configurations. Further, the framework of an almanac provides options for autonomy and the next cycle of devotion to the idea of pasture.

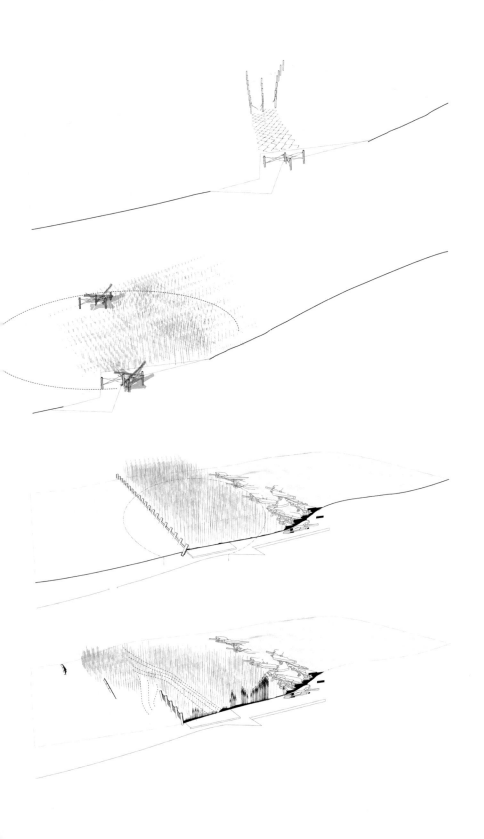

An excerpt from an interview with Farmer Alfred Nuckols III

ML: Headin' back to grass for a minute. Any other primary uses you have to import?

AN: Grass bedding. Thoroughbreds need to eat constantly. We have to bed down high quality edibles, and don't have the land to graze and produce what we need.

ML: With the increase in drought over the last ten years, how ya'll holdin' up?

AN: We try and get access to spring fed ponds if we can. We try and stretch a hose if we clear it with other owners. Free roaming foraging is the best way to grow stock—everything else is less desirable. Otherwise we buy pellets and outside hay. The feed costs are high enough to run you out of business. Pellets don't cut it, and horse growth is poor. Poor horse growth leads to bad returns at the sales. Ground hardness is a major issue—paying a ferrier and a vet to look at hooves and leg bones given the thoroughbred as a breed is a real problem.

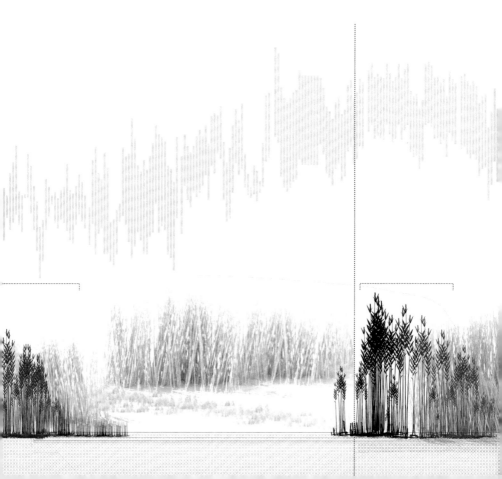

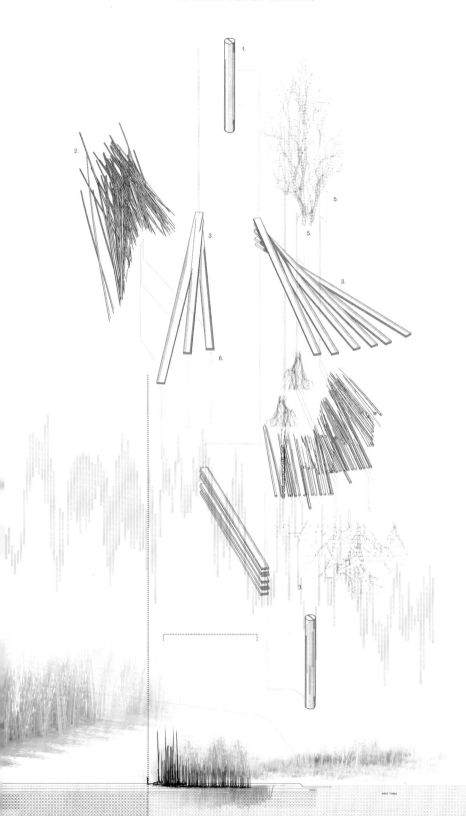

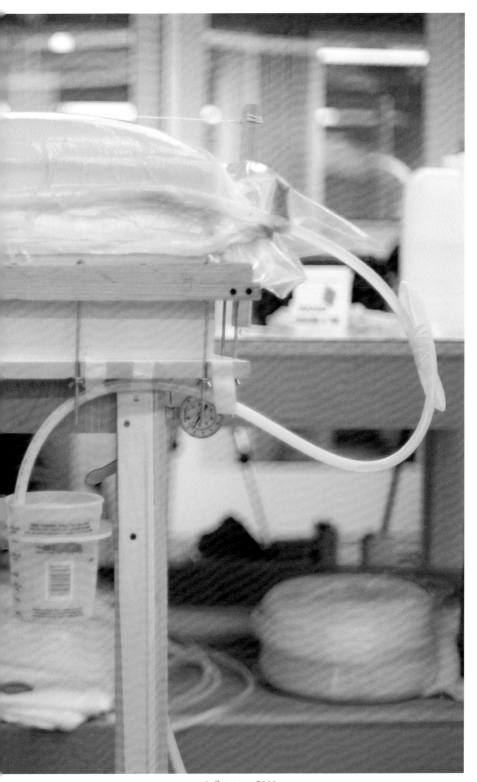

Inflatatron 5000
Kurt Fischer, Alexander Jacobson, Will Lambeth, Alfredo Pimental & Mark Rukamathu

FUN
PALACE

Students investigate the concept of fun and leisure in contemporary society and develop a "Fun Theory" as a basis for the design of their own "Fun Palace II." Students develop design strategies and goals based on this theory, developing a program and function, reasoning as a group or individually, and designing a project on one, two, or all three sites given. Projects will be located in Abu Dhabi, Bangkok, and Moscow, and students define their own locations within these cities.

Thomas Leeser

The educational goal is based on the understanding that students should be exposed to taking responsibility for complex decision-making processes in the development of architectural design, starting from taking an architectural (cultural) position, to siting, to programming and design. The reexamining and questioning of the status quo of all those decision and their "conventional" applications is a fundamental principle of this studio. The cultural understanding of leisure, fun, and entertainment will be examined as a starting point for a critique of our preconceived notions of social interaction and assumptions about one of the most important and possibly most misunderstood human needs, emotions, and experiences.

The horizon of Expanded Mechanisms/Empirical Materialisms (Andrew Witt) is bounded by the physics of materials themselves. The rules of material change—bending radii, elastic limits, viscosity, and so forth—are instrumental in machine design, becoming geometric laws and ultimately mechanical rules that shape elastic design ambitions. The machines operate on typical materials up to and perhaps exceeding their elastic limit to open the possibility for reconstitution in a transformed state. The specific tactile and textural qualities of the result are an integral part of the experiment.

continued on page 174 >>

Moojin Park

WX
Christian Ervin, Jose Luis Garcia del Castillo & Krista Palen

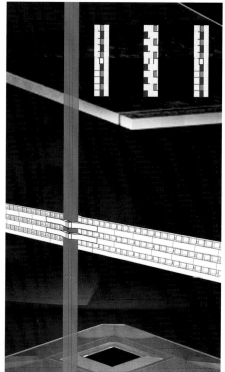

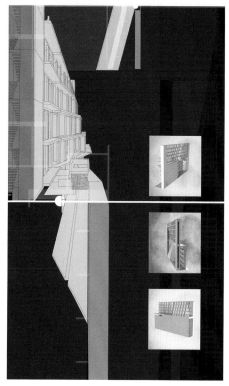

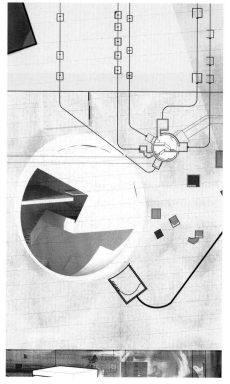

Through tapping into the surreal quality architecture can produce, the individual is at once enmeshed in the density of the city, and holds a privileged view point with respect to that city. This building is an egosphere in which the individual becomes outwardly focused. In exploring ways of using this particular social condition of aloneness to produce an extraordinary urban perspective, a surreal space of quiet, emptiness, and softness is produced in the middle of the frenetic, stimulating density of the urban.

<< Hal Wuertz

"It was really
exciting to realize
everyone's bored.
If you just do
something that
captures interest,
it's easier to do
something difficult."

Thomas Heatherwick
Open House Lecture
April 5, 2013

#DANCE
#HUMANEORIGINS
#CHEAPSHOES

What is architecture's role today in defining a society of the humane? Can the architecture discipline continue to sustain its unique ability to sponsor uncompromised difference in a world where the exceptional is redefined almost daily and the relationship between the singular and the collective is blurred of distinction in service to the integrative?

Mack Scogin

How can we discover when so much is so easily uncoverable? Can we now find comfort in simply reading between the lines? Can we relish never actually finding that word that's on the tip of our tongue? Can we dare to suspend our trust in science long enough to refine a belief in the power of personal intuition? Can we trust lateral interpretations to produce the strange but familiar that moves us beyond the rational? WHYCANTWEJUST-DANCE?? HUMANEORIGINSINNOCENTOB-SESSIONSANDCHEAPSHOES is like a gaggle of cavemen and cavewomen decorating themselves out of the cave.

"A pedagogical philosophy rises or falls on the merit of its ethical commitment to innovation and risk."

Sanford Kwinter
An excerpt from Instigations
continued on page 248 >>

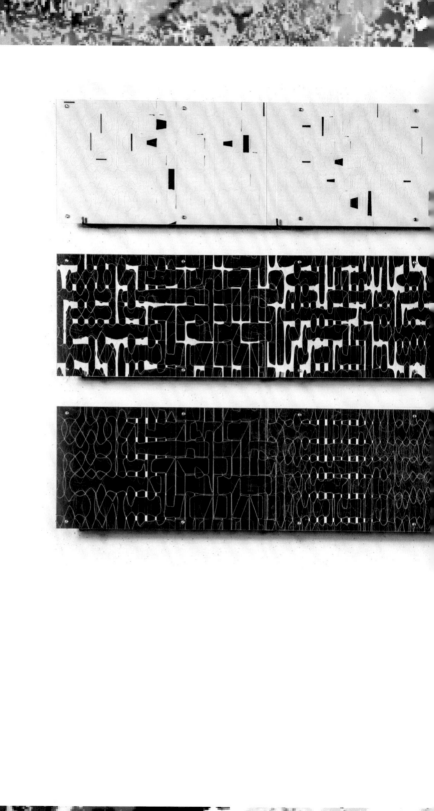

On Web-Based Learning: Lessons from the Rosetta Stone

Edward Eigen

Before there were test tubes there were trees;
before there were labs there were forests.

—Bruce R. Smith, The Key of Green: Passion and Perception
in Renaissance Culture (2009)

"The game ought to have been well and truly up," John Manning writes in *The Emblem* (2004), his study of those exquisitely compact and enigmatic bearers of ancient and modern meanings, "when one of Napoleon's soldiers turned up the Rosetta Stone during the Egyptian campaign."[1] In retrospect, this was to be expected, for the game—the exciting but unnerving work (or play) of interpreting complex visual and linguistic symbols—had been spawned on a "wrong-headed enthusiasm for hieroglyphic mysteries." Enter Antoine-Isaac Silvestre de Sacy, Johan David Åkerblad, Thomas Young, Jean-François Champollion and the magisterial campaign to decipher the stele's triscript decree in honor of Ptolemy V Epiphanes; exit the ghost of Horapollo Nilous, supposed Egyptian author of the *Hieroglyphica* (ca. 450–500), an exemplary work of syncretistic late-antique philosophy and erudition, a Greek manuscript of which was acquired in 1419 on the island of Andros by the scholar-traveller Christoforo Buondelmonti and brought to Florence where it was avidly studied by the humanists and Neo-Platonists.[2] But not just yet. The granodiorite stone turned up by the young *polytechnicien*, Lieutenant Pierre Bouchard, July 19, 1799, near the town of Rosetta (el-Rashid, in the Nile Delta), "exposed as vain centuries of erudite labor," Manning writes.[3] "By rights, the books that derived from so much misguided effort ought to have been swept away as mere cobwebs of learning, useless, erudite fantasies." Instead, the game began anew. "The realization of their fictive nature, their playfulness, has given a greater sense of freedom."[4]

The Rosetta Stone serves as an attractive pretext for the essay that follows. Its intended subject is the retrospective value of presently useless learning—the "cobwebs" of fantastical erudition. This historian, accustomed to stumbling over (his own) words as if they were obdurate blocks of half-buried meaning, is struck by the clarity of Manning's insight into the game of history itself. Once legibility was restored to hermetic emblems and hydrographical figures, the misguided lessons proffered by erudite scholars and pretended priests of ancient mysteries took on new value. In revisiting a question addressed with insistent frequency throughout the nineteenth century—namely, whether the roof beams and carpentry of medieval buildings were made of oak or chestnut—the present attempt is to observe the cob-webs of (questionably useful) learning as they gather in real time.

Do students of architecture and landscape architecture (I teach both their kind) need to study history? Is the embrace of such a need, like some form of moral duty, a prerequisite to greater inventive freedom? As befits the historian, I should and will respond to this broadly stated query by example and not by the philosopher's precept. The example chosen, spider's webs, or their alleged absence from oak roof beams (if those beams were in fact oak and not chestnut), serves to illustrate the special nature of "things that talk," to use Lorraine Daston's sterling phrase, or, in the words of Miguel Tamen, author of *Friends of Interpretable Objects*, those "hap-less lumps of matter" that become "important and meaningful, at least to those who feel compelled to talk about them."[5] What more can a history teacher do than gently compel students to talk more freely, to foster a certain kinship with unlikely objects of regard: things that lie dormant in a past still waiting to be invented.

Wyatt Papworth, architect, antiquary, and, briefly, Curator of Sir John Soane's Museum, considered it "more laughable than serious" that spiders might be "put forward as better authorities than ourselves in the settlement of what is oak or chestnut."[6] The potentially considerable epistemological value of laughter notwith-standing, the question remains, What do spiders know that we don't? Throughout the ensuing debate there was no discussion of the species of spider (from the large family of cobweb-spinning *Theridiidae*), though there was much consternation concerning the nature of authority *in se*. Papworth began his June 14, 1858, address to the Royal Institute of British Architects, "On the Assumed Use of Chestnut Tim-ber in the Carpentry of Old Buildings," by tracing the "confusion" to its probable origin in no less an authoritative source than John Evelyn's *Sylva, Or a Discourse of Forest-Trees, and the Propagation of Timber in His Majesties Dominions* (1664). The first publication to receive the imprimatur of the Royal Society of London for Improving of Natural Knowledge, the *Sylva* formed the corporation's response to the "Quæries" addressed to it by the Officers and Commissioners of the Navy "touching the Præserving of Tymber now growing and planting more in His Majesty's Dominions of England & Wales."[7] The "wooden edifice" that was Evelyn's *Sylva* was buttressed by the authority of the ancients while also serving as a bulwark against "servile submission of our noblest Faculties to their blind Traditions." In his *Natural History*, Evelyn writes, Pliny the Elder attests that the oak was held in foremost esteem by the Romans, citing the *corona civica*, a woven chaplet of oak leaves, the military decoration reserved for those who had saved another's life in battle. But it was Evelyn's direct testimony that caused so much difficulty with respect to the properties of various stocks of wood: "the use of the *Cheß-nut* (next the oak) one of the most sought after by the *Carpenter* and *Joyner*."[8] To John Claudius Loudon, in his *Arboretum et Fructicetum Britannicum; Or The Trees and Shrubs of Britain, Native and Foreign* (1838), it was evident that Evelyn "here falls into the common error . . . of confounding the chestnut with the oak."[9] To be in error was its own particular state of fallenness. The error was not, however, to be found in Evelyn's having read against the grain (of the wood), but was rather a interpretive misunderstanding re-communicated by his text. Through repetition it became a vulgar error.

The source of the difficult passage was William Fitzstephen's (*fl.* 1170) *Descriptio nobilissimae civitatis Londoniae*, according to disparate readings of which whole forests were caused either to flourish into or disappear from existence. In the concurrent French debate over oak and chestnut, the archaeologist Charles Lenormant observed that in his account of the additions to the abbey of Saint-Denis, the *Liber de rebus in administratione sua gestis*—the etymological roots of the word *liber*, referring to a book or the inward bark of a tree, are materially intertwined—abbé Suger indicated that its rafters were made of chestnut. What was remarkable, in Lenormant's estimation, was that the wood was taken from the ancient forest of Yvelines, where chestnuts no longer grew.[10] For there to be a forest, there must be (or once have been) trees.

"I had once a very large *Barn* neer the *City*," Evelyn personally attests in his discussion of chestnut, "fram'd intirely of this *Timber*: And certainly they grew not far off; probably in some *Woods* neer the *Town*."[11] The significance of Evelyn's statement depends upon a reading of Fitzstephen's topography of London. A retainer of Thomas Becket, Archbishop of Canterbury, Fitzstephen served as remembrancer in his chancery and sub-deacon at mass in his chapel. "I was witness of his passion at Canterbury," Fitzstephen writes in the preface to his *Vita Sancti Thomae*, where he carefully remarks, "many other things that are here written I saw with my eyes and heard with my ears; others I learned from the relations of those who knew about them."[12] The precociously Aquinian drawn distinction can be made to serve in judgment upon those who sought in his writing evidence of things past. "For in that description of *London*," Evelyn writes, "he speaks of a very noble and large *Forest* which grew on the Boreal part of it: *Proxime* (says he) *patet foresta igens, saltus nemorosi, ferarum latebrae, cervorum, damarum, aprorum, & taurorum sylvestrium, &c.*" (Beyond them an immense forest extends itself, beautified with woods and groves, and full of the lairs and covers of beasts and game, stags, bucks, boars, and wild bulls).[13]

Fitzstephen indeed describes a pleasant prospect, a *paysage riant* (from the verb *rire*, "to laugh") as the French would have it, happily calling to mind Evelyn's translation of Gabriel Naudé's *Advis pour Dresser une Bibliothèque* (1627). In this exercise in Baconian *historia litteraria*, Naudé compares libraries to "the Meadow of *Seneca*, where every living creature finds that which is most proper for him: *Bos herbam, Canis leporem, Ciconia lacertum* (the ox his grass, the dog its hare, the stork its lizard).[14] Yet while each kind had its wonted place in this fair meadow, the chestnut was not one of them. Papworth explains, "many writers, copying each other, have misquoted the above cited passage in Fitz Stephen, and declare that he states that the Spanish chesnut grew in great profusion in the forests near London."[15] It was the learned barrister, antiquarian, and naturalist Daines Barrington who sought to do justice to Becket's own judicial assistant. His amicus brief took the form of a letter, published in the *Philosophical Transactions* for 1769, addressed to William Watson, an early advocate in England of the Swedish naturalist Carl Linnaeus's botanical precepts, in which Barrington considered the "trees which are supposed to be indigenous in Great Britain."

Watson had sent Barrington a specimen of "supposed chesnut," taken from the old hall of Clifford's Inn, evidently suspecting that answers regarding its species and essence could be coaxed from the very substance of the wood. It was Barrington, after all, who had persuaded his faithful correspondent Gilbert White to compose *The Natural History and Antiquities of Selborne* (1789) from the unsupported evidence of "his own autopsia!"[16] The phenologist Rev. Leonard explained that for White this word was particularly used "to signify the observing things for oneself and with one's own eyes."[17] But before offering his observations on the habits and haunts of spiders, and the flies on which they fed, Barrington drew on the tolerable philological skills he had exhibited in his *Observations on the More Ancient Statutes* (1766). In that treatise he detected and pursued the "vulgar errors" perpetrated and perpetuated by just antiquated acts, many of which were shown to have been originally founded on questionable authority. The first deceptively obvious question was what constituted an indigenous tree. In consulting the "proofs which are commonly relied upon," which is to say the very passages from Pliny's *Natural History* cited by Evelyn, Barrington points to the purloined letter-like self-evidence of the name itself, "Spanish chestnut" (*Castanea sativa*), which necessarily raises "some doubts" as to its English origin.[18] Pliny suggests that the tree might not even be indigenous to Europe, having first been brought to Italy from Sardis.

Notable statements to the contrary appeared in Philip Miller's *The Gardners Dictionary*, a "comprehensive and massive repository of information" that the twentieth-century historian of botanical literature William T. Stearn has called the "most important horticultural work of the eighteenth century."[19] Miller, superintendent of Chelsea Physic Garden, endeavored to show that the Spanish chestnut once "grew in profusion" to the north of London. Such profuse growth was in fact one of Barrington's criteria for identifying indigenous species. Miller's authority for this claim was of course Fitzstephen. Yet Barrington points out that the medieval topographer speaks only of a *saltus nemorosi* ("dense forest"), "without either the chestnut or any other tree, being specified."[20] Miller does not solely rely on book knowledge, but he is led by his sources to make some unreliable claims on his own account. "There are some Remains of old decy'd *Chesnuts* in the old Woods and Chases not far distant from London," he writes, "which plainly proves, that this Tree is no great Stranger to our Climate as many People believe it to be."[21] Barrington, the publisher of *The Naturalist's Journal*, a blank book for "keeping daily register of observations on the weather, plants, and animals," regretted that Miller did not "particularize the spot, and it should seem therefore, that he had received this information from others."[22] All such hearsay was subject to probative cross-examination. The justice to the text done by Barrington did not go unnoticed. In his 1772 edition of the *Description*, Rev. Dr. Samuel Pegge writes that the respected barrister "justly exculpates Fitz-Stephen."[23]

Considering the problems latent in Evelyn's *Sylva*, which was only the first of the numerous more or less reliable texts consulted by Papworth, it is perhaps not surprising that he sought other (nontextual) means to answer the governing question: "How is chesnut, then, to be distinguished from oak?"[24] As if recovering the material evidence, the grainy natural particulars that had served as the prompt for Barrington's investigation, Papworth presented to the Society "specimens of the actual wood under discussion." Arthur Ashpitel, architect and author of *The Reign of Humbug: A Satire*, obtained for him specimens of oak and chestnut both grown in the same woods in Kent, "which suffice not only to show how close is the resemblance between the two woods when young, but also how the difference between them is to be observed."[25] One method contemplated by Papworth was to subject the specimens to an experimental ordeal, driving an iron nail into the wood while fresh; in the oak a black stain is produced, but not in the chestnut. This experimental ordeal inevitably bears comparison to the question posed by the dazzlingly learned Belgian humanist and Tacitean scholar Justus Lipsius in *De Cruce libri tres* (1593), and debated by others long thereafter: of what wood was the cross of Christ made? (Bk. 3, chap. 13) In supposing it was oak (*Quercus*), Lipsius indicates that is was once plentiful in Judea.

Another possible approach considered by Papworth was to weigh a portion of the wood in question with reference to the tables published by the engineer Thomas Tredgold indicating their specific density. But for all the mechanical accuracy Tredgold (with the help of Peter Barlow) applied to the dense blocks of wood, in his *Elementary Principles of Carpentry* he let stand unremarked the prevalent misreading of Fitzstephen's claim regarding London's boreal forest of chestnuts.[26] In any case, the results Papworth obtained were inconclusive.

Failing these measures, why not consider what spiders have to say? "We are told," Barrington offers, "that the roof of Westminster Hall and many others consist of chestnut; not because any one hath found it to be so on examination, but because there are no cobwebs upon such roofs."[27] Not for the first time the parties to this debate are forced to judge the reliability of that which "we are told," especially in the absence of further or prior examination. Fitzstephen neatly distinguished the evidence of his own eyes and ears from what he had at second-hand, without however weighing the relative merits of one or the other. Barrington, for his part, oppugned Miller's account of the remains of old decayed chestnuts found outside London because he had "received this information from others." He had failed at autopsia. No matter who had conducted the "examination" of Westminster Hall, there remained the problem of interpreting the evidence of an absence of cobwebs, and with it all the logical hazards of an *argumentum ad ignorantiam*. Barrington writes, "It is supposed that the timber is not English, but Irish oak; in short, recourse is had to any extraordinary and uncommon material, to solve the singularity of there being no cobwebs on these roofs."[28] Spanish chestnut is one thing, and English oak another, that is if and when they can be positively distinguished from each other. But Irish oak?

Papworth is suitably alarmed by the invasion of this species into an otherwise neat but unresolved material dialectic. Yet it is the reputed absence of spiders in Ireland tout court that leads him into another venue of investigation. Papworth, it seems, was a "constant contributor" to *Notes and Queries*, the self-styled "medium of inter-communication."[29] Founded in 1849 under the editorship of William Thoms, deputy-librarian to the House of Lords, and author of *Human Longevity: Its Facts and Fictions* (1873), its intention was the asking and answering of its variously well-informed readers' questions. The necessarily imperfectly corresponding "Notes" and "Queries," each bearing a date, volume, and page number, record in exemplary fashion the life history of facts and related fictions. Papworth's particular interest was aroused by a "Query" submitted by Cuthbert Bede, B.A., under the heading "Spiders and Irish Oak."

In [John] Pointer's *Oxoniensis Academia* (1749), is the following, in his account of the curiosities of Christ Church College: 'The Roof of the afore-saide Hall is remarkable on this Account that, tho' it be made of Irish Oak, yet it harbours Spiders, in Contradiction to the vulgar Saying. Tho' I am apt to think that there may be some Pieces of English Oak amongst the Irish; or else probably that particular Smell that proceeds from that Sort of Oak, and is perhaps so distasteful to that Sort of Vermin, may be spent through Age, or disguised by Smoak, and so that common Saying may stand good still. 'What was this common saying?'[30]

Is it possible that Cuthbert Bede, pen name of the noted humorist Rev. Edward Bradley, was ignorant of the discussion of this very question in Sir Thomas Browne's *Pseudodoxia Epidemica: Or, Enquiries into Very Many Received Tenents and Commonly Presumed Truths* (originally published 1646). It is far more likely to suppose that Browne's work of all-pervasive skepticism was the prompt for his witting query.

To illustrate his discussion of the "different productions in several countries, which we impute unto the action of the sun," Browne juxtaposed England and Ireland, writing, "The sun which with us is fruitful in the generation of frogs, toads, and serpents, to this effect proves impotent in our neighbour island."[31] One of Browne's attentive readers, Christopher Wren, Dean of Windsor, father of the archi-tect of Saint Paul's Cathedral, London, noted that this phenomena was not limited to the "to Irish earthe, but to the timber brought hence, as appeares in the vast roof of King's College Chappel in Cambridge, where noe man has ever saw a spider, or their webs, bycause itt is all of Irish timber."[32] Wren's marginal annotations to his copy of *Pseudodoxia Epidemica*, preserved in the Bodleian Library, were tran-scribed by the literary scholar and entomologist Simon Wilkin for his 1835 edition of Browne's *Works*. Reluctant to allow a vulgar error to persist in his own scholarly apparatus, Wilkin penned his own query, addressed to a friend in Cambridge, "requesting that some inquiry might be made as to the matter of fact."[33] His corre-spondent obliged his request by making a "personal enquiry and examination." He interviewed the chapel's curator, who had never "heard of the circumstance," but who nonetheless wished for him "to go up to the roof and examine" for himself, assuring him that that "no trouble was taken to sweep it over at any time." This friend of truth did not succeed in discovering the "least appearance of a cobweb," which the otherwise regrettable lack of housekeeping would have left intact. The curator promised to bring him a spider or web if he could find one, and "seemed much pleased with the, to him, novel information."[34] In the very act of receiving this information, an essentially time-sensitive commodity, the curator was enlisted in the campaign to evaluate its rational worth.

Wilkin's footnote is a little sub-floor laboratory of Brownian skepticism. In drawing an elaborate distinction, sometimes nearly hidden in maze-like digressions, between things "naturally examined" and those "hieroglyphically conceived," Browne contributed to the demise of the emblematic worldview of the late Renaissance. According to William B. Ashworth, Jr., this is one in which "everything is seen as a sign or symbol *of* something else"[35] (emphasis added). The newly conceived project of establishing what things are in and for themselves was made all the more challenging, in this instance, by the difficulty of distinguishing one thing *from* something else—the oak (be it English or Irish) from the chestnut. The presence or absence of cobwebs was the needed sign, if in fact it was symptomatically reliable. Wilkin was apparently unable to test the matter directly. As is fitting to the footnote, he ultimately becomes caught in what Bacon called the "labourious webs of learning." The reference is once again to Barrington's letter that appeared in the *Philosophical Transactions*, and his report that after examining several ancient roofs he was not "able to detect any spider's webs." Was this a simple failure of detection? Barrington accounts for this telltale absence, Wilkin writes, "on the principle that *flies* are not around in such situations, and therefore spiders do not frequent them."[36] To test the supposed antipathy of spiders to this or that species of wood, it might then be necessary to admit flies to King's College, perhaps tempted there by the unswept crumbs of the curator's lunch, and observe what ensues.

Question asked, question answered. Cuthbert Bede's "Query" was met with a "Note" supplied by Rev. Jonathan Eastwood, best known, if at all, for his *The History of the Parish of Ecclesfield, in the County of York* (1862), where he held the curacy. A notice in *The Gentleman's Magazine and Historical Review* generously described the volume as a "complete and useful specimen of local history." Eastwood himself was not a "very profound or scientific antiquary in any branch," it continued, but it was precisely his lack of specialization that recommended his approach, such as it was. An architectural antiquary, or a documentary antiquary, each learned in his "particular line," might well have "despised a great many details which Mr. Eastwood has inserted, and which have an use of their own."[37] There can be no better statement of the value of those otherwise uncollected and perishable details whose use is limited if not entirely obscure. "What was this common saying?" Bede had asked. We will leave to the specialists the (fruitless?) task of attributing the source and precise inspiration of that maxim of Warburgian adoption: *Der liebe Gott steckt im Detail* (God is in the detail).[38] As for "Spiders and Irish Oak," Eastwood adverts to an article "On Vulgar Errors," one in a series that originally appeared in *The Gentleman's Magazine and Historical Review* and was later incorporated into an edition of John Brand's *Observations on Popular*

Antiquities: Chiefly Illustrating the Origins of Our Vulgar Customs, Ceremonies, and Superstitions (1843) compiled by British Museum librarian Henry Ellis. There it was asserted, contrary to what was popularly held, that the spider "is found in Ireland too plentifully. That it has no dislike to fixing its web on Irish oak."[39] What Brand did not reproduce, however, and what might thus have remained unknown to Eastwood, was that "H.," the author of "On Vulgar Errors," supported his claim on Barrington's findings.

What good would it have done? Immediately following Eastwood's "Note" appeared another submitted by Mackenzie Walcott. The clergyman and antiquarian reported as follows: "The common saying at Winchester is that no spider will hang its web on the roof of Irish oak in the chapel or cloisters: and it holds good. Chestnut is said to possess the same virtue."[40] It was another several weeks before Algernon Holt White, grandnephew of Gilbert White, expressed his exasperation with the whole matter. Faithful to his family motto, *Plus vigila* ("Be more watchful"), Holt White was as attentive to the biography of natural facts as his son Rashleigh Holt-White was in composing his *Life* of his forebear, the parson-naturalist of Selborne.

> I thought the chestnut wood theory was by this time extinct, and the more probable one of Sessiliflora oak [Durmast oak] now was generally admitted. That 'N. & Q.' may not help to keep alive this old fiction, let me ask whence and why did our ancestors import chestnut wood when English oak was to be had almost for the cutting? I doubt there being a single specimen of chestnut in any old building whatsoever.[41]

The notion of an extinct theory, or rather a theory of extinction, can of course be considered in terms of its then increasingly familiar bio- and geo-historical sense. But another interpretive burden is imposed by the endemic nature of vulgar errors, by the way in which they are inherited and cherished. The work of alienating these unchallenged presumptions is not essentially different from that performed by genealogists animated by the entitled interest of lost possession. The threat of extinction was central to the legal practice and antiquarian pursuits of Timothy Christopher Banks, whose Dormant Peerage Office, John Street, Pall Mall, undertook the conduct of genealogical claims. And while he allowed himself greater sense of freedom, to borrow Manning's phrase, in his own self-fashioning, Mr./Sir Banks's unimpeachable bequest to history was his *Stemmata Anglicana; or, a Miscellaneous Collection of Genealogy*. It merits attention here if only and precisely for its title. A *stemmata*, via Latin from the Greek *stemma*, for "wreath," is a genealogical table. The term was given critical currency in the work of the Lucretius scholar Karl Lachmann, in the form of the *stemma codicum*. Thus Lachmann, with a large unacknowledged debt to the brilliant Jewish philologist Jacob Bernays, imagined a family-tree of extant witnesses (manuscript versions), which could be traced to a lost authorial "*archetype*."[42] Identifying family traits were found in errors of transcription, redaction, and other conjectural contaminants passed from one generation on to the next. It is the fact that errors persist that maintains the improbable hope and desire of seeing them exposed and corrected. The purpose here, as we draw to a conclusion, has not been to inquire into the origin of things, even if Evelyn's *Sylva*, which unwittingly provided faulty witness, served as a point of departure. Rather it was to consider the genealogy of one particular question, oak *or* chestnut, and what a number of responses to that question reveal about the order of things, itself subject to renovation. In short, the attempt was to write a small history of a largely inconsequential historical process that was revealingly unaware of its own (foregone) conclusions. Only the spiders knew for certain.

For now, just one more "Note" to document the state of things at the moment we leave them. Following Holt White's call for extinction, the question was resurrected by H. T. Ellacombe, curate of Bitton. An antiquarian who specialized in the history of church bells, Henry Thomas Ellacombe was perhaps particularly alert to the necessity of periodically recasting the materials of history. By now it almost goes without saying that he begins his "Note" with reference to Evelyn and Fitzstephen, only then to call for further scrutiny of the matter.

> There is a fine old roof at Torner's Court, in the parish of Cold Ashton, Gloucestershire, four miles from Bath, perfectly free from cobwebs . . . The timber is said to be chestnut, and why not? for the tree is considered by Evelyn and others to be a free-born Briton. He speaks of his own farm, and other buildings about London where it was much used in days gone by. A forest of such trees is known to have existed in the neighbourhood, *temp.* Henry II. Is not the roof of Westminster Hall of this timber? and it may easily be known whether it is kept free from cobwebs by the brush or the antipathy of the spider to the material used.[43]

If H. T. Ellacombe was not aware of Barrington's conclusions, evidently his son was. In one of the essays on historical and literary botany published in *The Garden*, Henry Nicholson Ellacombe allowed that the chestnut is "one of our handsomest trees, and very useful for timber." But he was under no illusions regarding the respective efficacy of the brush or the spider's antipathies in sorting out the matter. "[A]t one time," H. N. Ellacombe writes, "it was supposed that many of our oldest buildings were roofed with Chestnut. This was the current report of the grand roof at Westminster Hall, but it is now discovered to be of Oak, and it is very doubtful whether the Chestnut timber is as lasting as it has long been supposed to be."[44] It is what was reported about the different essences of wood, in truth and in error, that proved more lasting than even the most venerable of trees.

One year later after H. N. Ellacombe's essay was published, on April 15, 1878, Thomas Blashill addressed, once again within the halls of the Royal Institute for British Architects, "The Question of Oak or Chestnut in Old Timber Roofs." Wyatt Papworth himself was in attendance and eagerly responded to Blashill's not altogether new assertions regarding this "long disputed point in the history of our ancient buildings."[45] The likelihood that the matter would be resolved that particular Monday evening might be judged upon the evidence presented. "In the Museum at Kew Gardens," he indicates "there has long been exhibited a piece of the most palpable oak . . . labeled as 'Spanish Chestnut from an old beam in Windsor Castle.'" For Blashill it served as an exhibit that there was still more work to be done. What he insisted on, finally, was the unmistakably typical medullary plates seen in cross-sections of oak. But this feature was known to any skilled artisan in ornamental wood inlays or parquetry.[46]

Perhaps the missing evidence was not to be found in the roof beams but underfoot, with the unmysterious and non-hieroglyphic meaning of the "emblem." The original sense of the term appears in the notes to Richard Bentley's "New Edition" of John Milton's *Paradise Lost*:

each bounteous flour,
Iris all hues, Roses, and Jessamin,
Rear'd high their *flourisht* heads between, and wrougt
Mosaic; under foot the Violet,
Crocus, and Hyacinth, with rich inlay
Broider'd the ground, more colour'd than with stone
Of costliest Emblem [4: 697–703]

Bentley's ambiguously generous cornucopia of emendations and elucidations includes the following: "*Emblem* is here in the *Greek* and *Latin* Sense for inlaid Floors of Stone or Wood, to make Figures Mathematical or Pictural: *Arte pavimenti atque emblemate vermiculato* (With checquered emblems like a pavement marked).[47] The citation, from the Roman satirist Gaius Lucilius, appears in Pliny's *Natural History*. So, as a teacher of history, I can only implore my students, Come and walk with me a bit. We will start out from the syllabus, its own sort of Rosetta Stone, and see what uncommon places we stumble upon. Cobwebs are nothing to fear.

1 John Manning, *The Emblem* (London: Reaktion Books, 2002), 107.

2 Anthony Grafton, "Foreword," *The Hieroglyphics of Horapollo*, trans. George Boas (Princeton: Princeton University Press, 1993), xiv.

3 Manning, 107. For research on the stele's material composition, see Andrew Middleton, Dietrich Klemm, "The Geology of the Rosetta Stone," *The Journal of Egyptian Archaeology* 89 (2003): 207–216.

4 Manning, 107.

5 Miguel Tamen, "Lorraine Daston, ed., Things That Talk: Object Lessons from Art and Science," *Common Knowledge* 15 (2009): 520 [520–521].

6 Wyatt Papworth, "On the Assumed Use of Chestnut Timber in the Carpentry of Old Buildings," *Papers Read at The Royal Institute of British Architects, Session 1857–58* (1858): 196 [192–199].

7 Beryl Hartley, "Exploring and Communicating Knowledge of Trees in the Early Royal Society," *Notes and Records of The Royal Society* 64 (2010): 229–250.

8 John Evelyn, *Sylva, Or a Discourse of Forest-Trees, and the Propagation of Timber in His Majesties Dominions* (London: Jo. Martyn, 1664), 25.

9 John Claudius Loudon, *Arboretum et Fructicetum Britannicum; Or The Trees and Shrubs of Britain, Native and Foreign* (London: Longman, Orme, Brown, Green, and Longmans, 1838), III, 1992.

10 "Étude des Monumens," *Bulletin du Comité Historique des Arts et Monumens* 1 (1840): 90 [89–90].

11 Evelyn, 25.

12 Fitzstephen, *Vita Sancti Thomae*, cited in Michael Staunton, *Thomas Becket and His Biographers* (Rochester, NY: The Boydell Press, 2006), 57.

13 *Fitz-Stephen's Description of The City of London*, trans. and edit. by Rev. Samuel Pegge (London: B. White, 1772), 26.

14 John Evelyn, *Instructions Concerning Erecting of a Library* (London: G. Bedle, 1661), 21.

15 Papworth, 192.

16 Gilbert White, *The Natural History and Antiquities of Selborne* (London: T. Bensely, 1789) 129.

17 Leonard Jenyns, *Observations in Natural History: With an Introduction on Habits of Observing, as Connected with the Study of that Science* (London: John Van Voorst, 1846), 4.

18 "A Letter to Dr. William Watson, F.R.S. from the Hon. Daines Barrington, F.R.S. on the Trees which are supposed to be indigenous in Great Britain," *Philosophical Transactions* 59 (for 1769): 24 [23–38].

19 William T. Stearn, "Miller's Gardeners dictionary and its abridgement," *Journal of the Society for the Bibliography of Natural History* 7 (1974): 125 [125–141].

20 Barrington, 25.

21 Philip Miller, *The Gardeners Dictionary* (London: C. Rivington, 1735), I, s.v. Castanea.

22 Barrington, 25 [23–38].

23 *Fitz-Stephen's Description of the City of London*, trans. and edit. by An Antiquary [Rev. Dr. Samuel Pegge] (London: B. White, 1772), 26.

24 Papworth, 196.

25 Ibid., 196.

26 Thomas Tredgold, *Elementary Principles of Carpentry* (Philadelphia: E. L. Carey, 1837 [1st American from the 2nd London ed.]), 256.

27 Barrington, cited in Papworth, 193.

28 Barrington, 30.

29 ["Death of Mr. Wyatt Papworth"], *Notes and Queries* ser. 8, *vol. 6* (August 25, 1894): 160.

30 "Spiders and Irish Oak," *Notes and Queries* ser. 2, *vol. 4* (September 12, 1857), 209.

31 Simon Wilkin, ed., *Sir Thomas Browne's Works, Including His Life and Correspondence* (London: William Pickering, 1835), III, 239.

32 Ibid., 240, n. 9.

33 Ibid., 240, n. 9.

34 Ibid., 240, n. 9.

35 William B. Ashworth, Jr., "Natural History and the Emblematic World View," in David C. Lindberg, Robert S. Westman, ed., *Reappraisals of the Scientific Revolution* (Cambridge: Cambridge University Press, 1990), 312 [303–332].

36 Wilkin, 240, n. 9.

37 "History of Ecclesfield," *The Gentleman's Magazine and Historical Review* ser. 2, *vol. 13* (October 1862): 398 [398–405].

38 See, Giovanni Mastroianni, "Il buon Dio di Aby Warburg," *Belfagor* 55 (2000): 413-442.

39 John Brand, *Observations on Popular Antiquities: Chiefly Illustrating the Origin of Our Vulgar Customs, Ceremonies, and Superstitions*, ed., Henry Ellis (London: Charles Knight, 1842), III, 206.

40 Mackenzie Walcott, "Spiders and Irish Oak," *Notes and Queries* ser. 2, *vol. 4* (October 10, 1857): 298.

41 A[lgernon] Holt White, "Spiders and Irish Oak," *Notes and Queries* ser. 2, *vol. 4* (November 7, 1857): 377.

42 See Sebastiano Timpanaro, *The Genesis of Lachmann's Method*, edit. and trans. Glenn W. Most (Chicago: University of Chicago Press, 2005), 104–106.

43 H[enry] T[homas] Ellacombe, "Spiders and Irish Oak," *Notes and Queries* ser. 2, *vol. 4* (November 21, 1857): 421.

44 Henry Nicholson Ellacombe, "The Plant-Lore of Shakespeare," *The Garden* 11 (April, 14, 1877): 296 [296–298].

45 Thomas Blashill, "The Question of Oak or Chestnut in Old Timber Roofs," *Sessional Papers Read at the Royal Institute of British Architects 1876–1877* (1877): [231–234]; "Discussion on Mr. Blashill's Paper—Oak or Chestnut," *Sessional Papers Read at the Royal Institute of British Architects 1876–1877* (1877): 236 [235–239].

46 A. Aikin, "On Ornamental Woods," *Transactions of the Society, Instituted at London, for the Encouragement of Arts, Manufactures, and Commerce* 50 (1834): 159 [156–170].

47 Richard Bentley, *Milton's Paradise Lost. A New Edition* (London: Jacob Tonson, 1732), 132.

It is thrashing side to side. It is bulging with muscle. It is over and over. It is showing you off. It is beaming with pride. It is nudging at your feet. It enacts the waking dream. It will leave you weak at the knees. It is engulfing. It entangles you with a rush of wonder. It is stitching together circles. It is screaming without stopping. It runs you through with spectacular. It is unfulfilled eternal. It is the flatness of the multitude. It is your family. It is chiseled out of stone. It is steadily growing. It is cleaner than a hospital ward. It turns and turns and turns. It is flocks, it is in flocks. It is made once and over and over and over. It sharply bites the air. It is full of uses. It is everyday. It slips from your fingers. It is also infinite. It is also already expanding beyond your grasp.

Gavin Robb

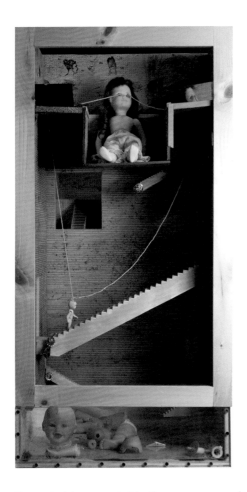

The project is suspended in the uncanny space between reality and dream. The personal obsession of dream interpretation is a daily source in the production of reality, one that is constantly producing images relying on symbols, signs, and relations—narrating the past, wondering in the present, and, predicting the future—an obsession that moves one through an alternative time frame. This unreal reality has manifested itself within the space of a doll factory, through the intertwined production of dolls, dreams, and the body, the spaces they all inhabit and the dual relations between the real and the unreal, becomes the architectural mode of their existence.

Sara Tavakoli

KALEIDOSCOPIC JOURNEYS
PROTO-CINEMATIC SPACES

Savinien Caracostea, MArch II

Advisor
Sanford Kwinter

Our existence is framed by the spaces we live in and our mental projections. Today, as virtual spaces attempt to connect the two, the physical realm is challenged by virtual interfaces. Cultural and social spaces are transitioning to new forms closer to cinema. These bodiless interactions, Juhani Pallasmaa writes, "give the viewer back his or her body, as the experiential haptic and motor space provides powerful kinesthetic experiences." As architects we must wonder: Can architecture become more "real" than cinema?

Early cinema, or *proto-cinema*, emerged with paintings on Paleolithic caves who seemed to move on its undulating walls, and has permeated history with devices such as the magic lantern, mirrors, the kaleidoscope—games of sorts to externalize mental projections and in so doing articulated the threshold or passage from inside to outside. Architectural typologies that imbricate the outside in the inside, such as the theater, department store, or hotel, best articulate the surface between our physical environment and our experiencing self. Alchemical, proto-cinematic devices, they become thresholds from wakefulness to dream, real to imaginary, space to time.

This project investigates the transition phenomena within these combined typologies—all sources of inspiration and meditation (the garden) as well as of consumption (the palace). This ambiguity of meanings, utilitarian and phantasmagoric, promotes transition as it expands the visitor's mental projections into proto-cinema—custom experiences in the "theater of our minds." The amalgam

of department store, hotel, and theater accentuates this transition phenomena—the department store as a backstage for theater, hotel rooms as changing rooms, theater stage as atrium. Both the visitors and the architecture become actors of these "projections".

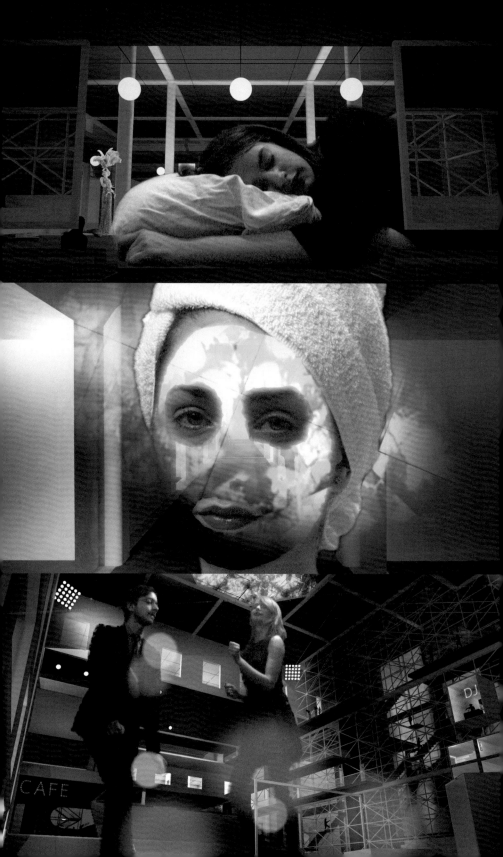

Marina Abramović

"It is very important for the public to understand and feel for themselves."

Marina Abramović is an artist based in New York City, and has pioneered the use of performance as a visual art form.

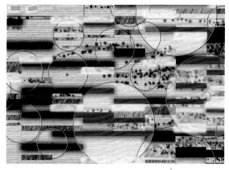

1 Eri Yamagata
2 Marissa Angell
3 Hillary Archer

CORE I
LANDSCAPE ARCHITECTURE

Core I Landscape Architecture problematizes issues of orientation and experience, scale and pattern, topographic form, canopy and climatic influences, and varied ecological processes that help define urban public space. As the first of a four-term sequence of design studios, the course helps students develop spatial literacy, critical design thinking, and proficiency in diverse modes of representation in landscape architecture. The first studio exercises investigate a set of typological models of space rooted in historical and contemporary precedents. These undergo sequential transformations aimed at devising hybrid solutions to common conceptual design problems: conditions of stasis, movement, and change over time. Later in the semester, these studies are examined through a program on a site at the edge of Harvard's campus that reimagines productive social intersections between university culture and civic life in Cambridge. Throughout, emphasis is placed on the design studio as a performative venue for conceiving, interrogating, and elaborating concrete ideas about the role of the biophysical landscape as a vital, sustaining force in urbanization and urban life.

Gary Hilderbrand
Jane Hutton
Silvia Benedito
Zaneta Hong

Materials and Construction (Danielle Etzler and Mark Mulligan) introduces students to fundamental properties and behaviors of buildings and other structures. Principles of design and construction are discussed in a comprehensive manner involving conceptual, historical, and technical analyses. Students learn to evaluate empirically various types of constructs and use analytical skills to enhance their design capabilities.

continued on page 198 >>

Inspired by organisms that develop slowly and accumulate over time, this project is about life left in the wake of swift forces, the distortion that occurs with these happenings, and the balance between them. The designed public space reflects modest characteristics of plant colonization and works with the rhythm of the site, such as the continuous fence surrounding Harvard Yard, establishing a new harmony within the incongruities that exist within the current site.

Eri Yamagata

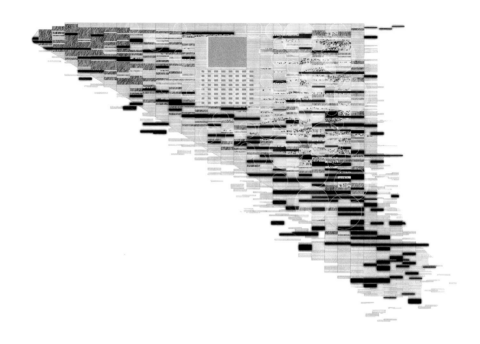

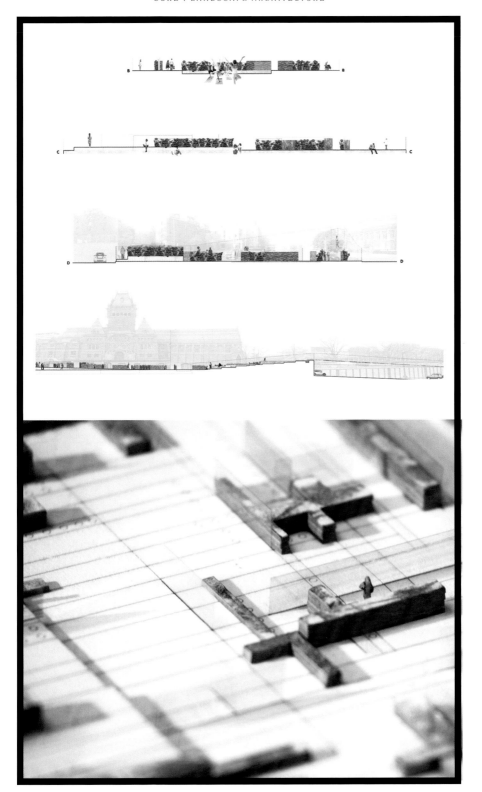

NOTHING, SPECIFICALLY

Kevin Lamyuktseung, MArch I

Advisor
Florian Idenburg

This building is an experiment in contradictions, but absent of style; instead of a singular or pre-emptive reading, it seeks a conflation of those contradictions. Seeking a method that does not begin and end with a critique and does not presume an end through its initiation, it instead attempts a suspension between legibility and affect, through a quantity of disciplinary techniques and quotations. Through this, the thesis seeks to privilege the architectural problem of wall, of room—over the identities attached to each individual move.

This is a sincere project that assumes responsibility, believing that in certain programs born of contemporary complexities, singular architectural responses are both naive and culturally irresponsible. The site for this project is the American embassy, which one could say is a mixed-use building, with too much program (the program of an entire self-supporting country) and too much identity, both in conflict with one another. Through the inherent complexities of this program, the project seeks an architecture of conflation.

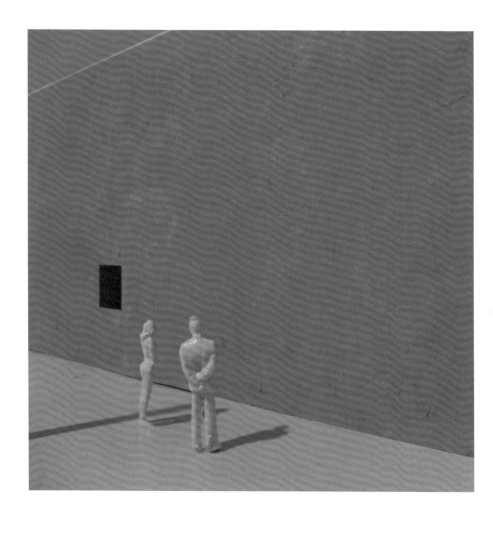

Christian Kerez

Contrast & Continuity

The models on display reveal the set of rules that determine how architectural spaces within buildings will be defined. They are more like models used in science, constructed to explain and visualize relationships, than small-scale representations of the actual appearance of an architectural space or the exterior of a building. Like workshop models, they offer a first rough impression of the everyday experience that would result from the execution of an initial concept.

The models resemble machines in the way that their appearances are conceived as an assemblage of elements, not simply an indication of the shape or material of a volume. Most of the models emphasize a system inside the building—the bone structure—instead of a skin. This structural system is intended as only the starting point for delineating interior architectural spaces, through the application of a conceptual rigor that is meant to be evident during all incidental uses within everyday life. A sense of this future daily interaction is created by unpolished images of handmade movies, shown in the exhibition, featuring only parts of building structures—in deliberate contrast to the idealized representations seen in animations done for clients.

Christian Kerez is the 2012–2013 Kenzō Tange Visiting Chair in Architecture and Urban Design at the Harvard University Graduate School of Design.

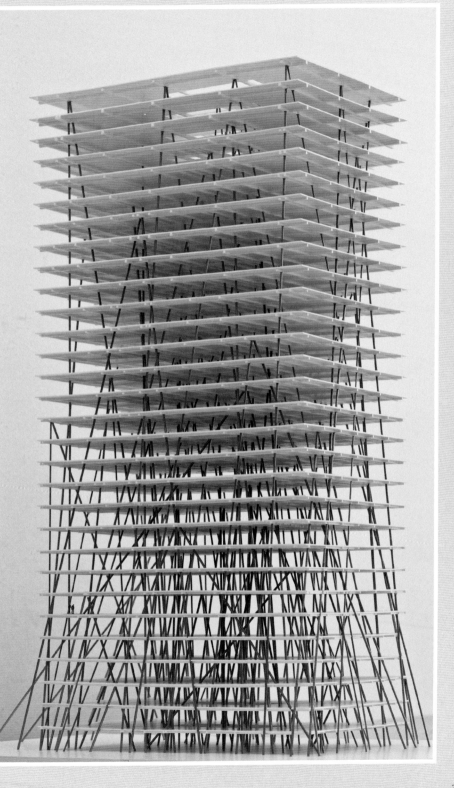

FIGU RAT ION

PURSUING

Lawrence Scarpa
Brian Healy

In a story, the narrative is captured in the telling; it is the selective details and descriptive moments that evoke a tone or mood. The plot is what actually happens, and a good plot can produce countless stories. We are interested in an architecture that suggests an equivalent multiplicity of tellings, and in plots that suggest narratives that are complex and layered. We look for the stories within stories. Architecture is made not of intentions but of works. There is no such thing as a good idea, only good expression. In its very essence, it involves a renunciation of words and an engagement with the physical. Architecture students develop ideas about architecture and how architects can create environments that promote occupation. Pursuing Figuration: Questions of Process, Structure, Scale, and Enclosure focuses on the translation of those ideas into legible architectural form that engages plot and narration.

With the rise of digital culture, ornament is back. Its return has been accompanied with recurring interrogations regarding the need to redefine tectonics, and more generally to revisit critically the link between architecture and structure. Once thought essential, this link appears weaker today. Paradoxically, while the fundamental role that modernism had attributed to structure is being challenged, the relation between architecture and infrastructure has intensified. Many contemporary projects play on the blurring of the frontier between architecture and infrastructure. Structure, Infrastructure, and Ornament (Antoine Picon) will examine the past and present interactions between these components of architecture and the built environment. The play between these notions enables us to raise some fundamental issues regarding the way architecture is to be understood.

continued on page 210 >>

207

Given rising concern about the origins of food, a new attitude toward consuming locally raised products has become a means to achieve full disclosure of the products ingested into one's body. To help lead this effort in thinking of different venues of cultivation, this project aims not only to provide a series of living exhibitions that examine potential methods of farming within an urban scale, but also to serve as an icon that can raise awareness of food and its origins.

Alfredo Pimentel

excerpt from <u>The Productive Thinness of the Line</u>
Rola Idris

Through academic writings and mani-festations of architecture, I propose that ornament is read through the line in three ways: in profile, in depth, and in formal. The analysis of the line that allows for these three interpretations is largely linked to means of structural realization through time from pre-frame to frame construction and further to a proposed 'beyond the frame' reading. Furthermore, I propose six specific readings of the ornamental line, named here Cases A–F. Additionally, each case has general attributes of whether the line is articulated as linear or non-linear. These cases do not aim to be all encompassing but they do cover the precedents studied in this paper. A further description of each case is as follows.

Case A Structure and the exterior wall formed one thick entity before the advent of frame construction. Ornament was applied as elements on the facade many times obscuring the structure. On some occasions, the ornament was also struc-tural, as in the case of ornamented columns. Structure was linear and ornament was an articulated profile line.

Case B With frame construction, structure is separated from the exterior 'free' facade. However, there were cases that applied ornament in the traditional manner as a supplement on the wall. Structure and the outer wall were linear, while the ornament was non-linear.

Case C With the Modern movement, a reversal of line attributes occurred within frame construction. In some buildings, the structure became a curvilinear plastic mass while the ornament remained a linear,

carved, or extruded imprint within the mass.

Case D During the twentieth century, structure and skin were mostly linear. The facade hung like a curtain or became an envelope, taking the form of one continuous volume. The facade became the ornament either through its texture or its form as a whole.

Case E Contemporary architecture and digital technology express a collapse of structure and skin. Thin surfaces are articulated as linear or non-linear forms that usually twist or fold, their topology becomes ornament.

Case F Other cases of contemporary architecture (but not limited to the con-temporary) express structure in an almost sublime way. The forces around the form and its tension create a field or space that imbues itself as ornamental.

Cases A and B are what I call ornament 'in profile' based on the articulation of the line of ornament applied to the frame or face. Cases C–E I call ornament 'in depth' based on the idea that although the advent of frame construction allowed for the realization of thin superficial surfaces, the line between interior and exterior has to be read deeply for its effect beyond the surface. Case F is ornament that I call 'in formal'; it operates beyond frame construction to defy grids and containment and achieve 'informal' structural feats that most often create a sublime or spiritual field or orna-mental space. Moving from case A through E (not strictly linearly) encompasses four types of progression: time; construc-tion methods; pre-digital to digital; and measured control to measured chaos.

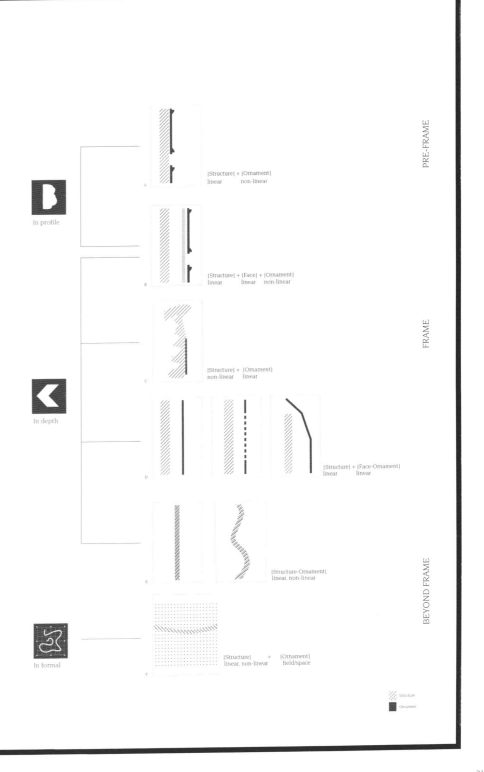

VAC BOS

January 23, 1957

Le Corbusier
Atelier Le Corbusier
35 Rue de Sevres
Paris 6, France

Dear Corbu:

It was nice to get your letter of December 18.
We are now expecting Michel any day in this School.
I will be glad to hear further about Pierre's
friend, Mr. Malhotra, who you say will apply here.

Of course, the person we want to see in this part
of the world is yourself. Is there any chance of
getting you to come here sometime next fall or
spring? On what conditions would you be willing
to pay a visit to Cambridge? Both M.I.T. and this
School are willing to do their best to get you to
come here. It is a long time since you have
visited this country, where, as you know, you have
many good friends. If you can, in your very busy
schedule, manage to spend two weeks here, we can
guarantee a grand reception; and from that there
are chances that other things may develop.

With my best to you and Yvonne,

                              Amities,

                              Jose Luis

JLS:jsc

cc: Dean Pietro Belluschi
    School of Architecture and Planning
    Massachusetts Institute of Technology

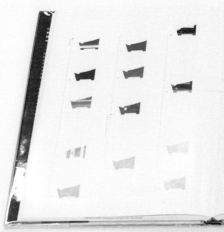

OFF THE EVERYDAY LIFE

Lap Chi Kwong, MArch I

Advisor
Florian Idenburg

This thesis looks at the interior of the suburban house. The plan is selected from the top-selling house under 2,000 square feet by builder.com. The top model home is designed by Frank Betz Associates, Inc. I looked at each room very closely to revisit the everyday life in the suburban house. There is a huge selection of suburban house plans, but the pattern of the suburban house is more or less the same. Its programmatic arrangement maintains a certain sequence of everyday life. This thesis proposes an intervention, to make a slightly curved diagonal cut across the initial home plan, which serves as an enfilade to the house. Each of the rooms remain in the same placement but by inserting this enfilade, a new circulation sequence is provided within the house. By reworking the existing pattern of the model home plan, the everyday is accentuated.

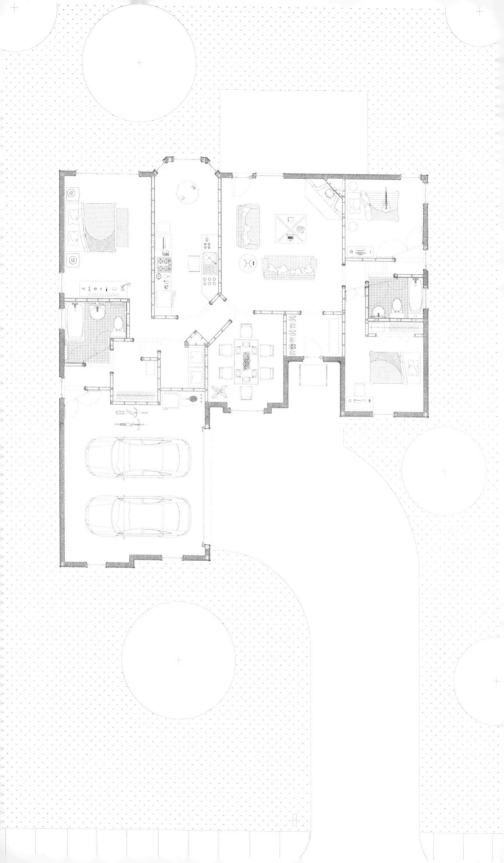

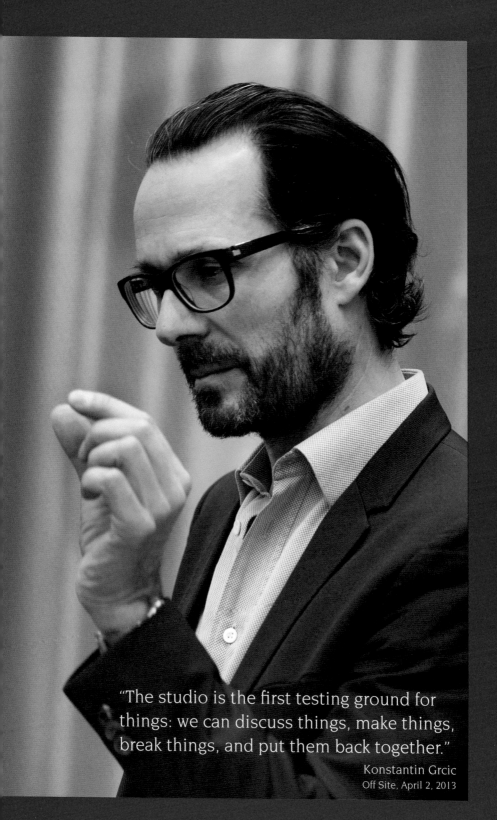

"The studio is the first testing ground for things: we can discuss things, make things, break things, and put them back together."

Konstantin Grcic
Off Site, April 2, 2013

ROTTER**DAMO**

In spite of a century of globalization, the range of architectural typologies and Rem Koolhaas the common understanding of the elements of the discipline may have diminished. At the same time a consensus is emerging about architecture's "final" typological repertoire. As control of architectural production and discourse shifts back from west to east, this studio attempts to reassess the repertoire and the tools available to architects everywhere. The Elements of Architecture is a study abroad program, hosted by Office for Metropolitan Architecture.

The studio generates an inventory of the individual components of architecture through history—an effort that is already underway in recent studies on the history of the corridor, the false ceiling, and the fluorescent tube, for example. Students study the ways in which typological richness has been eroded over time, leaving us only the extremes: very flat or very vertical buildings.

The inventories are underpinned by political and historical study. It is widely accepted that the number of available architectural languages has shrunk drastically in the past century. However, the transition from a specific language to an international language is a richer process than we typically recognize, involving significant encounters and influences between cultures. The reconstruction of this history, taking in the period 1918 to the present day, uncovers within globalization the unique features that could be cultivated by individual cultures in the coming period of international collaboration.

BALCONY — Heather Dunbar

The Elements of Architecture
BALCONY From One to Many
Heather Dunbar
Fall 2012
AMO

FALSE CEILING — J. Arthur Liu

The Elements of Architecture
CEILING Architectural Superhero
J. Arthur Liu
Fall 2012
AMO

CORRIDOR — Max Wong

The Elements of Architecture
CORRIDOR The Panic Room
Max Wong
Fall 2012
AMO

DOOR — Beth Eckels

The Elements of Architecture
DOOR Stretched Threshold
Beth Eckels
Fall 2012
AMO

FACADE — Ellie Gentleman

The Elements of Architecture
FACADE The Rise and Fall of the Curtain Wall
Ellie Gentleman
Fall 2012
AMO

FLOOR — Patrick Hamon

The Elements of Architecture
FLOOR Immutable Element
Patrick Hamon
Fall 2012
AMO

HEARTH — Will Lambeth

The Elements of Architecture
HEARTH Machine for Warming
Will Lambeth
Fall 2012
AMO

PARTITION — Nicholas Potts

The Elements of Architecture
PARTITION Encrustation's Meltdown
Nicholas Potts
Fall 2012
AMO

ROOF — Jelo Lu

The Elements of Architecture
ROOF The Birthplace of New Regionalism
Jelo Lu
Fall 2012
AMO

STAIR — Jenny Hong

The Elements of Architecture
STAIR Endangered and Dangerous
Jenny Hong
Fall 2012
AMO

TOILET/BATH — Kurt Nieminen

The Elements of Architecture
TOILET/BATH Triumph of the Apparatus
Kurt Nieminen
Fall 2012
AMO

WINDOW — Tiffany Oloser

The Elements of Architecture
WINDOW Climate Controlled
Tiffany Oloser
Fall 2012
AMO

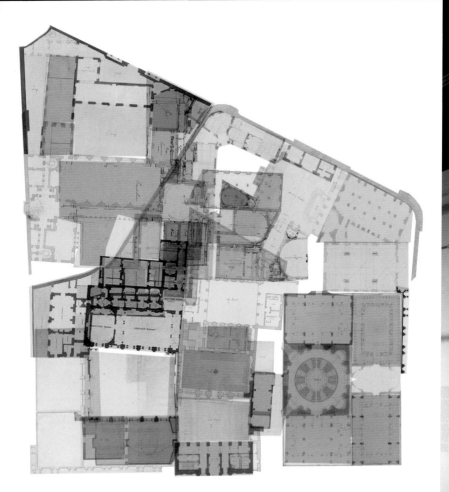

Mediator of adjacent intimacies, the partition is a tool of aggregation through autonomy. Its horizontal extensity somewhere broke free from architecture and its overarching dimensional tools: the section, the elevation, the frame, the shelter, the cosmos: its politics of negotiation enable indeterminacy through immediacy. Privacy (aural, visual, thermodynamic) becomes a tool of megalomaniacal multiplication. It belongs to nobody but itself, its codified systems (sound transmission coefficients, material toxicity, fire and smoke ratings) manage only what happens on each side of the membrane, yet bind it from chaos. The partition is no longer a part of the architecture—it's subsumed it.

Nicholas Potts

Rotterdam Studio Panel Discussion

Stephan Trüby: We don't have a cultural history of the roof. We don't have a cultural history of the floor in architecture. How is it that we, on the one hand, know so much and, on the other hand, know so little about architecture? This was the starting point in thinking about the role of elements in architecture, architecture theory, and architecture history. We are very interested in the role that an architect today could play in the evolution of, for example, windows or floors. Our hope is that when we look at architecture, we realize that some of the architecture and buildings are mainly driven by the roof or by the floor.

Tom Avermaete: There is a relationship between elements and systems, or elements and pedagogy. There is a topological discourse embedded in our discussions on elements.

Rem Koolhaas: That is the whole point of this exhibition; you could say it will have two possible endings: there could be a desperate ending, where all the wealth of architectural civilization, architectural history, architectural thinking, architectural theory is emanating a utilitarian repertoire of very few limited topologies. Or perhaps, by going in the other direction and undoing part of those simplifications, we can discover new complexities. The reason to make the entire effort public is to actually test the hypothesis, and since this is quite a young audience, I would like to particularly ask if you are all incredibly happily engaged in your kind of parametric dream? Are you not worrying about particular and separate issues, such as the status of the floor, the ceiling? What kind of situation is this, where we have become oblivious to the parametric problems persisting in the old-fashioned building of architecture?

Tom Avermaete is an Associate Professor of Architecture at the Delft University of Technology.
Rem Koolhaas is the founding partner of Office for Metropolitan Architecture and Professor in Practice of Architecture and Urban Design at the Harvard Graduate School of Design.
Stephan Trüby is a lecturer in the Department of Architecture at the Harvard Graduate School of Design and Course Director of the Master of Spatial Studies Design program at the Zürcher Hochschule der Künste.

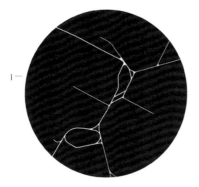

1 Lauren Bordes, Gillian Chang, Chris Espers & Brian Haulter
2 Natsuma Imai, Aja Jeanty, Kait Kurs & Kevin Murray
3 Jim Peraino & Lily Wubeshet

CORE IV
ARCHITECTURE

Architecture in the city is the "temporary" outcome of a continuous dialogue between individual or semi-collective aspirations and our collective "public" positions and convictions. These attitudes are mostly secured and communicated through codes, laws, decrees, and other organizational systems. Although in constant flux and informed by societal trends, these organizational systems form the framework within which one operates in the city.

Florian Idenburg
Danielle Etzler
Eric Höweler
Jinhee Park
Renata Sentkiewicz
Spela Videcnik

Core IV Architecture explores the design of relationships and regulations in order to carry forward the ongoing experiment that is architecture in the city. The work of the studio will be to constitute a piece of urban fabric in New York City, understood and realized as a relational system, and to design architectural elements, also governed by explicit rules, within this structure. These elements will be architectural objects that through their design are able to convey ramifications outward into the codes that structured them and into their relationships with other objects that surround them. To this end, the work undertaken in the studio is collaborative throughout, with each project realized in negotiation with other designed elements. From the scale of collective urban configurations to specificities of position, shape, and image, the mode of design will be the formulation and manipulation of codes. The goal is not to confirm the priority of existing structures of regulation but to produce, through architecture, new sequences of code that formulate a future of the city.

"Cities are often layered, but they rarely exhibit the characteristics of vertical succession, as defined by spatial stacking. Cities, more often than not, do not pile up."

Preston Scott Cohen
Successive Architecture
April 23, 2013

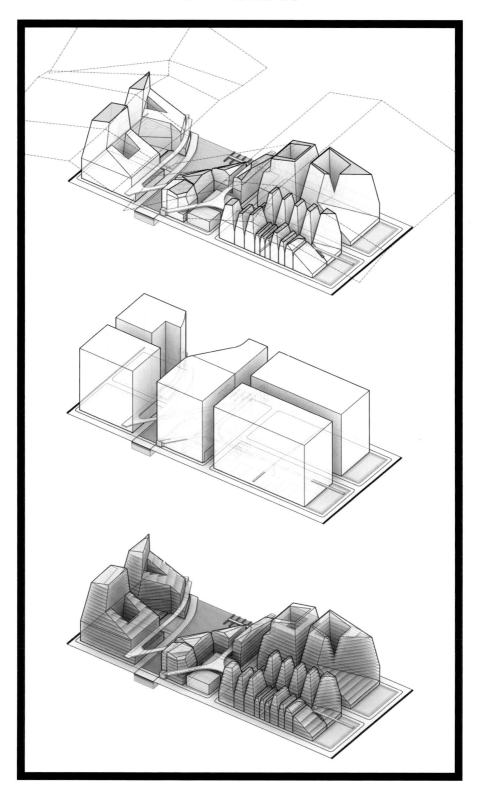

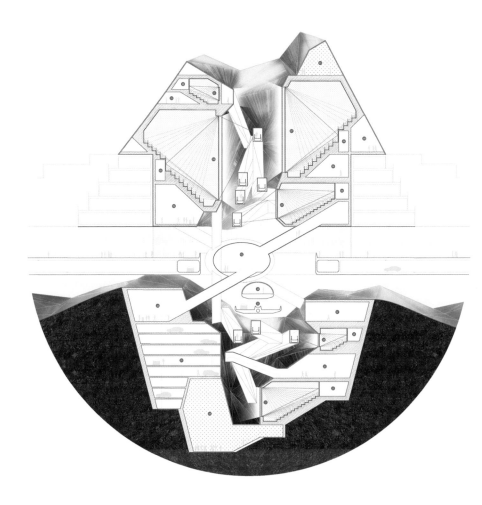

The formal composition of a dunescape provided the methodology for space making. Importing this landscape into Gowanus and imposing upon it the existing Brooklyn street grid produced an urbanism of new geometries and scales, and a new system of relationships among built urban forms, causing moments of low and high density, programmatic intersections, and the continuity of systems. Simultaneously, the landscape acted as a singular organic surface, a series of hills and valleys to remediate water and soil contamination and serve as flood control. This project focuses on the topographic layering of systems to produce micro and macro urban-scapes. These systems compound into a vertical network of operations that frees the built from the natural landscape, maintaining the sinuousness of the dunescape in both form and function.

Natsuma Imai, Aja Jeanty, Kait Kurs & Kevin Murray

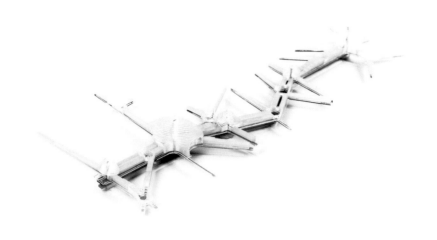

Zaha Hadid

Mohsen Mostafavi: What is next for you? You're at the point where some of the things that seemed to be almost impossible—you've realized them. So, what is there?

Zaha Hadid: I still think that on the level of urbanism, we still have a long way to go. Not on the scale of the whole city—but on the scale of very large segments of the city, we're still dealing with the normal street pattern. The basic idea of transportation has not really changed very much, for example. I would say that this would be the next level of investigation on an urban level. In terms of the building itself, as far as I can see, all the fragmentation—all that chaos on the level of the city that was shown in the [Peak Project] was sucked into the building, and turned out to be a much more fluid morphology as opposed to fragmentation.

Zaha Hadid is the founder of Zaha Hadid Architects, and the recipient of the 2004 Pritzker Prize.

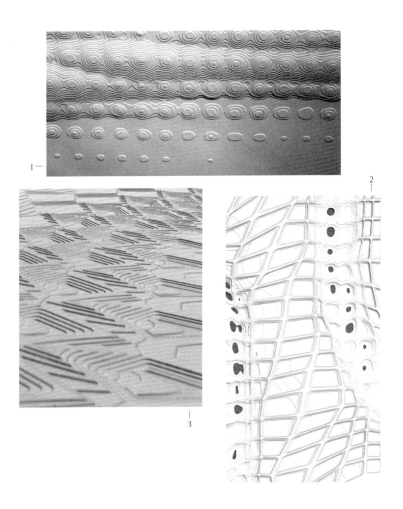

1 Anya Domlesky & Justin Jackson
2 Jason Brain & Lauren Hamer
3 Zhewen Dai & Takuya Iwamura

CORE IV
LANDSCAPE ARCHITECTURE

Most traditional Western cities are founded on principles of stability and permanence: change or uncertainty—often in the form of rich and complex landscape systems—are typically erased, filled, leveled, denuded, marginalized, or stabilized.

Chris Reed
Leire Asensio-Villoria
Silvia Benedito
Zaneta Hong
David Mah

Core IV Landscape Architecture takes a different approach to city-making—or, in this case, to urban renovation: the studio assumes change as the baseline. In doing so, the studio builds on ecologists' reconceptualization of their field over the past quarter-century, in which classical Newtonian concerns with stability, certainty, and order give way to more contemporary understandings of dynamic, systemic change. With this reconceptualization comes the related phenomena of adaptability, resilience, and flexibility—phenomena applicable not only to ecological systems (whether native or adapted), but also to city systems, infrastructures, and urbanism writ large. The studio also explores multiple development scenarios (assemblies and deployments) over time, rather than a singular and totalizing plan; these scenarios operate according to a set of rules or parameters, but can be programmed to respond to a range of differing inputs across time. In this way, our proposals aspire to a level of resiliency with regard to long-term environmental, social, political, and economic shifts—and therefore can be rendered truly sustainable (responsive, adaptable) over the long term. More broadly, the studio addresses fundamental questions of what it means to be urban, what urbanism is, and how ideas of the city and city-life can be informed by and actively engaged with ecological change.

"For the Dutch, defending their country from water either by soft or by hard measures is absolutely a sine qua non, or a condition for existence, and that means that by definition, it is a collective issue, which also means that the Dutch are much more oriented towards prevention than in repairing something that is already broken. Given that America has not yet embraced water as a collective issue, we need citizen participation, regional design, landscape architects, designers, engineers and also governments to help us face the challenges that are ahead."

Tracy Metz
Sweet and Salt: Water and the Dutch
April 2, 2013

Like other urban estuaries around the world, Jamaica Bay has been the site of land filling, garbage dumping, massive highway infrastructure, and port development plans. This history is used as fodder to think about the forces shaping and reshaping land and water: processes of aggregation, processes of transport, and processes of dispersal. Our project proposes not rebuilding in high risk areas, but migrating in response to events at a time when rebuilding after disaster was very much a part of the larger urban discussion.

Anya Domlesky & Justin Jackson

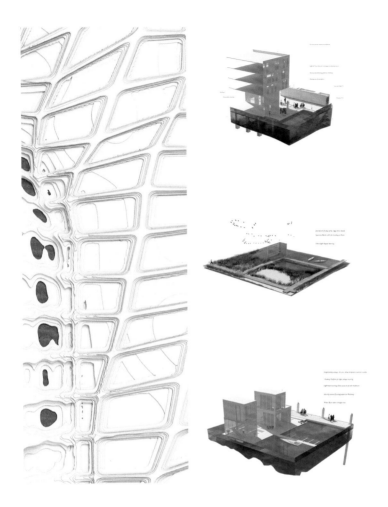

As a landscape urbanist intervention, this project preserves the precarious ecological conditions of an Atlantic saltmarsh while also facilitating seasonal inhabitation and recreational activities. By not destroying the saltmarsh or tidal flats with foundations and heavy infrastructure, the buoyant city allows endemic tidal flushing to persist, rehabilitating the environment. Structures within the city are moored according to season and individual leasing, providing a highly flexible ordering of urban fabric that can respond to natural disasters by vacating the site altogether, or simply rearrange itself according to the desires of those who live there.

Jason Brain & Lauren Hamer

<< " I hope that we will not have to all build our own dykes in the future."

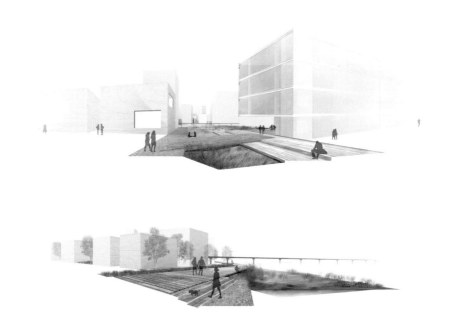

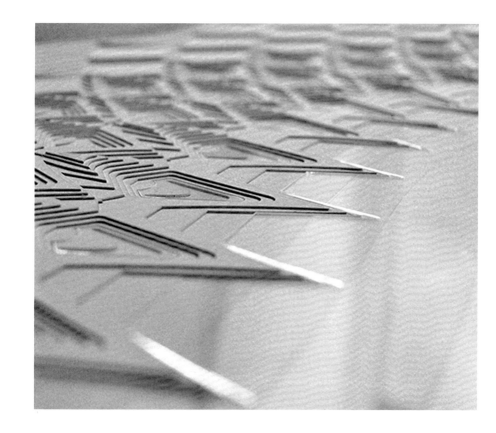

Design & Knowledge

By Sanford Kwinter

A pedagogical philosophy rises or falls on the merit of its ethical commitment to innovation and risk. It has become a cliché of staggering universality and consensus that it is a university's duty to provide what the social and economic machinery of our world requires, rather than to conceive, invent, and test alternatives and variations that both challenge and transform what is. No discipline within the modern university has a stronger mandate or responsibility to mix imagination and knowledge, and to produce a fully scientific hybrid of this mixture, than the design disciplines. In many ways this fact has provided the first opening and historical opportunity for design to claim a priority with respect to the arts and sciences, as the fields that *thinks* the social integration of knowledge with life.

Three fundamental convictions have guided some of the more radical (and successful) of the design programs, and these reflect very deliberate commitments that are sustained, even if less explicitly, throughout the school's pedagogy and culture.

The first is the unflagging commitment to the ethical primacy of the city in every aspect of design practice, at all scales and across all modalities of thought and practice. The word *city* of course is almost purposely overused today, but the effect of this broad use is still beggared by the necessity that never ceases to exceed it: the need to understand the collective, the social, the integrated, and the connective dimensions of the life of forms. The city is the place where history is unfolded, where form becomes historical, political, liberatory, or inhibiting. The city is the ground on and in which the processes of modernization are made concrete—palpable, visible—and where we in turn discover the forces that, in the end, compose (and modernize) us too. The city animates the form and transforms it into *praxis*.

The second is the extraordinary importance and relevance of hybrid and especially art practices for the present and future development of architectural and spatial practice and invention. Throughout the twentieth century, as art shed its transcendent meanings and sources of mystique, it began increasingly to engage with the ways in which transforming an environment could directly shape or transform experience itself. Relationships began to take precedence over objects, and problems of direct physicality and temporality took on both a fascination and a charm that only the figure could claim previously. Today this freedom and rigor has been widely adopted by architects and designers. Additionally, the commission of *actions* in and on space and time have become means to directly engage broad publics and the social realm in ways that were only hinted at in the most radical of modernist design philosophies, but which are today providing extraordinary new surfaces for design speculation and acts.

The third conviction that guides research and experiment is the ineluctability of nature as an actor and shaper of the context of design. The problem of nature is one that we seek to aggravate and multiply at every turn, to grasp the fundamentals of its processual forms as central to the thinking through of our own "cultural" ones. The logic of nature and life systems is not only inescapable, it is also an incredibly rich and mysterious model for renewing thought about all aspects of design, from the central importance and position of evolutionary and developmental problems of form to the radical and complex economics introduced by its energetic and thermodynamic organization and processes. Nature connects, envelops, and also limits, and each of these affects represents productive forces and influences that have always been there, but have only of late emerged into visibility within the purview of design thinking. The irrefutable facts of nature force upon us some of the most rigorous philosophical and methodological discipline that design practice has ever encountered—not only the concept of the "balance sheet" but of interaction, feedback, integrative thinking, and a great deal more besides.

Each of these three adjacencies are, by force of the efforts of our curricular tooling, no longer considered adjacencies at all but as necessary parts of the "expanded field" of design pedagogy, and especially of our emerging worldview and our attempt to project a plausibly rich and dynamic image of the future of design.

Sanford Kwinter is Professor of Architectural Theory and Criticism in the Department of Architecture at the Harvard Graduate School of Design.

This essay was excerpted from *Instigations: Engaging Architecture, Landscape, and the City*, eds. Mohsen Mostafavi and Peter Christensen (Zürich and Cambridge, MA: Lars Müller Publishers and Harvard Graduate School of Design, 2012): 226–231.

V/A LDEN

Last year Rem Koolhaas provocatively announced his legendary U-turn at the Harvard Graduate School of Design, proclaiming that he was abandoning urbanism to focus on the countryside: the territory becomes an area for work and speculation; it is "the next big thing." Following in the illustrious footsteps of Rem, our studio takes a series of field trips to the great outdoors, making base-camp at the legendary Walden Pond, 15 miles west of Boston. Walden Pond is significant for its association with Henry David Thoreau, the polymath philosopher, poet, and naturalist who built a small cabin near the shore, where he wrote *Life in the Woods*, which appeared in 1854.

Bridget Baines
Eelco Hooftman

Parallel Walden: A Landscape of Civil Disobedience acts as a laboratory to develop new ideas and concepts for nature and wilderness in the twenty-first century. After a forensic autopsy of Walden Pond, students are invited to produce a new manifesto for a parallel Walden and transform a 35-acre former landfill adjacent to Walden to act as catalyst for change. The intent of the studio is to re-activate the notion of Walden as cultural manifestation and provide an expression of emerging concepts of hyperecology.

In recent years, there has been a movement in anthropology toward a focus on objects, while design and planning have been moving toward the understanding of objects as part of a greater social, political, and cultural milieu. Design Anthropology: Objects, Landscapes, Cities (Steve Caton, Gareth Doherty) explores their common ethnographic ground. The course is about both the anthropology of design and the design of anthropology. The goals are to learn thick ethnographic observation and description; the application of theoretical concepts in making connections between ethnographic data; and how to move from ethnography to an understanding of how context informs design—as well as asking why we design in the ways that we do.

continued on page 255 >>

The Sociological Imagination

Diane E. Davis

From Plato's ideal republics to Aristotle's treatises on politics to the utopian visions of Robert Owen, Charles Fourier, Ebenezer Howard, Frank Lloyd Wright, Lewis Mumford, Le Corbusier, and Paul Goodman, imagination as embodied in physical, discursive, or experimental renderings of a desired state of affairs has been key to the design disciplines. The *Garden City* by Ebenezer Howard and *Ville Radieuse* by Le Corbusier are iconic examples of the application of imagination to twentieth century architecture and urbanism. While critiques of utopian excess have been levelled against these and other futuristically prescriptive projects, a commitment to imaginative "social dreaming" as a tool for recasting the built environment nonetheless remains defensible.[1] For all who aim to construct more sustainable environments, produce more equitable cities, fabricate more inventive structures, or create more desirable urban spaces, the starting point must be imagination as much as technical knowledge or pragmatism. The aim of this brief essay is to underscore the role of imagination in the design and planning lexicon and to offer some analytical principles for cultivating and deploying imagination as a "method" for generating new forms of knowledge and action.[2]

Although the task of imagining new possibilities may inevitably be grounded in design aesthetics and planning principles, it also requires decidedly sociological sensibilities built on an understanding of the ways that individuals live in space and time, the values they hold, how they will react to change, and what larger social, political, economic, or institutional dynamics are at play that might enable or constrain imaginative design and planning interventions. For C. Wright Mills, who coined the concept of the sociological imagination, this sensibility is liberating because it enables a vivid and reflective awareness of the relationship between experience and the wider society, making it possible for individuals to understand how larger social structures, social conditions, and power relations influence their everyday lives.[3] Once such sociological sensibilities are marshalled in the study of the built environment, they provoke new ways of seeing how social conditions and relations impact physical form and urban space—whether in the form of individual interactions in streets, the uses of buildings, the production of landscapes, and so on. Yet the sociological imagination is much more than an analytical tool. It also is a normative construct, one that asks us to pull away from routine perceptions and think from alternative points of view, looking at things "from anew" rather than through conventional or hegemonic lenses of comprehension.[4] Think of it as cultivating and adopting the perceptual "agency" to imagine something different.

For scholars like C. Wright Mills and Anthony Giddens, the sociological imagination is understood as the first step towards enabling a better future.[5] It reveals to individuals how their biographies are linked to history and makes them conscious that social context constrains personal options, thus motivating collective action for change. Such a mandate also drives many in the design and planning professions, who use their talents to ingeniously craft and enable far-reaching changes in the built environment that may elude the grasp or imagination of individuals. Yet if individuals have suffered from a lack of imagination in recognizing larger social constraints and pushing beyond them, planning and design professionals often suffer from an excess. To counter-balance this tendency, designers and planners must cultivate a greater appreciation of social context and how it writes itself on the material world. Such sensibilities not only give design professionals a sense of the real, preventing overly cavalier, utopian lapses only into the ideal. They also allow an engagement with ethics and social responsibility. As Zygmunt Bauman reminds us, "(t)o think sociologically can render us more sensitive and tolerant of diversity... to think sociologically means to understand a little more fully the people around us in terms of their hopes and desires and their worries and concerns."[6] This knowledge can be a starting point for planning and design professionals who seek to acknowledge and build on such dreams in their proposed interventions, making themselves the handmaidens of change in a process where peoples' own desires are brought to life by the constructive action of design and planning professionals.

So how does one cultivate such sensibilities? Anthony Giddens and others have identified three epistemological fundamentals that together comprise the sociological imagination. First, one must develop *historical and geographical awareness*, or the recognition that all places and times are different and thus interventions and imagined possibilities must be grounded in the political, social, and economic specificity of place. For designers and planners, this has not only meant grounding studio and class work in architecture, landscape, urban design, and planning history. It also means focusing attention on the territorial scale and on the geo-physical and spatial correlates of any location or site under study, and placing both sets of knowledge in a macro-sociological context. Second, one must acquire an *anthropological aptitude*, or a commitment to a deeply grounded understanding of how everyday life is experienced by individuals and communities. Once we understand how people live and are in interaction with whom, we can acquire a better knowledge of what their problems are. The third is the adoption of *critical thinking*, which means looking for the essence of a phenomenon rather than its surface appearance, and reaching out to identify the unfamiliar rather than framing one's observations and actions through the familiar. This last sensibility is particularly important for designers and planners who are working on problems closer to home, where the tendency to make assumptions can get in the way of "seeing" the authentic. One of the best ways to instill critical thinking is to embrace the study of foreign cultures, locales, and settings. Such experiences will by their very nature require one to confront normative assumptions, thus activating critical reflection and a sustained *telos* of questioning.

But even these sensibilities can only take one so far if concern with the built environment is the intended starting point, as it will be with most of the design professions. In order to translate the sociological imagination directly into design and planning practice, it also is necessary to develop a more precise analytic for the application of temporal, anthropological and critical thinking. Several additional principles serve in this regard. The first applies to *the perception of space.* Designers must ask how sites are perceived by those who seek to transform them, as well as by those whose lives would be affected by such transformation. Are there certain assumptions about what is or is not "appropriate" for certain spaces; are they historically tied to time, place, or peoples; and how might such assumptions actually be laid bare by design interventions in ways that allowed for new spatial perceptions and new sociological sensibilities? Likewise, are there sociological expectations that certain spaces are to be determined by use value, exchange value, or some other normative aim? Some of the most intractable and enduring contestations in and over space owe to the assumption that gains for one set of users will produces losses for others. One way to overcome such a stalemate is to design interventions that can create alternative properties of place or uses of space that will hold the potential to transform sociological perceptions of a site in ways that can create common cause among those use it.

A second principle that can help instil sociological thinking builds on a closer examination of the *subjects—or stake holders—*of any proposed action. Who are those who will be most affected by a particular intervention, in both positive and negative ways, and what scope do these subjects have to insure they are not exploited or unduly disadvantaged by the transformation of a site. Such questions bring to the surface the issues of equity, and the fact that different actors and institutions can have different priorities for a site that may be good for some but not for others. It may worth underscoring that the call to imaginative practice as a concept echoes the work of the political philosopher John Rawls who was were deeply concerned with universal rights. Rawls argued that any attempts at organizing society should be undertaken from a "neutral" position in which any single individual may not know at which social class or station they will be experiencing the effects of a given intervention. Such thought exercises maximize the likelihood that interventions will be better for the collective whole. To achieve universality in thought and deed, and to increase the likelihood of achieving a socially inclusive and just future, designers would need take into account all whose lives would be affected by changes in a particular site both as individuals and as a collective. In more specific terms, this means that the task of imagining a different landscape or built environment must be grounded in a deeper sociological understanding of stake holders at a variety of scales and temporalities: from individuals to institutions and those whose fate is tied to the present as well as the future.

Raising questions about scales of determination leads to a third principle that informs the sociological imagination: critical examination of *the territorial boundaries* of any proposed vision or imaginative intervention. What are the spatial or territorial contours for the creation of equitable and socially just urban experiences, and why are some territorialities preferred over others? A version of this question was raised by the French philosopher Henri Lefebvre, whose claims about the "right to the city" were intended to shed light on the multiple localities and various social collectivities that constituted society in its entirety, not merely on the concerns of residents of a particular bounded site. When Lefebvre argued for "the right to the city," he was not preoccupied with any particularly city or only with clearly identifiable urban spaces. He was interested in universal rights that expanded beyond any single territorial unit to embrace all of society. His propositions and critiques about how urban space was organized were intended to reveal an understanding of how power, authority, and economy worked more generally. In a similar fashion, design professions can deploy their critical, historical, and geographical sensibilities to understand the larger societal interest and conflicts at play in any given site, using this more expanded sociological knowledge to frame their own imaginative visioning of novel interventions that could have universal or societal impact beyond the circumscribed territory, neighbourhood, or landscape at hand.

With concerted efforts to integrate this wide array of sensibilities and principles into design and planning pedagogy, future professionals will be better positioned to display an understanding of real world institutional and political-economic constraints while also transcending them, thus nurturing the hope that the future can be better. Such vastly humanist aims cannot always be readily achieved by conventionally pragmatic methods. A vibrant sociological imagination will also be key to such outcomes. As Lefebvre asked, "[W]hy should the imaginary enter only outside the real instead of nurturing reality?...[t]he imagination is also a social fact."[7] Social facts, both "real" and imaginative, have and will create the built environment, yet the purposeful deployment of a sociological imagination through design and planning practice holds even greater potential to uncover new spheres of possibility and multiplicity.[8] It is my firm belief that this calls for neither a naïve celebration of utopian thinking nor a futile exercise in futurism, but rather, serves as a methodological tool to enable the production of new ideas in the form of non-routine social, political, and spatial arrangements that are engaged enough with context that they may in fact have a chance at being adopted. Armed with both critical insight and a wider template of possibilities, designers and planners are better positioned to produce novel ideas and new interventions in ways that may not be immediately obvious and that may, in fact, transcend conventionality to support new futures.

1 For further reading on utopian visions in western architecture and planning, see Nathanial Coleman, Utopias and Architecture and Robert Fishman, Urban Utopias in the Twentieth Century. For criticism of utopian visions in architecture and planning, see Manfredo Tafuri, Architecture and Utopia and Rowe, Colin, and Fred Koetter, Collage City.

2 This essay draws heavily on my own experience while running an international design competition for the city of Jerusalem (Jerusalem 2050: Vision for a Place of Peace), and on writings about that competition and imagination produced jointly with my colleague Tali Hatuka. For an overview of the role of imagination in the Jerusalem design competition, see Diane E. Davis and Tali Hatuka, "The Right to Vision: A New Planning Praxis for Conflict Cities,"   Journal of Planning Education and Research, vol. 20/10 (2011): 1-17. For focused discussion of imagination as a research method, see Diane Davis and Tali Hatuka, "Imagination: A Method for Generating Knowledge of Possible Urban Futures." In Elisabete A. Silva, Patsy Healey, and Neil Harris (eds.), Research Methods in Planning, Royal Town Planning Institute, in press.

3 C. Wright Mills, The Sociological Imagination. London: Oxford University Press, 1959

4 Anthony Giddens. "Sociological Imagination." Introduction to Sociology . New York: W. W. Norton & Company, Inc, 1996.

5 The Sociological Imagination, originally published in 1959 by Oxford University Press, is considered to be one of the seminal texts of sociological discourse of the twentieth century. Written by Charles Wright Millsas a continuation of his arguments in White Collar and The Power Elite, the book is known for its instigation of the 'New Left' within society, arguing for an engagement of the public and political spheres through connecting individual experience with larger societal relationships. This relational understanding gives the individual the ability to situate him or herself within a historical framework, and ultimately allows them to cope with understanding contemporary structural transformations. Mills taught as a Sociology professor at Columbia University from 1946 through 1962.

6 Zygmunt Bauman and Tim May, Thinking Sociologically. Hoboken, NJ: Wiley Press, 2001.

7 Henri Lefebvre, "The Right to the City," P. 167 in E. Kofman and E. Lebas (eds.),Writings on Cities, Oxford, UK, Oxford, Malden, Mass: Blackwell, 1996.

8 For more theorizing on the ways that imagination opens up new spaces for action, see Doreen Massey's For Space. London: Sage Publications, 2005.

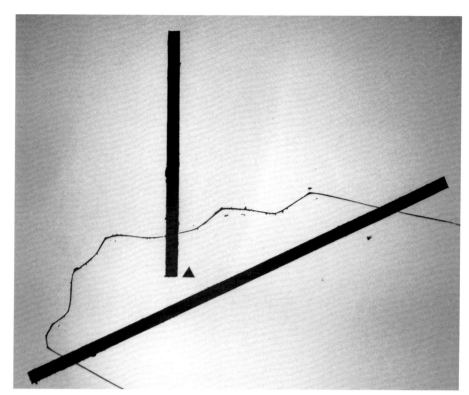

Field Notes—Williams Town, Little Exuma, Exumas, Bahamas
Tamer Elshayal

excerpt from <u>Landscapes of Exchange:</u>
<u>Cartography and Representation in the *Itinerario* of Jan Huyghen van Linschoten</u>
John Davis, PhD candidate

Some historians have suggested that Jan Huyghen van Linschoten's Itinerario represents the first Dutch encyclopedia.[1] The subject matter of the book is indeed broad, and Linschoten aspires to comprehensiveness. Encompassing a variety of fields, the Itinerario includes sailing instructions, ethnographies, notes on various plant species, and descriptions of fortifications. However, it is not an intellectually abstract attempt to represent the entirety of the world. The work is deeply pragmatic, and in many cases, deeply personal. This personal pragmatism is in turn revealing of the situation in the sixteenth century of that other attempt to describe the world—cartography.

The *Itinerario*, however, is not solely a guidebook to the untold riches of the East. The book was met with great demand when published; historians believe, for instance, that the more rote sailing instructions, which may have simply been translations of materials Linschoten had acquired, were published separately and were onboard the ships of van Neck's expedition to the Indies in 1596.[2] The larger Itinerario encompasses more than the bare minimum of instructions needed to trade successfully. Yet in its expanded field it remains relentlessly commercial. Linschoten was working within a tradition of both description and drawing that allowed him little room for innovation or personal expression; the demands of his audience and the world of trading activity defined the ways and means by which he could transport his experiences home.

Portuguese nautical cartography was a mature and established practice at the end of the sixteenth century, and Linschoten worked within this adopted tradition. Late-Renaissance Portuguese nautical charts are distinguished by concentration on the depiction of a latitudinally accurate coastline crowded by names, an ocean of clearly marked shoals and navigational hazards, but devoid of sea-monsters or other mythical elements.[3] Precise and lacking frills, these maps were all business, meant to be used by pilots at sea. Professional map-makers were also skilled mechanical craftsmen, whose duties not only included drawing maps and making plates but constructing navigational instruments such as astrolabes and compasses.[4] Pilots bound for India and the king's pepper would be supplied with a folio of navigational aids. Navigational charts could be supplemented by two other aides meant to assist pilots when approaching unfamiliar or treacherous ports. Profile drawings of landforms, called *conhecenaças*, were meant to assist pilots in determining their location once within sight of shore. These drawings of the *conhecenaças* were accompanied by a written report of compass bearings and distances, called the rotiero.[5] It is almost certain that given Linschoten's long service in the East, he was at least familiar with these materials, not discounting the probability that he had acquired his own copies.

His motif of pushing the expressive capacity of the emphasized landform,

arguably derived from his familiarity with the *conhecenaças*, manifested through plants, demystified in their commodification, holding little expressive power. Shorn of their vegetation and amplified, Linschoten's drawings of landscapes deliver the exoticism he wished to convey about his "second homeland."[6] Constrained by the conventions of commercial writing and the ambition to represent as much as possible, Linschoten afforded himself little room for expression beyond the odd note of terror, ambivalence, melancholy, or awe scattered throughout the text. His drawing techniques, both fantastic and pragmatic at the same time, could be interpreted as resistance to the constraints of the form, or simply the appropriation of commercial techniques by a mediocre draughtsman. Either way, the drawings themselves are a narrative that touches on subjects not immediately present if one relied just on the text—a way to see past the lists of produce and cloud of ambivalence, and to understand another aspect of the "second homeland" he was trying to convey.

[1] Günter Schilder and Marco van Egmond, "Maritime Cartography in the Low Countries During the Renaissance," in *The History of Cartography*, ed. David Woodward, vol. 3 (Chicago: University of Chicago Press, 1987), 1410.

[2] Linschoten, Jan Huygen van. *Itinerario* (M. Nijhoff: 's-Gravenhage, 1910).

[3] Maria Fernanda Alegria et al., "Portuguese Cartography in the Renaissance," in *The History of Cartography*, ed. David Woodward, vol. 3 (Chicago: University of Chicago Press, 1987), 988.

[4] Ibid., 990.

[5] Ibid., 1010.

[6] Linschoten, *Itinerario*, 2:219–220.

Image: f STC 15691 (A), Houghton Library, Harvard University

Cartographic Grounds:
Projecting the Landscape Imaginary

Lead Curator, Jill Desimini

The exhibition Cartographic Grounds was initiated by Mohsen Mostafavi, Dean of the Faculty of Design and Alexander and Victoria Wiley Professor of Design, and Charles Waldheim, John E. Irving Professor of Landscape Architecture and Chair of the Department of Landscape Architecture. Jill Desimini is Assistant Professor in Landscape Architecture at the Harvard Graduate School of Design.

"The drawing of a parallel between cartography and architecture is instructive. Each lies in the field of the practical arts; each is older than history; and each, since its beginnings, has been more or less under the control of its consumers."

Arthur H. Robinson, The Look of Maps (1952)

The ascendance of "mapping" and data visualization in design culture has changed the way architects, landscape architects and urban designers communicate ideas about buildings and landscapes, often privileging abstract forces and flows over the material conditions of the site. This exhibit reimagines the projective potential of cartographic practices that afford greater proximity to the ground itself. The approaches presented here seek to reconcile the precision and instrumentality of the plan with the geographic and territorial scope of the map.

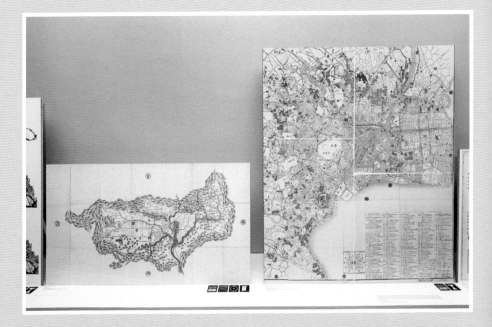

Cartographic Grounds investigates a range of surface conditions and representational tools, cutting across multiple disciplines. It follows the contour line from its origins in early European bathymetry to its terrestrial arrival in 19th century Parisian parks to its projective potential in the contemporary work of James Corner Field Operations. The stratigraphic column is celebrated as the means to create vibrantly colored geological maps and, by extension, to depict any subsurface condition. The work of Prussian geographer Alexander von Humboldt demonstrates the power of the section. He translated his field notes from an 1802 expedition to Mt. Chimborazo in Ecuador into an intricate rendering and cut-away— techniques that provided the opportunity to combine the physical characteristics of the surface materials with his botanical survey information. Lines, often deployed to delimit territory, are used instead to describe topographic morphology and to explore interfaces between surface and subsurface, land and water, earth and sky.

There are no absolute standards or conventions in cartography, but there are logics, systems, and precise techniques for describing the ground that are capable of transcending scales (from the body to the territory) and materials (from the aqueous to the terrestrial) without losing fidelity to the condition being depicted. In *Cartographic Relief Presentation*, Eduard Imhof reacted against loose cartographic practices and pushed for the careful rendering of terrain, the foundational layer of many maps and landscape plans. As design extends its purview to cartography, it is time again to look closely at maps and plans, to immerse ourselves in their beauty, but also to uncover their projective potential. We have an even greater challenge now, as our drawings are required to read at numerous scales, to be interactive, to make sense of big data, and to describe increasingly complex systems.

GATHERED MARGINS
INCREMENTAL EXCHANGE ALONG
THE MYSTIC RIVER

Senta Burton, MLA I

*"There are few public grounds which are not grossly deformed by the
imperfections of their boundaries."*

Charles Eliot, Metropolitan Park Work (1894)

<u>Advisor</u>
Jill Desimini

The margins of our lives accumulate trash, treasure, and memory—the edge is
materially different from the core. At the city scale, estuaries become marginal
landscapes: town borders often follow the water's edge, and the river receives
runoff from the city's minimally permeable membrane. The thesis argues
for the river as a working margin, where incremental pollution is met with
incremental cleansing.

In 1902, Charles Eliot refigured the Mystic River's industrialized waterfront
as a thickened band of open space, a key link in the Boston public park network.
Today, the Mystic Valley Parkway remains a system of open land at the edge of
densely populated towns. Yet the Mystic itself is a degraded estuary, swaddled
in pavement and dotted with combined sewer overflows. More than seventy
five percent of the surrounding surface material is impermeable; runoff is a
significant source of water pollution. The Mystic meets swimming standards
less than half of the year—least of all during the warmest months—and direct

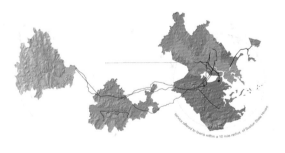

access to the water is limited. This
thesis develops a series of modular
cleansing pools that extract, filter, and
re-release water at selected moments
along the Mystic. The pools reengage
the river's edge as a site of reciprocal
exchange. Working across the margin,
the pools redirect resources upstream
and offer cleaner water and recreation
downstream, binding communities in
a coalition of stewardship.

1—

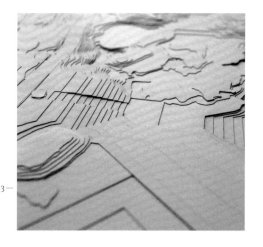

3—

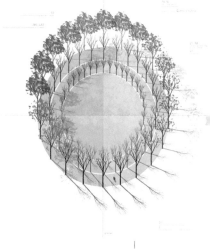

|
2

1 Peichen Hao
2 Lara Mehling
3 Michelle Franco

CORE II
LANDSCAPE ARCHITECTURE

Core II Landscape Architecture introduces the students to the challenges and opportunities of complex urban sites that have been designed and built many times over a long span of history. The sites reflect the traces of their previous histories—geological, material, programmatic, and topographical—that are embedded within, and contribute to, the present condition of the space. In addition, the various contexts that surround the site have also been transformed with time. Changing street patterns, codes and regulations, demographics, politics, economics, social practices—all have a profound effect on the urban landscape, causing it to continuously evolve. A basic assumption of the studio is that design is not a *tabula rasa* but a negotiation between past, present, and future projections of the site.

Anita Berrizbeitia
Jill Desimini
Luis Callejas
Rosetta S. Elkin

The emphasis is on understanding and reconceiving the three-dimensional interface between the designed landscapes and their evolving contexts. Plazas and parks are integral to urban environments; they support and shape the city's ecological, programmatic, and social functions. The edge between these designed landscapes and their surrounding urban fabric is a place of interaction, a threshold thick with material and programmatic complexity. This rich ground forms the foundation for a series of projective endeavors to expand, articulate, and enliven the interplay between a given site and its constructed milieu.

The interacting forces of globalization, urbanization and climate change are restructuring the environment in novel and unpredictable ways. One of the important questions facing the profession of landscape architecture is how to navigate the changes that are relentlessly bearing down on us. Plants for a Changing World (Peter Del Tredici) focuses on the nature of the interaction between plants and their environment and covers both the native and non-native species that grow in forested landscapes and natural areas as well as in designed and unmanaged urban landscapes. In this class the basic question is not so much how the plants can serve the needs of the landscape architect but rather how landscape architects can better meet the needs of plants.

continued on page 271 >>

This project seeks to open views of the park to create a feeling of ownership, while increasing the overall property value of the adjacent community. Franklin Park does not offer the neighborhood the possibility to gain visual access of its scale, size, influence, history, and character. Accordingly, adjacent buildings are proposed to be raised in height and scattered so as to obtain optimal visual connectivity with the park. Lookouts inside the park, as visual responses to the adjacent community, are proposed. They are emphasized by shrubs, evergreens, and canopy clumps. Seasonal bulbs are proposed to reveal the Olmstedian landform and provide flashing impressions.

Peichen Hao

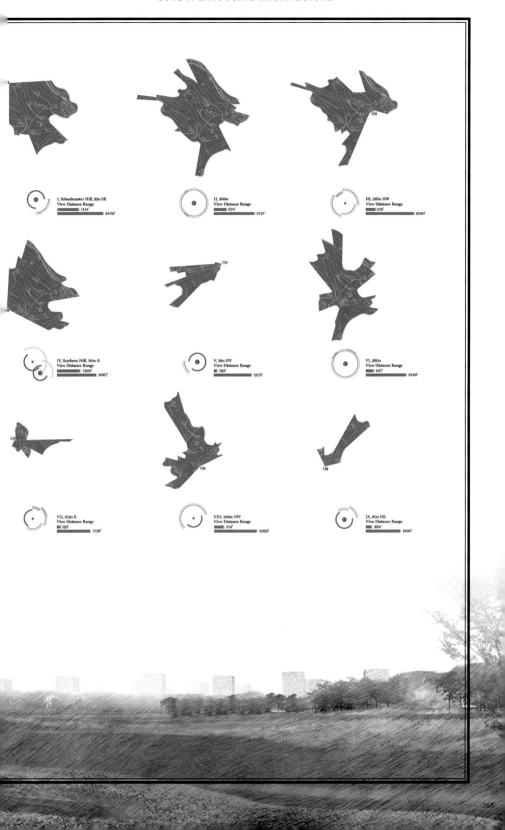

I, Schoolmaster Hill, 92o SE
View Distance Range
1141'   2409'

II, 36oo
View Distance Range
674'   2121'

III, 265o NW
View Distance Range
512'   2530'

IV, Scarboro Hill, 164o E
View Distance Range
1222'   2067'

V, 58o SW
View Distance Range
193'   1972'

VI, 36oo
View Distance Range
407'   2130'

VII, 213o E
View Distance Range
195'   1756'

VIII, 208o NW
View Distance Range
515'   2222'

IX, 60o NE
View Distance Range
334'   1820'

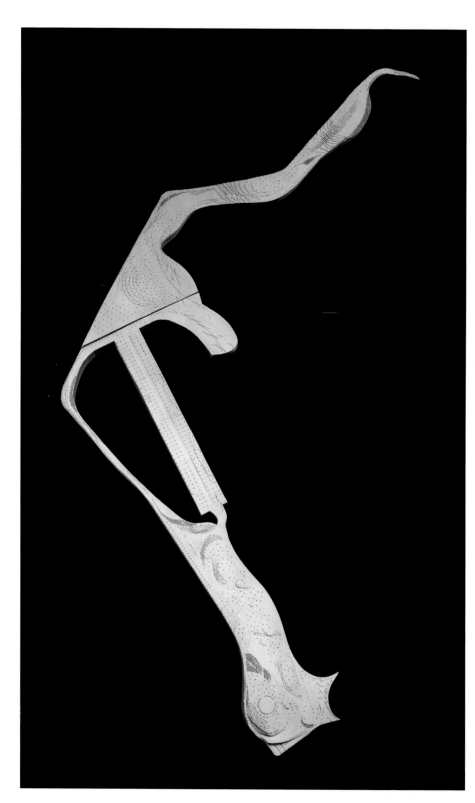

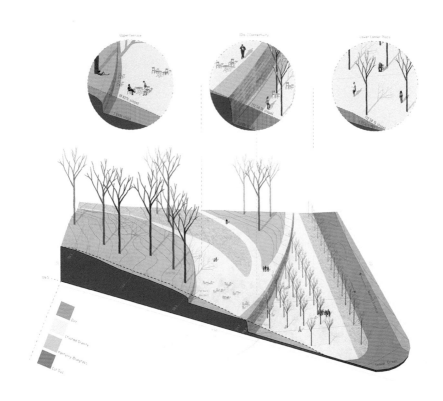

Franklin Park can be understood as a highly functioning and valuable urban wilderness. Despite the dynamic interplay between spontaneous vegetation and Olmsted's precisely designed parameters, the park's many lovely moments are held tightly within, distinct from the surrounding city. Through regrading at axes of potential visual access, new horizons of color and texture are created by a terraced ground, visible from a distance and piquing the public's curiosity. At times the earthworks are dramatic,intensifying the topography and revealing significant geologic moments. Still, the terraces remain open for myriad public activities, functioning variously as plazas, sports fields, courts, and amphitheaters.

Michelle Franco

"Every scale has its language and its solutions."

Michel Desvigne
Intermediate Natures
April 10, 2013

Botanical Illustrations
Christopher Myers

HORTUS EXTENSUS

Mara Kate Smaby, MLA I

Advisor
Rosetta S. Elkin

Enlisting the phyto-world of frankincense, the dried resin of a rapidly declining population of trees in the genus *Boswellia* in Ethiopia, and the oldest persistently trafficked aromatic in the world, this thesis proposes how a specific contemporary confluence of transportation, land use, and material processing can generate coordination between a legion of actors and landscapes across a wide and variegated terrain with a very small footprint of physical intervention.

Frankincense has been harvested domestically in Ethiopia for over a thousand years, since the era of the Aksumite Empire. The distributional range of frankincense, its management strategies, and patterns of consumption have proven persistent; there are still quarters of some cities where the smoke of incense obscures the hard lines of architectural forms and makes languid and non-specific the transition from inside to outside; there are still oil-anointed wrists and incense burned for the newly born and newly dead. Frankincense is still predominantly harvested in the dry season on foot, with a small iron blade called a *mingaff*, sorted by hand, and sent to the capital to be shipped in bulk to be processed elsewhere.

An abandoned early twentieth century train station, *Leghare*, situated in the geographic center of Addis Ababa, is reactivated as a multi-functional logistical node along an already emergent domestic rail network—a simple and systematically transformational lay-over in this millennia-old value chain. On-site, the three platforms of the species' enhanced diplomatic agenda—an essential oil distillery, a transit station, and a botanical laboratory, are nested into a cohesive public garden that affirms the viability of a vast and critical land-use pattern across the country.

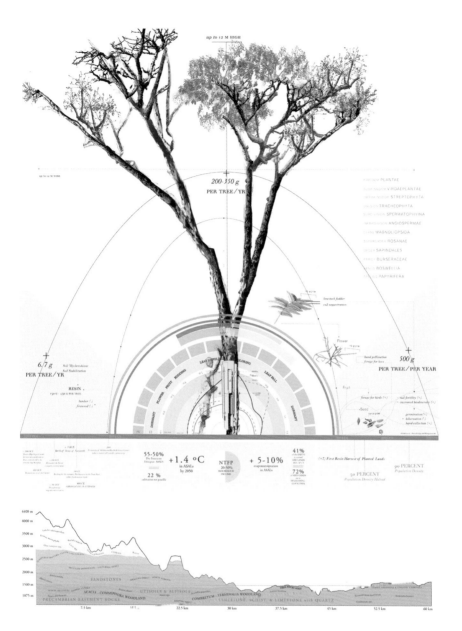

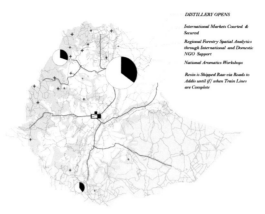

DISTILLERY OPENS

International Markets Courted & Secured

Regional Forestry Spatial Analytics through International and Domestic NGO Support

National Aromatics Workshops

Resin is Shipped Raw via Roads to Addis until if/ when Train Lines are Complete

SPECIES DIPLOMACY | SYSTEM ORGANIZATION

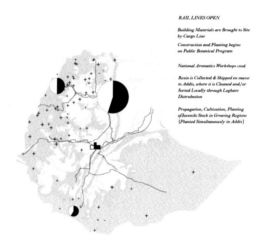

RAIL LINES OPEN

Building Materials are Brought to Site by Cargo Line

Construction and Planting begins on Public Botanical Program

National Aromatics Workshops ctnd.

Resin is Collected & Shipped en masse to Addis, where it is Cleaned and/or Sorted Locally through Leghare Distribution

Propagation, Cultivation, Planting of Juvenile Stock in Growing Regions {Planted Simultaneously in Addis}

INCENTIVIZED COLLECTION | INCREASED CULTIVATION

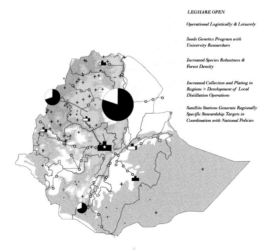

LEGHARE OPEN

Operational Logistically & Leisurely

Seeds Genetics Program with University Researchers

Increased Species Robustness & Forest Density

Increased Collection and Plating in Regions > Development of Local Distillation Operations

Satellite Stations Generate Regionally Specific Stewardship Targets in Coordination with National Policies

ECOTONE DIVERSIFICATION | DIFFUSED PROCESSING

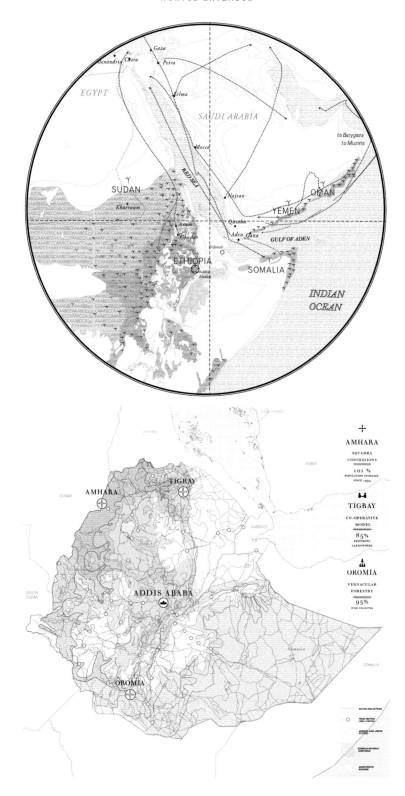

Pierre Hermé

with Sanford Kwinter

The Architecture of Taste

In his lecture, Pierre Hermé described the development of a series of his pastries from an original intuition to the elaboration of specific flavors, textures, and formal manifestations that give each its own character. A guided tasting of the pastries and conversation with Sanford Kwinter followed.

Sanford Kwinter: Everything delicious about food is derived form the *Maillard Reaction*[1]... It is the *Maillard Reaction* and those sensations of crispiness that remain the keystone of contemporary culinary arts.

    Architecture, like many formal arts, is haunted by classicism. It regularly repudiates classicism and its oppressive forms but we also constantly go back to them, with a certain regularity as a ritual of simplification or recalibration. A great deal of culinary culture since the 1970s consists of a repudiation of the principles of classicism and it valorizes innovation. You are definitely part of that tradition. Sometimes innovation is made simply for its own sake—I would add. You took the inherited idea of *le gâteau*[2] and you even talk about going beyond *le gâteau* and renounce it.

Pierre Hermé: *Pour pouvoir être créatif, il est indispensable de connaître les classiques de la pâtisserie[3] et les maîtriser. J'ai pu ainsi, au fil des années, m'en détacher progressivement et créer mon propre style, à partir de mes envies.*

"To be creative, you have to know the classics definitively. I was able over the years to detach myself progressively from what I have learned, and to interpret my own style, based on my own desires."

[1] *Maillard Reaction* - designating or relating to a reaction between reducing sugars and proteins or amino acids which yields brown-coloured products and occurs naturally when certain foods are stored or heated
[2] *gâteau* - cake, cookie, Dodger
[3] *pâtisserie* - pastry, confectionery, cake, French pastry

Known as the 'Picasso of Pastry', Pierre Hermé is a pastry chef and founder of Pierre Hermé Paris.
Sanford Kwinter is Professor of Architectural Theory and Criticism at the Harvard University Graduate School of Design.

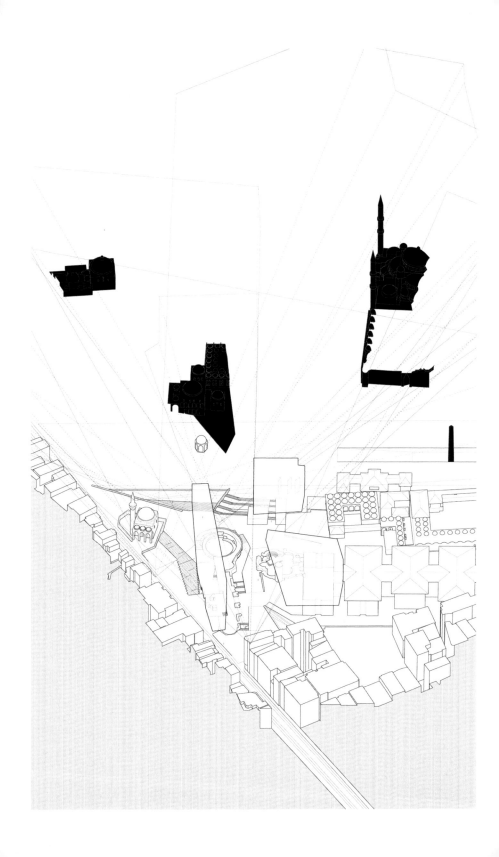

3 ORDER
1 ON
2 THE
4 OF
5 OBJECTS

On the Order of Objects: Mediating between Monuments, Museums, and Mega-liths is set in the area around the old Byzantine hippodrome in the historic center of Istanbul. Here an accumulation of buildings and groups of buildings over time provides strong evidence that architectural objects could produce effective urban orders between them.

Hashim Sarkis

The studio explores how objects, whether by accumulation or orchestration, have the ability to develop inter-relational qualities. It also seeks to extend this proposition from the discrete confines of the architectural project to the scale of urban ensembles. Instead of the monument and fabric conception of urban form by postmod-ernism that excepted monuments against the city fabric ordered by streets, and instead of the modernist object that highlighted the object's radiant order against urban systems, the studio explores other possibilities of medi-ating between monuments, urban equipment, and ordinary buildings.

"The city is a complicated technology that needs to be understood on its own terms. A city is not simply a gathering of many people living in one place; a city contains cityness.

There is in the city a kind of DNA that even when you're looking at a very small slice of the city, it is still imbued with cityness."

Teju Cole
The City as Palimpsest
November 7, 2012

By investigating both urban and architectural scales using two general design frameworks—arrival and framing—the projects rethinks the role of the ensemble through an order among objects. This order emerges in response to the need of making and understanding the city and its opposing force, urbanization, through the very finite nature of architectural form. Programmatically, the project manifests itself through a hybrid educational campus with controlled public access and a Byzantine gallery.

Victor Rico Espínola & Sarkis Sarkisyan

<< "The site was a palimpsest, as was all the city—written, erased, rewritten."

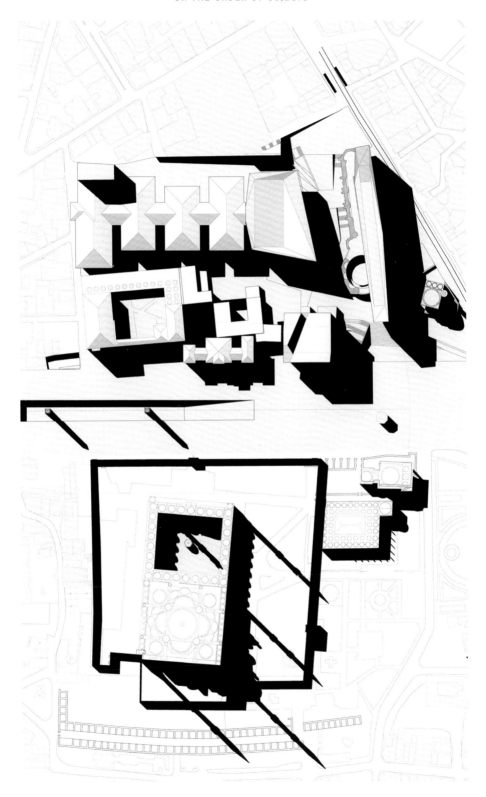

Under the rubric of cultural support space, this proposal intends to recuperate the urban possibilities of Sedad Hakki Eldem's unfinished composition, especially in relation to frontality, arrival sequence, and public space. As such, the primary architectural strategy features a bridge/ bar that completes the fragmented campus, provides a gateway to a new shared courtyard, and creates continuous outdoor circulation to unite the park at the top of the site of the site with the hippodrome at its base.

Jack Becker & Maynard Leon

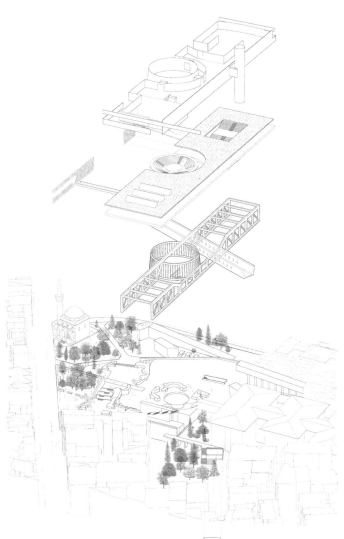

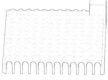

THE MEMORY PALACE
ARCHITECTURE AS A MNEMONIC DEVICE

Jungon Kim, MArch I

Advisor
Ingeborg Rocker

Memory, both personal and collective, is strongly linked to the concepts of space and imagery. Thus, architectural space and the image that it provides can serve as a remedy for today's tendency of personal and social amnesia.

The essence of the so-called memory palace technique consists of a certain idiosyncratic spatial configuration that has a striking image projected onto it that serves as a mental reminder. Collective memories strongly link to a sense of place and image. A certain space or place within a society—like a

structure of the city—can serve as a memory palace of the collective memory of the society.

Pyongyang is the only city of North Korea that the country will officially expose to international media. Almost like a showcase city, Pyongyang is filled with monuments and iconic architecture that are purposefully built to show off the superiority of Socialism and the glorification of their dictating leader. This thesis is manifested as an inhabitable gridded structure in Pyongyang, North Korea, as a view port that frames the vista of the city, becoming a focal point of all the city's icons and vignettes. As a spectator of the city, the building highlights the importance of the existing city, landscape, and its imagery, and brings it together to a culminating point.

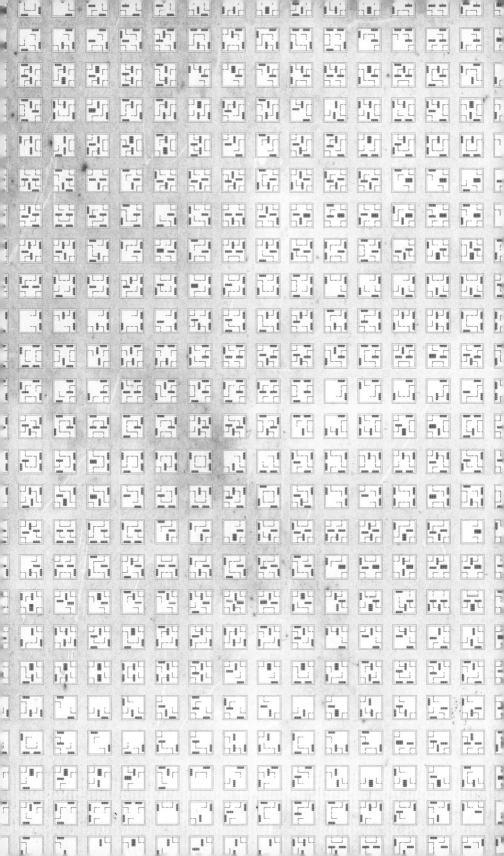

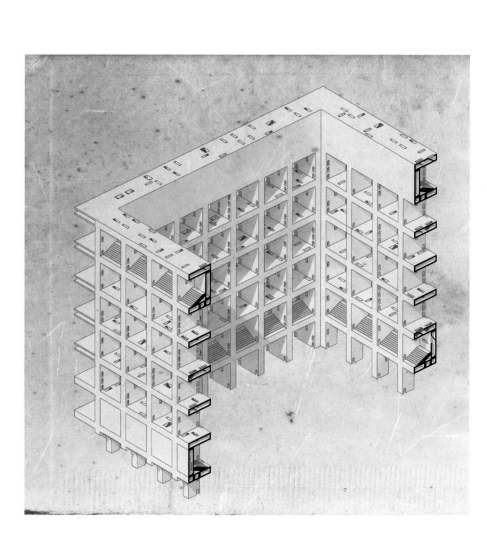

RUINS
MEMORY

In no other time as in the present have we have found architecture in such a perplexing contradictory relationship with history: on the one hand the practice of architecture is under intense social and political pressure to relate positively to "a history" (be it to its own, to the history of a given context, or to that of a narrative—just to name the most common cases that dominate the field), while on the other, the discipline of architecture has become utterly indifferent, even oblivious to history itself. This is a studio in which such a disconcerting dichotomy between a social demand for concurrence and an intellectual stand of divorce is dealt with by direct engagement with the discourse, polemics, and techniques of conservation and heritage policy. In other words, each design takes a critical stand vis-à-vis theory, ideology, and technology.

Specifically, we are intervening in a vast, multilayered territory in the Northern Neck of Virginia, whose dense architectural, natural, and historical significance needs to be reinterpreted by design interventions to reveal its stories to all. Ruins, Memory, and the Imagination requires students to situate and design a conservation research laboratory, a visitor's center, and a river harbor, as well as the design of all elements necessary to structure and present the site narratives to the visitor.

Jorge Silvetti

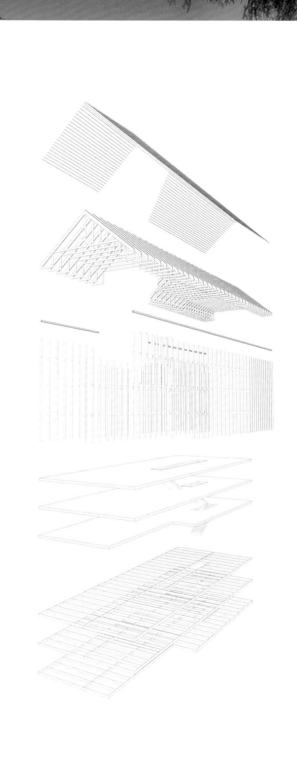

Xin Li

Menokin, an eighteenth-century Virginia plantation site, is characterized by the presence of ruins which are the medium of such abstraction. To that end, the intervention considers the ruin not as architecture but as an object laden with the inert matter of history and memory. This inert matter must be activated by architecture to become an operative medium of imagination.

Carmine D'Alessandro

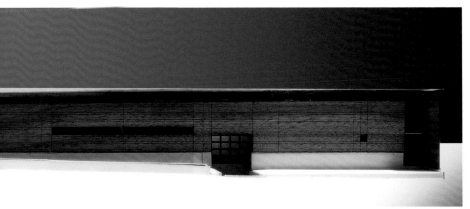

PYROGEOGRAPHY
THE POTENTIAL OF DISTURBANCE IN TERRITORIAL CLEARINGS

Savina Romanos, MAUD

Advisor
Hashim Sarkis

Regarding wildfires in the Mediterranean region, the World Wildlife Foundation reports: "land-use changes have been accompanied by severe land-use conflicts. Fire has been consequently used as a tool to convert rural land into urban land, or to appropriate land—mainly in countries where property boundaries are not clearly established." Wildfire occurrence can also be attributed to the Mediterranean "rural exodus" that began in the late 1960s. With new industries, infrastructures, private investments, and economies, populations shifted to the metropolis—towards development—and villages were slowly abandoned and city fringes were left vulnerable: terrains were deserted and left unmaintained for decades, and thus, significant quantities of biomass fuel accumulated, and the growth project of the city became a sprawling one in that fire used to change land use and foster development.

Just as a set of urban values shape the city's form, can a new set of metrics and rules be extracted from fires affecting the urban-wild interface? Can new dimensions or modules be used to establish better management of the land? This thesis aspires to synthesize the territory using fire metrics; it proposes a network relating form with geography; it looks to project new urbanities and synthesize the territory using fire metrics.

Iceland is facing increased pressure in a geopolitical situation where energy policies lead to infrastructural development and ecological adaptation. Plugged In Territories I: Icelandic Energy Landscapes (Luis Callejas) investigates the spatial and ecological implications of the recent shifts in the cultural perception of energy exploitation and recreation—and how the two can be integrated—in this geologically active territory. This seminar looks at the current plans for new geothermal and hydropower plant infrastructure and possibilities for effectively linking new forms of public realm with the capacity to act as buffer zones between exploitation and the delicate Icelandic environment.

continued on next page >>

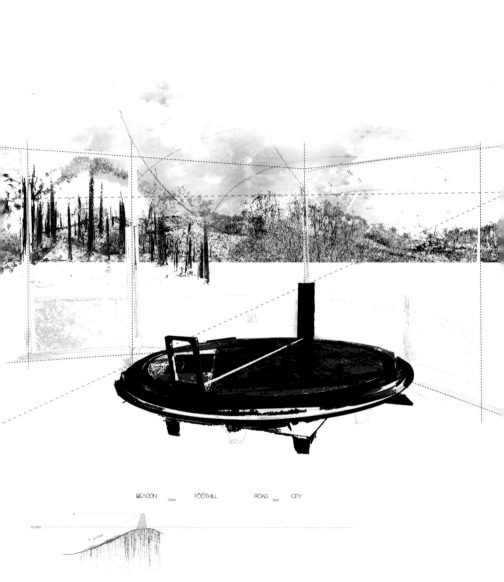

BEACON   FOOTHILL   ROAD   CITY
                15km   5km

1074m

30.90km

220m

Aphrodite Stathopoulos

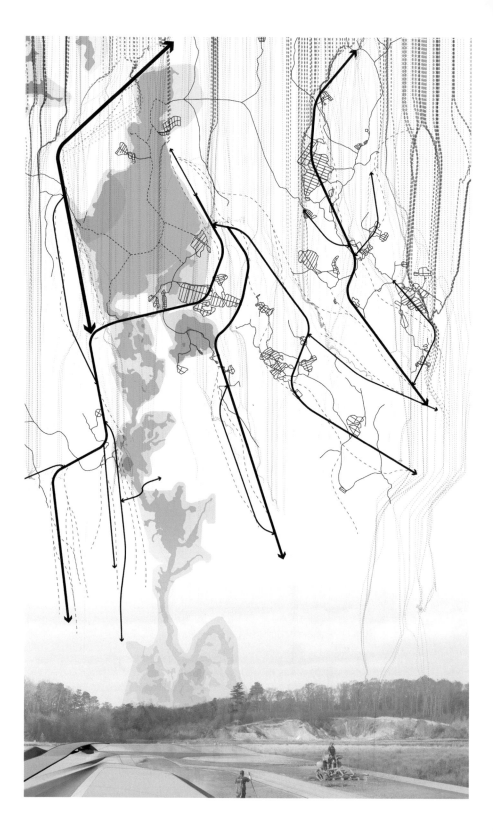

TERRI
TORIAL
ISM

The territorial scale and the form of the territory are today the fundamental basis for understanding the contemporary city and the important changes that occur in its spatial, economic, and social structure. The centrality of landforms and of their dynamics inspires less abstract and more situated approaches, "a new modernity" in which the agency of natural elements is integrated. The urban field is changing and ecological rationality can offer fundamental opportunities to intersect and integrate the various territorial layers—a means of directing or redirecting attention toward the territorial support in contemporary landscape architecture and urbanism.

Paola Viganò
Laura Abrahams

Territorialism: Inside a New Form of Dispersed Megalopolis investigates the role of design as knowledge producer, as an active research tool in the understanding and construction of the contemporary territory. It will be concentrated on operations of conceptualization and on the elaboration of scenarios, crossing different scales (from the regional to the scale of strategic projects). Territorialism focuses on the need of new spatial and processual concepts to deal with time, new problems, and varied perspectives.

Infrastructural Ecologies: A Projective Urbanism (Chris Reed) explores cultural ideas of ecology specifically as they relate to life in the contemporary metropolis. The projective possibilities of the unique and often bizarre interactions among the infrastructural systems, emergent and adapted environmental ecologies, and social and jurisdictional relationships are investigated along two infrastructural lines of water in the greater Los Angeles region: the L.A. Aqueduct and the L.A. River.

continued on page 303 >>

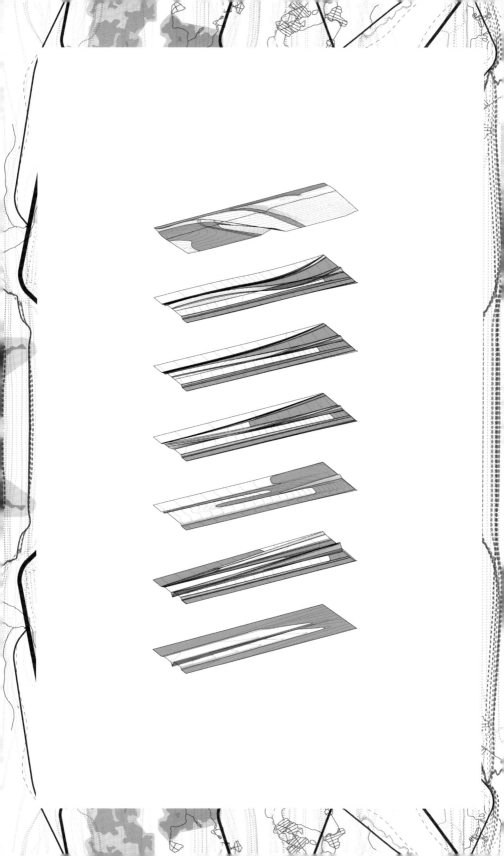

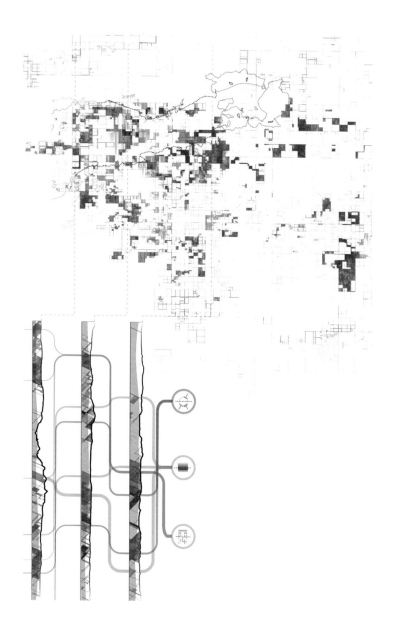

"I do not accept reality. I fight everyday against reality. That is fundamental for designers."

Paola Viganò
Modification. Texts and Projects
October 24, 2012

The complex metabolic matrices of wetland, cranberry bogs, aquacultural habitat, sand and gravel extraction, "lifestyle" residential development and decentralized hydrologic infrastructure that characterize the Buzzards Bay watershed region of Southeastern Massachusetts provide a contextually unique yet operationally paradigmatic case of the fringe condition. A close study of the metrics of this metabolic matrix refigures how we may respond to pressures of transformation—a rising saline gradient, nitrification, changing cycles of seasonal labor and inhabitation, among others—through contextually responsive, functionally agile, and technically replicable design tactics. It is the autonomy of the fringe, not its geography alone that is annexed by the megalopolitan economy, framing a political ecology of design at once localized and territorial.

This embodied political energy cannot be effectively exported or displaced, and constitutes a fragile endemism of its own.

Alexander Arroyo &
Michael Luegering

Beginning in 1913 the City of Los Angeles began diverting water from the rivers and streams for the L.A. Aqueduct. Due to this diversion, Owens Lake in Inyo County is now the largest source of dust pollution in the country. This project utilizes the network of wind and temperature sensors currently in place on the dry lakebed to inform a system of water misters, automatically turning on the water devices when the wind velocity and temperature reaches a certain level. Rather than using the current framework of constant shallow flooding, the new network of water misters allows vegetation to re-establish as a means to control the dust pollution.

McKenna Cole >>

Digital Landscape 3.0

By Charles Waldheim

Over the three-quarters of a century marked by the Harvard Graduate School of Design's recent seventy-fifth anniversary, two paradigm shifts have transformed landscape representation. Both signified profound changes within landscape architecture as professed at the GSD and radically altered the theoretical and representational frameworks of their respective eras internationally. Equally, they shed light on the role of computational environments and ecological thinking in the education of designers across disciplines at the School. The first major shift began just after the GSD's twenty-fifth anniversary in the mid-1960s and was associated with the conceptualization, development, and articulation of computer mapping. The second occurred just after the fiftieth anniversary in the early 1990s and was related to the import of collage and montage practices from the historical avant-gardes and architectural culture.

The intellectual implications and practical application of geographic information systems (GIS) for landscape representation are now evident worldwide. Since its origins in the 1960s at Harvard, GIS has enabled designers, planners, developers, public agencies, and communities to make better decisions about the shape of urbanization and its impact. Two contributors to the early research and development of GIS from the Department of Landscape Architecture played a particularly significant role. Carl Steinitz, now Professor Emeritus, focused on environmental analysis and theoretical frameworks for planning. Jack Dangermond, MLA '69, joined the Laboratory for Computer Graphics at the GSD in 1967 and aided in developing SYMAP. At the time, Harvard had one supercomputer, and Dangermond had to assemble unwieldy stacks of punch cards for processing, succeeding in printing his first computer map after a month of night work. Computer mapping and GIS as developed at the GSD represented one of the first genuinely digital applications of landscape representation and changed the culture and practice of landscape architecture internationally.

Various alternatives to the paradigm of digital modeling of empirical knowledge in service of planning practice have emerged in the context of postmodernism and landscape architecture, including techniques of collage and montage. Beginning in the late 1980s and early 1990s, leading schools of landscape architecture began to experiment with what would become a dominant mode of landscape representation, the collage view. The import of collagic techniques and modes of thought from architecture and the arts shifted the focus of studios and representation courses away from models based on scientific method (associated with the social sciences) toward multiple scenario-based temporal studies (associated with the design disciplines and fine arts). Much of this work argued for a conflation of empirical evidence with cultural references that would come to inform a postmodern sensibility of landscape representation.

In recent years, the Department of Landscape Architecture has been engaged in a series of discussions regarding the history and future of digital media in landscape representation. These conversations and their cognate pedagogic experiments are intended to open up multiple avenues of exploration. They collectively represent a desire to de-stigmatize the digital within landscape culture and claim a broad field for experimentation and testing of various ways forward. The foundations for these lines of investigation have been recently rebuilt, with the reorientation of the four-term core studio sequence, the renovation of the three-term representation sequence, and the construction of a range of optional and elective coursework.

Based on these preliminary experiments, it would be premature to claim anything resolved. It would be equally problematic to venture a prediction of the future trajectory of landscape representation based on these few lines of inquiry. Given the history of this conversation within landscape architecture, and the two major paradigm shifts over the past half century at the GSD, it might be possible to conclude with a sketch of the present predicament for landscape representation, with an eye toward apprehending where and when the next truly transformative practice might come.

It seems inarguable that landscape architecture will persist, and perhaps accelerate, over the medium term in its ongoing process of adoption of digital culture and computation. It seems reasonably likely to assume that as in allied disciplines, landscape architecture will continue to move toward the performative as information and data flows will likely drive form-making toward more responsive, measurable, and predictable outcomes. If so, landscape architecture may rather quickly come to rehearse several profound shifts that architecture is currently experiencing or anticipating. First, as already evident in the "performative turn" in landscape architecture over the past decade, there is likely to continue a shift away from taste-culture appearance toward performative metrics expressed in landscape forms. Second, one could expect that landscape architecture will increasingly find itself embedding information from multiple data streams, and sensors for its dynamic systems and infrastructures. Third, it is reasonable to assume that this tendency, combined with ongoing trends toward mobility and ubiquity in computing, will mean that the urban-minded landscape architect will be expected to manage increasingly complex models of urban form and ecological process. Fourth, as architectural culture has recently experienced, landscape architecture may move more completely to connect performative measures with fabricational outcomes, short-circuiting design and omitting representation altogether. Finally, some have argued that the ascendency of digital culture in architecture may very well decenter if not replace the culture of tectonics and craft. Although it is too early to tell whether either of these more disruptive and transformational outcomes will come to pass, they are certainly in the realm of possible, if not probable, outcomes of the ongoing digital revolution in landscape representation.

Charles Waldheim is John E. Irving Professor of Landscape Architecture and Chair of the department of Landscape Architecture at the Harvard University Graduate School of Design.

This essay was excerpted from *Instigations: Engaging Architecture, Landscape, and the City*, eds. Mohsen Mostafavi and Peter Christensen (Zürich and Cambridge, MA: Lars Müller Publishers and Harvard Graduate School of Design, 2012): 444–461.

FRONTIERS LAST

Colonizing Last Frontiers: Energy Landscapes in the Chilean Patagonia explores the material and ecological processes and byproducts of the highly controversial *Proyecto Hidroaysén* (PHA), a series of five dams in the Baker and Pascua Rivers in southern Chile that are to supply about 93 percent of the country's future demand for electricity.

Anita Berrizbeitia
Kelly Doran

The construction of the dams, their lakes, and the 1,400 miles of transmission lines generates, engages, and has repercussions on a series of material, spatial, and ecological processes that have not been, and rarely are, explored in this type of infrastructural project. Rather than assume either the position of environmental groups (that the project should not be built at all) or of the government (that it is the most efficient of all projects of this type in the world—a sufficient argument to have it built as proposed), we focus our investigations on the material and ecological byproducts themselves, deploying their productive, economic, aesthetic, and ecological potential to turn a monofunctional infrastructure into a multivalent landscape. Our working hypotheses, then, is that the operations associated with the development of an energy corridor are opportunities for synthesis and hybridization.

On Collaboration: The South America Project

The South America Project (SAP) —a transcontinental research collaborative focused on evaluating rapid urbanization across South America's hinterlands—was launched in response to the region's rapid urbanization and to the Initiative for the Integration of the Regional Infrastructure of South America (IIRSA), the most wide ranging intra-continental mobility integration network ever projected for the continent. While IIRSA's plans are meant to integrate regional infrastructures, they completely overlook the spatial and environmental ramifications that new highways and intra-continental shipping canals will have across the continent.

continued on page 313 >>

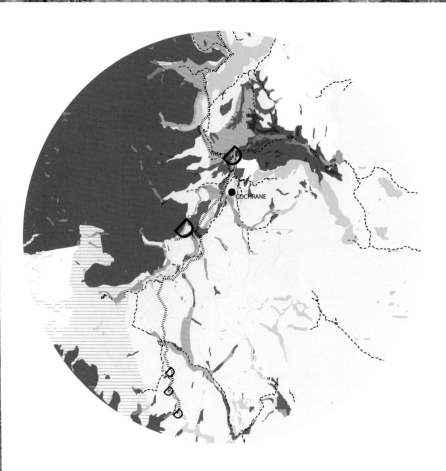

COCHRANE

With the addition of new infrastructure—including the dams and transmission lines, human and wildlife connectivity, and circulation—will be dramatically altered and habitats significantly impacted. The landscape in the Aysén Region has witnessed high levels of deforestation, road construction, and urbanization, resulting in fragmented habitats and diminishing populations of several species that play significant roles in the local ecosystems. This project aims to improve the interface between energy infrastructure and habitat connectivity through a series of strategies ranging from the regional scale down to the scale of the deer.

Emily Milliman

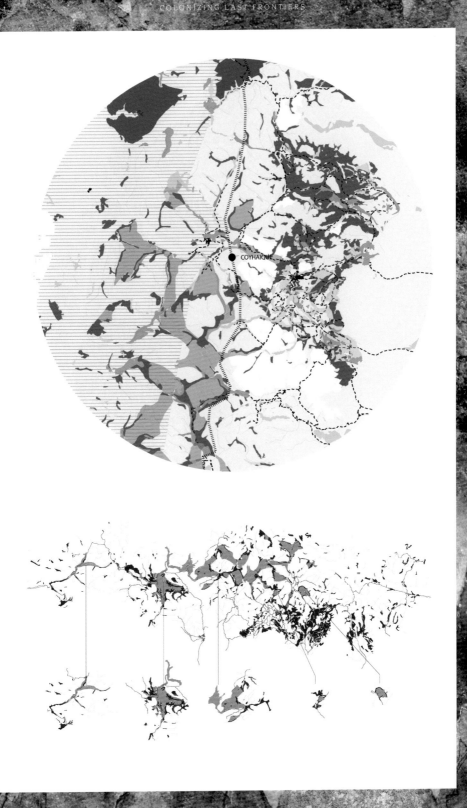

COYHAIQUE

Pedro Bermudez & Oscar Malaspina

>> continued from page 311

The region's hinterlands—most notably the Amazon River basin—are being rapidly inscribed with new patterns of spatial occupation, primarily characterized by major resource extraction facilities, agro-industrial clusters, and new entropic settlements along the recently opened roads. In response, SAP explicitly tackles the new urban configurations that have appeared and will continue to materialize as a result from the region's new transnational networks. In bringing together over 131 participants from across the Americas, who are leading 23 collaborative projects in 11 countries, under the auspices of 43 public and private sponsors, SAP's focus is to research and develop new spatial syntheses for alternative physical and experiential identities in South America's heterogeneous hinterlands. By drawing together individuals who work in different disciplines from across the Americas, SAP combines diverse design methodologies that can create alternative models to not only visualize and evaluate the effects of fast-paced urbanization, but also to propose specific pilot projects for the region.

Of the many objectives of SAP, three themes emerge. The first involves moving beyond well-defined disciplinary boundaries in search of productive overlaps among architecture, landscape architecture, urbanism, and engineering. Such overlaps can cut across scales, locating newly integral and synthetic possibilities. Second, the participants' multi-national backgrounds allow for members to share and learn from each other's unique cultural experiences. Third, the collection of multiple individual projects—diverse in ambition, scale, and scope—unite these otherwise dispersed proposals within a single organization, and articulate a range of alternatives to the region's current culture of development. As development pressures continue to transform the hinterlands across the globe at an unprecedented rate, it has become more crucial than ever for design to actively engage and conceptualize alternative futures for decentralized geographies and unbound territories in the traditionally remote hinterlands of South America (particularly the Amazon basin, a strategic territory that deserves close attention as its urban frontiers count among the most expansive in the world). As many of our research topics coalesce into design proposals, work from SAP will continue to gain significant attention from local authorities, national governments, and the private sector as alternative yet viable initiatives for more integral modes of urban development.

Felipe Correa is Associate Professor in the Department of Urban Planning and Design and Director of the Urban Design Degree Program at the Harvard Graduate School of Design.

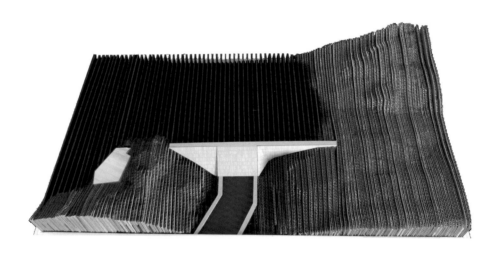

The Baker River in the Aysén region of Chile has an extensive logging tradition that dates back to the 1900s. In order to acquire land for pastureland, intensive modifications of the native forest communities were made. Today, erosion and sedimentation poses a threat to many tree species, while the logging industry in the Baker region is simultaneously affected by the Hydroaysén. The town of Tortel depends on the production of timber products derived from native species and needs a secure wood input. The damming of the river presents an opportunity to recover the lost forest and enhance local culture by serving as catalyst through which the forest is re-colonized with a silviculture strategy and local loggers are given a wood source and new saw mill station.

Hugo Colón Acevedo

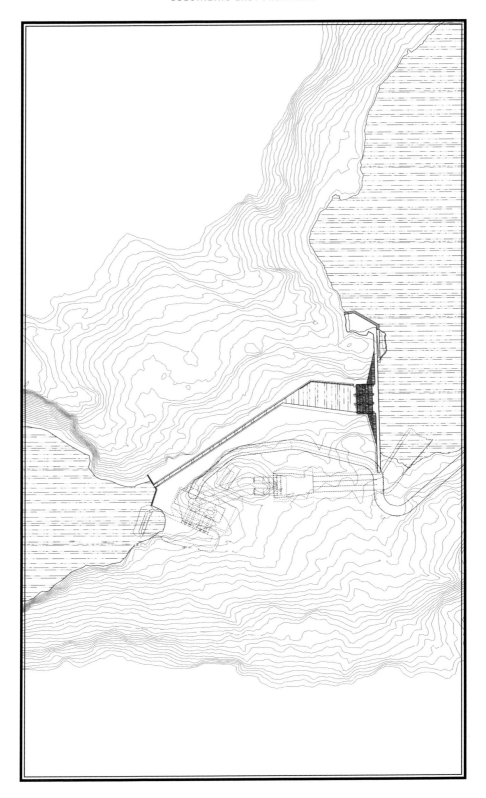

REDRESSING THE TYRANNY OF DISTANCE
URBAN FUTURES FOR THE SOUTHEASTERN SEABOARD OF AUSTRALIA

James Whitten, MAUD

Advisor
Hashim Sarkis

In an exploration into the forces shaping patterns of urbanization on the Island Continent, this thesis explores these dynamics through the lens of a proposed High Speed Rail (HSR) project. There are competing models of urbanization in Australia—the Metropolitan and the Regional—that are brought into tension by the HSR project. After the construction of HSR, these two worlds that presently define patterns of urbanization in Australia will be juxtaposed in unexpected ways as their divergent imaginaries for the hinterland collide. An 'arc' of settlements occupying a dense network of transportation infrastructures in Southern New South Wales could leverage HSR to grow a regional city. There is significant scope for urban design to engage with the HSR project by exploring and rendering the forces held in tension by the territory that will be exacerbated by the new rail system, and establishing strategies for settlements to appropriate the project as a significant form within an evolving cultural landscape.

THE NOMAD, THE TECHNOLOGIST
A TWENTY-FIRST-CENTURY STEPPE FABLE
Xiaowei Wang, MLA I

Advisor
Pierre Bélanger

Somewhere from 2030, a woman recounts how Mongolia became the center of the Asian economy. Unearthing an arc of history from a single point in 1990, a land of nomads, deep ecology and open pastureland seems diametrically opposed to emerging resource extraction, urbanization, and infrastructure building.

What have the men of science and technology overlooked? To answer this, an ambitious young geographer proposes an economy of time that so carefully aligns with the steppe's ecology. His Ten Year Plan identifies 133 free trade zones that exist seasonally, dependent on water availability, location to seasonally appropriate pasture, wind direction, and topography. Within these

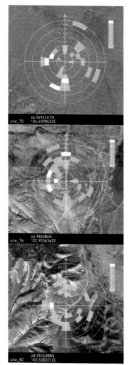

free trade zones, a careful circuitry of ecological infrastructure propels temporary airfields and ice shields for water storage, bathhouses, and agile infrastructures of hangars. As the Ten Year Plan nears completion, the young geographer discovers that his plan has cycled through—Mongolia has become the key logistics corridor between Russia and China, a stronghold of inland trade. The model of steppe urbanization spreads to other countries in Central Asia, a model predicated on careful timing, mobility, and restraint of trade events with meteorological ones. China's own infrastructure building has slowed down, and its economy begins to lag in contrast to its nomadic neighbor—a neighbor unconvinced of patriarchal utopias and the sheer poetry of data and parameters. In all cycles, the young geographer realizes, time becomes distanced from the linear. As his plane takes off from one of the temporary airfields he has designed, he begins to write his letter to the woman, a woman who will recount the events that have unfolded. His letter is nothing else but a resignation to the impermanence of things.

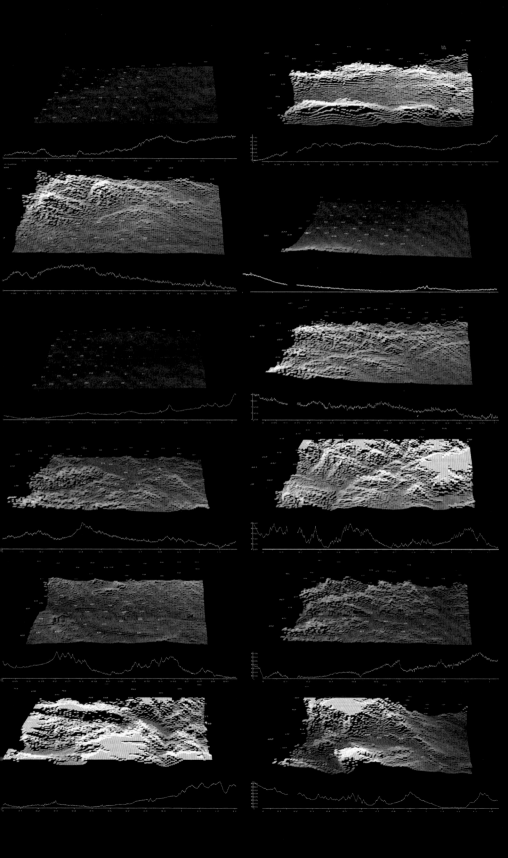

Editing Pedagogy

Rosetta S. Elkin

The text does not gloss the images, which do not illustrate the text...
—Roland Barthes, Empire of Signs

When Roland Barthes wrote Empire of Signs,[1] his ambition to distill an entire country into a series of vignettes or signs was not just ambitious but unprecedented. The act of publishing selective fragments to represent the whole of Japanese culture was not without criticism, but in its totality the book offered an engagingly aggregated exploration: signs, symbols, excerpts, and artifacts. It was a form of portraiture, one that was highly literary in style and fundamentally spatial or place-based in ambition. For Barthes, it was not only critical to leave out the obvious but to explore the nuances, the connections, and the materials that amalgamate across scales.

Editing a book that concerns itself with a year of intellectual production is akin to composing a similar kind of portrait. The sites are equally multifarious and varied although the rendezvous is certainly less exotic and definitely more repetitive. The act of compiling matter in itself draws out suppressed emotion from its subjects, creating compositions that are difficult to control, while endorsing a perspective that is seemingly limited but actually expansive. From the outside, the result is a highly synthetic, staged review, but it is the subject's perspective that can change dramatically, as depiction creates new frames of reference, offers altered perceptions. *Platform 6* is a portrayal of our present knowledge, shorn of elaborations and complications, as the work it contains is inherently varied and complex—embedded with its own particular brand of signs and artifacts.

You will be characterized by your content and liable for the trends from the year of production; your content will be composed of (1) projects that are not formatted or conceptualized as linear or sequential, (2) a selection of existing publications that are wholly complete unto themselves, (3) events that are valued through direct experience, and therefore resist print media.

Platform 6 is a book about how education is shared and knowledge gained. The process begins with an archetypal ritual: the dissemination of the brief, the confrontation of the task, and finally, the tested response. This ritual is our pedagogical commons, an established form of investigation, akin to a contract. By accepting the brief, the student agrees to make a determined attempt to either answer its query or reveal its deficiencies. Lessons are learned along the way, ground is won or lost, and effort is exerted in supporting or dismantling the brief. *Platform 6* opens a theoretical discussion regarding this exacting kind of education, as students experience it. Their collective experience of learning deserves particular attention because it may differ from the one that is designed and campaigned for by the faculty, or even from the one that is experienced by the instructor in the same context. These pages are an archive of those efforts, deciphered by revealing the questions asked and answers given. Metacognition—how information is administered and processed—in some ways is the true subject of *Platform 6*.

You will be responsible for establishing perspective across programs, using annotation and hyperlinkage to establish connections that map layers of stimulus onto pedagogic experiences.

The editorial concept of *Platform 6* relies on presenting the range of outcomes that manifest through this exchange at the GSD. As with most design education, knowledge is acquired and tested in a studio environment. Studio-based learning is essential to each design discipline, acting as a laboratory for experiential scholarship. Working in studio offers solitary designers a chance to interact; it is a hands-on model, organized around the investigation and attempted resolution of the suggested variables. This approach to learning embraces problems as possibilities and challenges as opportunities, placing emphasis on iteration and experimentation with risk. Correspondingly, no such environment is without conflict and no ecology can endure without disturbance—a characterization that reflects Gund Hall's place as an ecosystem, a community of living organisms. According to Frederick E. Clements, who first initiated the study of vegetative succession, ecology can never be represented as a permanent condition.[2] The notion that a community might go through dynamic yet orderly stages is aptly applied to the feeling of studio life in "the trays," which unifies each year of production—continually expiring and renewing in front of us. The trays are our habitat, our workplace and our classroom—a space of close cooperation and friendly competition.

Platform 6 is structured around studio, as experienced through the sequence of core pedagogy and options, embraced or supported by seminars, lectures, and events. Outside of graphic devices, and beyond discriminations of style, the reader will find perhaps surprising correlations between disparate projects and a deliberate undoing of any perceived segregation between studio-based learning and significant peripheral influences. Studio offers a model of non-prescriptive teaching and strategic thinking, supporting the student's ability to adapt to changing conditions.[3] If metacognition is the subject of this volume, the design of instruction is its substructure.

You will be remembered for what you leave out or neglect.

This system of transformation is taken seriously on these pages, each image offering a sampling of a larger endeavor. The work in this compendium is far from complete, just as most projects work with models that must be continually adapted to changing environments or as statistics are transformed by new inputs. Advanced projects are refined and iterated over extended periods of time and in ways that don't often fit neatly into an annual investigation. Our work is in a constant state of modification, as feedback and criticism are offered to make the outcomes more robust. The majority of projects are tested and iterated through this critical exchange.

Within this sometimes chaotic domain, knowledge spills over, flowing into the classrooms, spreading ideas and dispersing expertise while fostering incidental conversations.[4] Frequently these encounters yield collaboration, absorbing diverse characters and their particularities into complex explorations. The contributors to this knowledge environment are a combination of faculty, students, staff, and guests, each adding successive layers of disturbance and regeneration. The Graduate School of Design becomes a matrix of chance meetings, accidental intersections, and competitive tensions; the feeling of being new mingles with the competent airs of being established. The sequence of pages borrows from this exchange, where the reader will find that opinions and people overlap and associate freely, in surprising ways.

You might be analyzed for structure, but you will be read for content.

Some of the most interesting relationships are reflected in material presented alongside studio-based work, found at the intersection of disciplines and pedagogies. The purpose of this editorial treatment is not to reaffirm our multi-scalar, multidisciplinary approaches but rather to develop a more profound understanding of the genealogies that underpin our present. Witness the compelling current that can be felt as Toyo Ito discusses the future of the village by referencing Kiyonori Kikutake's Metabolism, as the page turns to reveal an architecture thesis that questions the autonomy of the urban dwelling (offering an aggregated alternative), while the next page uncovers an urban planning studio in Burkina Faso that studies innovative typologies for constructing modular housing in Ouagadougou. These associations are not made lightly but offer a powerful tool for revealing emergent patterns that operate across public event, individual thesis, and global narrative.

In 1993, *Studio Works 1* included a series of conversations between students and faculty in an effort to document the issues being discussed at the Graduate School of

Design.[5] One of those questions was: "What is the GSD's particular pedagogy and what will it be like in five to ten years?" If we consider that most of the varied replies could easily be reprinted with today's date, then the question becomes: "Where have we seen significant change in the pedagogy of the GSD?" One of the clearest signifiers lies in the space between disciplines. As Alex Krieger replied at that time, "I believe we are heading into a period when rethinking is a kind of collective rather than a discipline-by-discipline thinking. I think we will see more interactive attempts to teach, to think through how we need to re-tool or re-direct, not so much within the three traditional disciplines but in-between them, or in relationships with one another. *Platform 6* confirms this projection, as these aspirations have been realized and are taking shape daily in Gund Hall. The appeal to categorization, classification, or theme that organized past presentations of research and production is withdrawn, the need for common terms obsolete. The emphasis on connections and exchange has been transformed by our own pedagogical evolution. Nowhere is this more articulated than in the faculty essays that punctuate this book. Each text is significant in its intention to explore methodology over pedagogy, and creativity over obligation—ambitions made manifest in the passion of their words. When research reaches the cultural or structural level, methodologies must engage with ideas and relationships over disciplines.

You are a printed book. You will be handled, manipulated, and flipped through.

Which brings this discussion back to the material artifact in design, the scope of which is now so diverse that it becomes difficult to define (observe the predominance of concept over form, process over site, and simulation over experience). The physical artifact has taken an extreme form: either as a display of pure craftsmanship, tactility, and dedication to uncorrupted materials, or completely dematerialized as a computational consequence, moving image, big data, or parametric projection. Contemporary conditions in the academy reinforce this output, as pedagogy enables these disparate conditions and their evolution. As the multi-scalar, territorial, and global become our grounds, the devices used to describe it must also be tested. If student production can be projective of future practices, then there is no doubt that videos are replacing the static model and that narrative is still the most compelling framework for sharing ideas. It would seem that the typical but disparate deliverables of iteration (sketch) or rendering (polish) are diminishing, to be replaced by approaches that evoke future conditions, scales, and issues, critiquing current paradigms of production. This volume is a testament to the students who are testing, trying, and the bearing responsibility for their motivations and risks.

1 Roland Barthes *The Empire of Signs* New York: Hill and Wang, 1982.

2 Clements, Frederick E. *Research Methods in Ecology* New York: Arno Press, 1977. [c.1905]

3 Cassidy Schmidt, Maribeth and Timothy Newby "Metacognition: Relevance to Instructional Design" *Journal of Instructional Development*, Vol. 9, No. 4 (1986) p.29-33

4 see Jacobs, Jane. *The Economy of Cities*. New York: Vintage Books, 1961.

5 *Studio Works 1*, ed. Linda Pollak (Cambridge: Harvard Graduate School of Design, 1993). P.37

Jack Dangermond

GIS and Geodesign in Transition

All cities basically do the same thirty-two spatial things. These tasks or workflows are common generic geo-processing things. This was the birthing of a kind of language, like proximity analysis, we needed to carry out each of these thirty-two things, a vocabulary of these little generic geometric tools. Some of the tasks were tabular; some were geometric. This matrix became the foundation for the first piece of software we wrote from scratch. We also discovered that these thirty-two different functions either used or created geographic data. Those thirty-two functions created base maps. This is the new kind of shared knowledge or infrastructure, and geography as a platform will open our world. The enabling of technology is now here, which will require new patterns to emerge—new patterns of design, new patterns of science, new patterns of communication. It's going to go very, very, big.

1 Acquire/Dispose Property	17 Conduct Area Districting
2 Process/Issue Permits	18 Manage Survey Facilities
3 Preform Inspections	19 Manage Inventories
4 Issue Work Orders	20 Manage Resources
5 Issue Licenses	21 Administer Zoning Bylaws
6 Conduct Street Naming	22 Prepare Official/Secondary Plans
7 Manage Mailing Lists	23 Conduct Engineering Design
8 Review Approved Site Plans	24 Conduct Drafting
9 Review Approved Subdivisions	25 Maintain Topographic Database
10 Perform Street Addressing	26 Manage Drawings
11 Perform Event Recording	27 Disseminate Public Information
12 Dispatch Vehicles	28 Conduct Development Teaching
13 Perform Vehicle Routing	29 Respond to Public Inquiries
14 Conduct Traffic Analysis	30 Conduct Title Schemes
15 Allocate Human Resources	31 Bill/Collect Taxes and Fees
16 Site Facilities	32 Manage Database Systems

Jack Dangermond is the co-founder of the Environmental Systems Research Institute (ESRI), the largest GIS software developer in the world.

SHAPESHIFTER

Shapeshifter will use Stanislaw Lem's novel *Solaris* to reflect on the figure of the architect. As progressively more "inhuman" elements are introduced into the design process, what are the remaining points of control? Architecture could be described as the control and organization of form; by definition, form is inextricably associated with matter. Yet even today the fundamental nature of matter remains an open question. The final project will apply the Solaris model to a program that reflects the heterogeneity of the material substance of form. Situated between the natural sublime of the Swiss Alps and the technological sublime of CERN's Large Hadron Collider, the Museum of Matter will be an archive of form and formal dynamics at a variety of scales. The architectural typology of the museum will confront the irreducible ambiguities inherent in the medium of form itself. In this context, we will use Solaris as a model for form generation—attempting to reconcile automatic processes with the traces of the architectural unconscious.

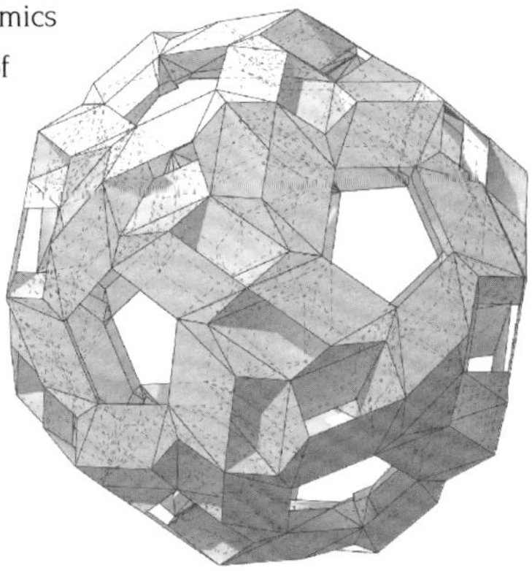

Luke Ogrydziak
Zöe Prillinger

continued on page 333 >>

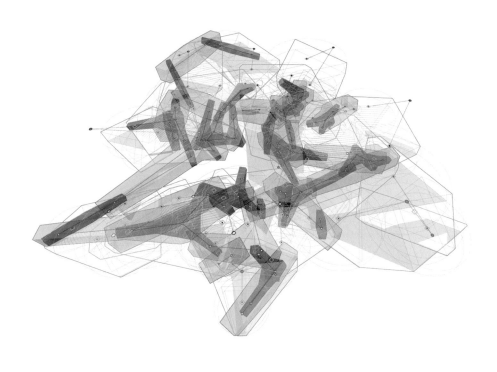

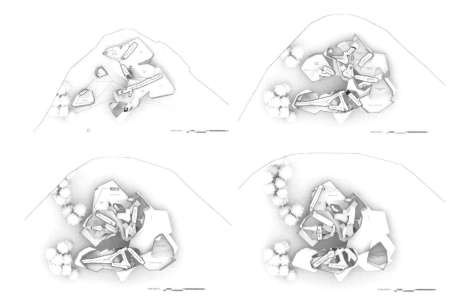

What are the elementary particles of architecture? What logic accounts for their behavior? Particle physicists seek answers to an unknowable question: What is matter? By necessity, they discretize, dividing the infinite domain of matter into finite particles described with knowable laws. Architects face a homologous question: What is architecture? This project proposes a homologous method: a lineage of discrete models for architecture. Each successive model reconstitutes its predecessor's behavior while developing further structural complexity.

<< Collin Gardner

Framed by a general ambition to develop explorations in digital design, fabrication, and parametric tools, (Re)Fabricating Tectonic Prototypes (Leire Asensio-Villoria, Hanif Kara) is informed and enriched by historical precedent while maintaining a speculative and novel outlook. Through employing digital design tools, associative design models for tectonic systems are generated to be tested, modeled, and prototyped at the digital fabrication facilities at the GSD Fabrication Lab. The primary focus is the development of conceptual skills and techniques as well as technical understanding of the application of digital processes and tools in the development of tectonic and construction systems in architecture.

Yun Fu, Chen Hao Lin, Ricardo Solar & Juan Yactayo

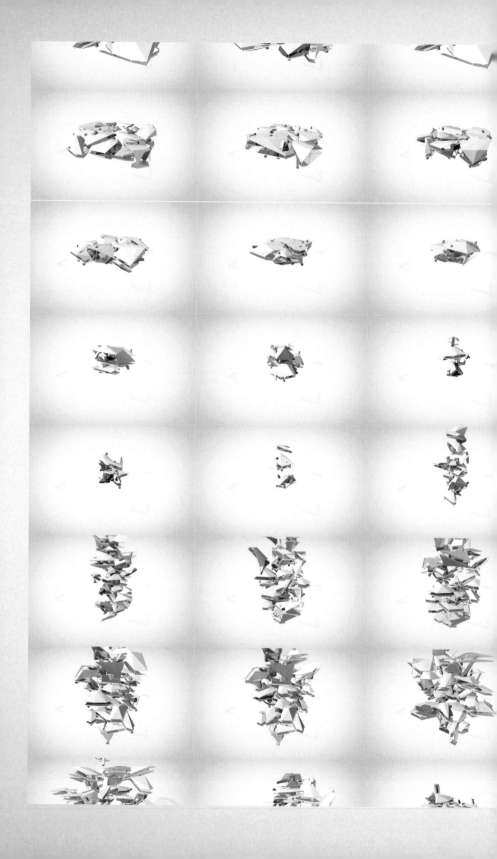

SMS.003
PARTICLE COMPONENTS OF A MASS

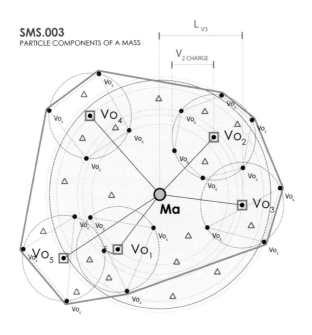

mass   ■ shaping point   ⬚ volume shape spread   ⬚ volume shape charge   □ Explicit Form

SMS.004
PARTICLE COMPONENTS OF AN EVENT

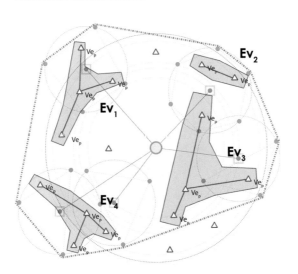

boundary from mass   △ active event particle   △ passive event particle   □ explicit Interior

REAL
+ iMAGiNARY
VARiABLES

Halfway between the socially responsive discourse of programmatic indeterminacy and the alleged futility of form giving, this studio explores architecture's
critical return to form. Our interest in the topic of form is neither aesthetic nor
ideological. Contrary to the notion of shape—with which it is often confused—
we understand form as a syntactic, procedural,
and (increasingly) technical problem, much
like the study of language in the 1970s, or the
more recent emergence of object-oriented
programming in the software industry. Our
past GSD briefs have systematically explored
the architectural potential of the variable
parametric surface, a vehicle chosen for its
relentless abstraction and relative resistance
to predictable questions of architectural
function and figure. The investigation continues. Real and Imaginary Variables II aims
to produce sophisticated, if counter-intuitive,
new formal prototypes—incorporated into
pragmatic urban and architectural proposals
located in a dense urban site.

George L. Legendre

Digital Media II (Andrew Witt) explores the design
and science of logical form making examined
through geometry, parametric control, algorithms,
and digital tools. The point of departure is a
cumulative sequence of fundamental topics and
problems in design geometry, which have recurring
impact on the history of form. These problems
provide a context and pretext for a rigorous
introduction to parametric modeling, algorithmic
automation, and the mathematical principles
underpinning them. These logical investigations
of modeling cultivate a certain objective approach
to form that explores the application of parametric
methods that are both deductive and empirical.
Thematically, the course fosters an integrated
understanding of topics such as parametric
geometry definition, surface geometry qualifica-
tion, and the converse dynamics of packing and
subdivision.

continued on next page >>

$X_{m,n} = A\sin(\sin(n)) + \cos(m) + m$

$Y_{m,n} = A\sin(\cos(n)) + \cos(m)$

$Z_{m,n} = A\sin(\sin(m))$

When two dependent variables are mapped against each other, the mathematical representation frees us from seeing the result as a simple topographic surface. To these base equations, constants were added and multiplied until they produced a form that was more than the sum of its parts. The form stays right on the boundary of interpretation. The mesh produces a figure eight ramp that connects to a horizontal slicing logic. It is a loop, a stacking spiral, and connected by open floor plates, introducing labyrinth-like circulation patterns. The bar building has compressed so much that it is a block building opening back up to the city. Eight museum typologies were identified. Each typology was analyzed as a transformation of the neighboring type and quantified with gallery efficiency, showing the cyclical nature of these transformations. In this project, three equations were used, each one contributing to the xyz components of a mesh.

John Morrison & Joseph Ross

The base screen is a system of minimal surface panels tiled onto a twisted surface. The panels provide an intricacy for the volumetric render, while the twisted surface gives the render an overall shape. The effect of multiple passes is a blurred reading of shape and component, regardless of scale.

Art Terry & Yang Dingliang

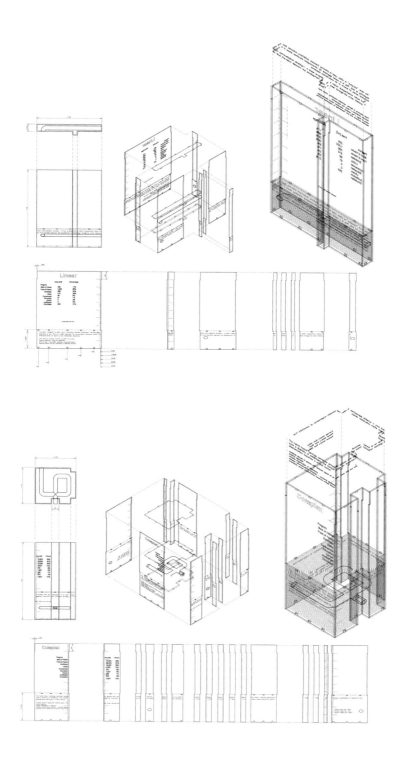

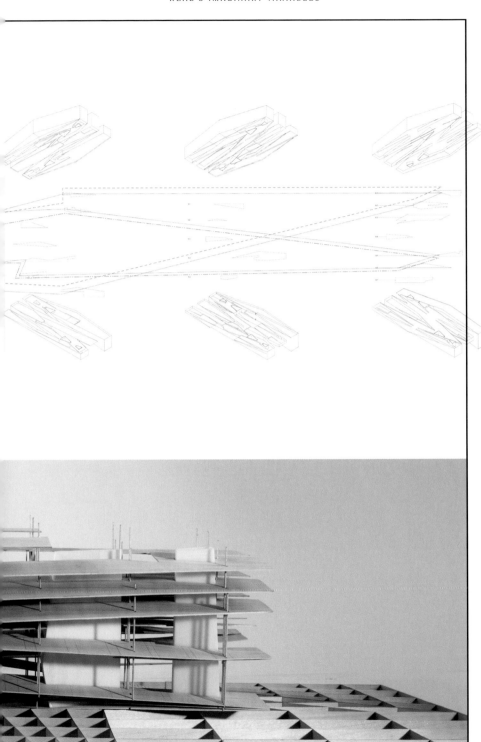

THE RULE
DERIVATIONS OF NATURE
William DiBernardo, MLA II

Advisor
Rosetta S. Elkin

Current methodology in landscape architecture can be seen in two parts: the definition of a problem, and the process used to, in some capacity, solve or mitigate that problem. While the former has seen a broadening of scope, the latter has failed to evolve simultaneously. New tools, namely big data, have seen their way into design methodology, providing us new lenses through which we define and view landscape. These new tools seem to only assist in defining our design problems though. In testing an evolved design methodology, this thesis holds the apprehension and interpretation of data as central to its thesis. Allowing these tools to dictate actual spatial intervention will reveal the strengths and weaknesses of a truer data-driven design method. More importantly though, is what an alternative design methodology says about our current design paradigms. Operating outside of these current paradigms removes us from a self-referential discourse. Can the crafting of data help us negotiate the space between virtual lens and physical condition?

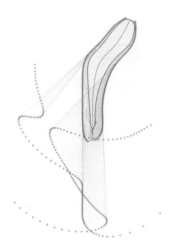

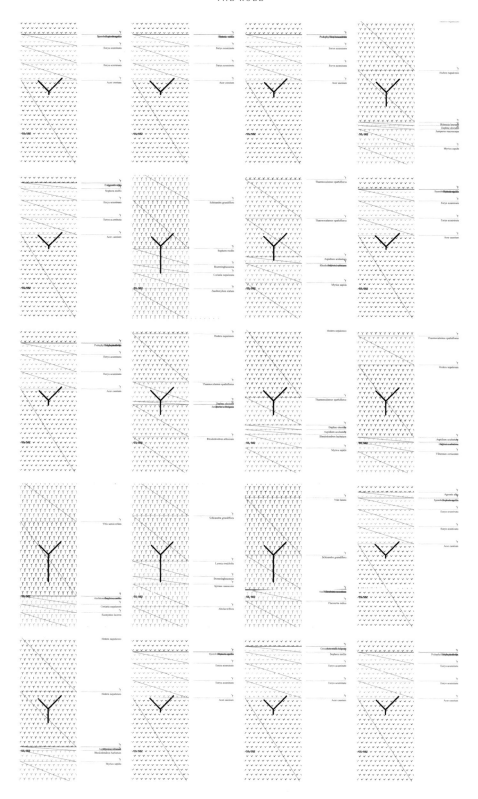

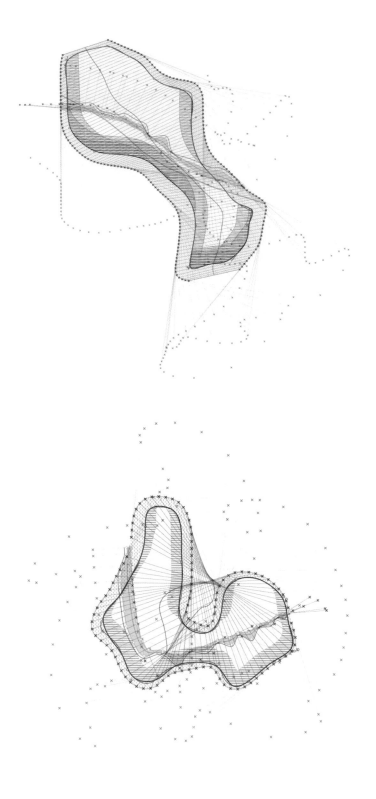

>> continued from page 13

The evolution of the atmosphere and outer space as a vertical territory is directly connected to enhancements in flight- and space-based technologies. Distance in relation to the earth's surface is vital to the production, acquisition, and exchange of terrestrial information—it is a remote-sensing operation owing itself to an Archimedean tradition insofar as it presupposes distance. Lacking the need for physical proximity, such remote-sensing technologies require an active appropriation of outer space to achieve a totalizing and dominating visualization of earth.

Outer space is such an extraterrestrial site where fixed investments, namely satellites, are placed and mobilized to ensure the return on capital—by way of trade/circulation of goods or information. It is on this basis that the binary opposition set up between mobility and fixity, and the privileging of the latter, is disrupted; the mobility of the vehicle breaks the liberal conception of the dichotomy between production and trade; information is simultaneously produced and traded in the case of low-Earth communication satellites. Furthermore, the idea of "production" being delimited within confined state borders is also fractured, given that the communication satellites now operate as "fixed capital" producing information and communication data from a non-terrestrial territory.

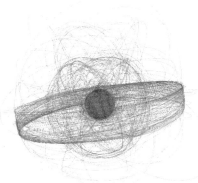

Robert Daurio &
Melany Sun-Min Park

Harvard University
Graduate School of Design 2012-13

Drew Gilpin Faust President of Harvard University
Mohsen Mostafavi Dean of the Graduate School of Design
Martin Bechthold Co-Director of the Master in Design Studies Program
Anita Berrizbeitia Director of the Master in Lansdcape Architecture Program
Preston Scott Cohen Chair of the Department of Architecture
Felipe Correa Director of the Master of Architecture in Urban Design and the Master of Landscape Architecture in Urban Design Programs
Ann Forsyth Director of the Master in Urban Planning Program
K. Michael Hays Associate Dean for Academic Affairs and Co-Director of the Doctoral Programs
Rahul Mehrotra Chair of the Department of Urban Planning and Design
Mark Mulligan Director of the Master in Architecture Programs
Sanford Kwinter Co-Director of the Master in Design Studies Program
Antoine Picon Co-Director of the Doctoral Programs
Charles Waldheim Chair of the Department of Landscape Architecture

Faculty of Design

Iñaki Ábalos Professor in Residence
Alan Altshuler Ruth and Frank Stanton Professor in Urban Policy and Planning and Harvard University Distinguished Service Professor
John Beardsley Adjunct Professor of Landscape Architecture
Martin Bechthold Professor of Architectural Technology
Pierre Bélanger Assoicate Professor of Landscape Architecture
Silvia Benedito Assistant Professor of Landscape Architecture
Anita Berrizbeitia Professor of Landscape Architecture
Eve Blau Adjunct Professor of the History of Urban Form
Neil Brenner Professor of Urban Theory
Joan Busquets Martin Bucksbaum Professor in Practice of Urban Planning and Design
Preston Scott Cohen Gerald M. McCue Professor in Architecture
Felipe Correa Associate Professor of Urban Design
Diane Davis Professor of Urbanism and Development
Peter Del Tredici Adjunct Associate Professor of Landscape Architecture
Jill Desimini Assistant Professor of Landscape Architecture
Sonja Duempelmann Associate Professor of Landscape Architecture
Ed Eigen Associate Professor of Architecture and Landscape Architecture
Danielle Etzler Assistant Professor of Architecture
Richard T.T. Forman Professor of Advanced Environmental Studies in the Field of Landscape Ecology
Ann Forsyth Professor of Urban Planning
José Gómez-Ibáñez Derek Bok Professor of Urban Planning and Public Policy

Toni Griffin Adjunct Associate Professor of Urban Planning
K. Michael Hays Eliot Noyes Professor of Architectural Theory
Gary Hilderbrand Adjunct Professor of Landscape Architecture
John Hong Adjunct Associate Professor of Architecture
Michael Hooper Assistant Professor of Urban Planning
Eric Höweler Assistant Professor of Architecture
Jane Hutton Assistant Professor of Landscape Architecture
Timothy Hyde Associate Professor of Architecture
Mariana Ibañez Associate Professor of Architecture
Florian Idenburg Adjunct Associate Professor of Architecture
Hanif Kara Adjunct Professor in Architectural Technology
Jerold Kayden Frank Backus Williams Professor of Urban Planning and Design
Niall Kirkwood Professor of Landscape Architecture
Remment Koolhaas Professor in Practice of Architecture and Urban Design
Alex Krieger Professor in Practice of Urban Design
Sanford Kwinter Professor of Architectural Theory and Criticism
Mark Laird Adjunct Professor of Landscape Architecture
Christopher Lee Adjunct Associate Professor of Urban Design
George L. Legendre Adjunct Associate Professor of Architecture
Jonathan Levi Adjunct Professor of Architecture
Judith Grant Long Associate Professor of Urban Planning
Rahul Mehrotra Professor of Urban Design and Planning
Panagiotis Michalatos Assistant Professor of Architectural Technology
Kiel Moe Assistant Professor of Architectural Technology
Rafael Moneo Josep Lluís Sert Professor in Architecture
Toshiko Mori Robert P. Hubbard Professor in the Practice of Architecture
Mohsen Mostafavi Dean of the Faculty of Design and Alexander and Victoria Wiley Professor of Design
Farshid Moussavi Professor in Practice of Architecture
Mark Mulligan Associate Professor in Practice of Architecture
Erika Naginski Associate Professor of Architectural History
Paul Nakazawa Adjunct Associate Professor of Architecture
Richard Peiser Michael D. Spear Professor of Real Estate Development
Antoine Picon G. Ware Travlestead Professor of the History of Architecture and Technology
Spiro Pollalis Professor of Design Technology and Management
Chris Reed Adjunct Associate Professor of Landscape Architecture
Ingeborg Rocker Associate Professor of Architecture
Joyce Klein Rosenthal Assistant Professor of Urban Planning
Peter Rowe Raymond Garbe Professor of Architecture and Urban Design and Harvard University Distinguished Service Professor
A. Hashim Sarkis Aga Khan Professor of Landscape Architecture and Urbanism in Muslim Societies

Allen Sayegh Adjunct Associate Professor of Architectural Technology

Matthias Schuler Adjunct Professor of Environmental Technology

Martha Schwartz Professor in Practice of Landscape Architecture

Mack Scogin Kajima Professor in Practice of Architecture

Jorge Silvetti Nelson Robinson Jr. Professor of Architecture

Christine Smith Robert C. and Marian K. Weinberg Professor of Architectural History

Laura Solano Adjunct Associate Professor in Landscape Architecture

John Stilgoe Robert and Lois Orchard Professor in the History of Landscape Development

Maryann Thompson Adjunct Professor of Architecture

Matthew Urbanski Adjunct Associate Professor in Landscape Architecture

Michael Van Valkenburgh Charles Eliot Professor in Practice of Landscape Architecture

Charles Waldheim John E. Irving Professor of Landscape Architecture

Bing Wang Adjunct Associate Professor in Real Estate and the Built Environment

Elizabeth Whittaker Adjunct Assistant Professor of Architecture

Jay Wickersham Adjunct Associate Professor of Architecture

Krzysztof Wodiczko Professor in Residence of Art, Design, and the Public Domain

Cameron Wu Assistant Professor of Architecture

Visiting Faculty

Lauren Abrahams Design Critic in Landscape Architecture

Ari Adler Lecturer in Architecture

Frank Apeseche Lecturer in Urban Planning and Design

Steven Apfelbaum Lecturer in Landscape Architecture

Leire Asensio-Villoria Lecturer in Landscape Architecture and Architecture

Bridget Baines Design Critic in Landscape Architecture

Vincent Bandy Design Critic in Architecture

Katy Barkan Design Critic in Architecture

Peter Beard Design Critic in Landscape Architecture

Eric Belsky Lecturer in Urban Planning and Managing Director of the Joint Center for Housing

Imola Berczi Instructor in Architecture

Andre Bideau Lecturer in Architecture

Adrian Blackwell Visiting Assistant Professor of Landscape Architecture and Urban Design

Sibel Bozdogan Lecturer in Architectural History

Jeffry Burchard Design Critic in Architecture

James Burns Instructor in Architecture

Luis Callejas Lecturer in Landscape Architecture

Bradley Cantrell Visiting Associate Professor in Landscape Architecture

José Castillo Design Critic in Urban Planning and Design

Steven Caton Professor of Contemporary Arab Studies, Harvard University

Jana Cephas Instructor in Urban Planning and Design

Lizabeth Cohen Affiliated Professor to the Department of Urban Planning and Design

Philippe Coignet Design Critic in Landscape Architecture

Betsy Colburn Lecturer in Landscape Architecture

Jürg Conzett Lecturer in Architecture

Salmaan Craig Lecturer in Architecture

Bradley Crane Lecturer in Architecture

Pierre de Meuron Arthur Rotch Design Critic in Architecture

Nathalie de Vries Design Critic in Architecture

Timothy Dekker Lecturer in Landscape Architecture

Theo Deutinger Design Critic in Landscape Architecture

Richard Dimino Lecturer in Urban Planning and Design

John Dixon Hunt Visiting Professor of Landscape Architecture

Daniel D'Oca Design Critic in Urban Planning and Design

Gareth Doherty Lecturer in Landscape Architecture and Urban Planning and Design

Kelly Doran Lecturer in Landscape Architecture

Diana Eck Affiliated Faculty to the Department of Urban Planning and Design

Farès el-Dahdah Visiting Professor of Architecture

Rodolphe el-Khoury Visiting Associate Professor in Architecture

Rosetta S. Elkin 2012-2013 Daniel Urban Kiley Fellow and Lecturer in Landscape Architecture

Stephen Ervin Lecturer in Landscape Architecture and Urban Planning and Design

Teman Evans Lecturer in Architecture

Teran Evans Teaching Associate in Architecture

Gerald Frug Affiliated Professor to the Department of Urban Planning and Design

David Gamble Lecturer in Urban Planning and Design

Ginés Garrido Design Critic in Urban Planning and Design

Andreas Georgoulias Lecturer in Architecture

Jeff Goldenson Instructor in Architecture

Christopher Gordon Senior Lecturer at Harvard Business School

Andrea Hansen Lecturer in Landscape Architecture

Ewa Harabasz Lecturer in Landscape Architecture and Architecture

Brian Healy Design Critic in Architecture

Ron Henderson Visiting Professor of Landscape Architecture

Michael Herzfeld Affiliated Professor to the Department of Urban Planning and Design

Jacques Herzog Arthur Rotch Design Critic in Architecture

Chuck Hoberman Lecturer in Architecture

Zaneta Hong Lecturer In Landscape Architecture

Eelco Hooftman Design Critic in Landscape Architecture

Christopher Hoxie Lecturer in Architecture

Richard Jennings Lecturer in Architecture

Paul Kassabian Lecturer in Architecture

Stephanie Kayden Visiting Professor in Urban Planning and Design

Brian Kenet Lecturer in Landscape Architecture

Francis Kéré Design Critic in Urban Planning and Design

Christian Kerez Kenzō Tange Design Critic in Architecture

Matthew Kiefer Lecturer in Urban Planning and Design

Eugene Kohn Lecturer in Architecture

Robert Lane Design Critic in Urban Planning and Design

Thomas Leeser Design Critic in Architecture

Robert Levit Visiting Associate Professor in Architecture

Jorge Francisco Liernur Visiting Professor in Urban Planning and Design
Nina-Marie Lister Visiting Associate Professor of Landscape Architecture
Enriqueta Llabres Design Critic in Landscape Architecture
Yanni Loukissas Instructor in Architecture
John Macomber Lecturer in Architecture
Kathryn Madden Design Critic in Urban Planning and Design
David Mah Lecturer in Landscape Architecture
Edward Marchant Lecturer in Urban Planning and Design
Sebastien Marot Lecturer in Architecture
Chris Matthews Lecturer in Landscape Architecture
Patrick McCafferty Lecturer in Architecture
Alistair McIntosh Lecturer in Landscape Architecture
Maria Alejandra Menchaca Lecturer in Architecture
Lars Müller Lecturer in Architecture
Nashid Nabian Lecturer in Urban Planning and Design
Ciro Najle Design Critic in Architecture
John Nastasi Lecturer in Architecture
Joan Ockman Lecturer in Architecture
Luke Ogrydziak Design Critic in Architecture
Thomas Oslund Design Critic in Landscape Architecture
Philipp Oswalt Design Critic in Landscape Architecture
Erkin Özay Lecturer in Urban Planning and Design and Aga Khan Fellow
Jinhee Park Design Critic in Architecture
Peter Park Design Critic in Urban Planning and Design
Katharine Parsons Lecturer in Landscape Architecture
Orlando Patterson Affiliated Professor to the Department of Urban Planning and Design
Rodrigo Pérez de Arce Lecturer in Urban Planning and Design
Hanspeter Pfister Visiting Gordon McKay Professor of the Practice of Computer Science
Robert Pietrusko Lecturer in Landscape Architecture and Urban Planning and Design
Linda Pollak Design Critic in Urban Planning and Design
Zöe Prillinger Design Critic in Architecture
Jason Rebillot Instructor in Landscape Architecture

Eduardo Rico Design Critic in Landscape Architecture
Jennifer Riley Lecturer in Architecture
Juan Manuel Rois Design Critic in Landscape Architecture
Thomas Ryan Lecturer in Landscape Architecture
Robert Sampson Affiliated Professor to the Department of Urban Planning and Design
Holly Samuelson Instructor in Architecture
Lawrence Scarpa Design Critic in Architecture
Deidre Schmidt Lecturer in Urban Planning and Design
Michael Schroeder Lecturer in Architecture
Renata Sentkiewicz Design Critic in Architecture
Jesse Shapins Instructor of Architecture
Gavin Smith Visiting Associate Professor in Urban Planning and Design
Susan Snyder Lecturer in Architecture
Kathy Spiegelman Design Critic in Urban Planning and Design
James Stockard Lecturer in Housing Studies
Belinda Tato Design Critic in Urban Planning and Design
George Thomas Lecturer in Architecture
Raymond Torto Lecturer in Urban Planning and Design
Stephan Trüby Lecturer in Architecture
Jose Luis Vallejo Design Critic in Urban Planning and Design
Ben van Berkel Kenzō Tange Design Critic in Architecture
Spela Videcnik Design Critic in Architecture
Paola Viganò Design Critic in Landscape Architecture
Günther Vogt Visiting Professor of Landscape Architecture
Alexander von Hoffman Lecturer in Urban Planning and Design
Rachel Vroman Instructor in Architecture
Emily Waugh Lecturer in Landscape Architecture
Ann Whiteside Lecturer in Architecture and Librarian
Simon Whittle Instructor in Urban Planning and Design
Andrew Witt Lecturer in Architecture
Kongjian Yu Design Critic in Landscape Architecture
Andrew Zientek Instructor in Landscape Architecture
Cino Zucchi John T. Dunlop Visiting Professor in Housing and Urbanization

Loeb Fellows

Ramiro Almeida
Jim Lasko
Karen Lee Bar-Sinai
Helen Marriage
LZ Nunn

Lynn Richards
Deanna VanBuren
Ed Walker
Ann Yoachim

Staff

Jane Acheson Dean's Office
Ashley Alberts Building Services
Joseph Amato Building Services
Nader Ardalan Architecture
Alla Armstrong Academic Programs Business Office
John Aslanian Student Services
Lauren Baccus Human Resources
Kermit Baker Joint Center for Housing Studies
Pamela Baldwin Joint Center for Housing Studies
Lauren Beath Finance Office
Eric Belsky Joint Center for Housing Studies
Preston Belton Computer Resources
Shantel Blakely Communications
Susan Boland-Kourdov Computer Resources
Sarah Bordy External Relations
Dan Borelli Exhibitions
Laura Briggs Development and Alumni Relations
Stacy Buckley Faculty Planning
W. Kevin Cahill Building Services
Bonnie Campbell External Relations
Joanne Choi Frances Loeb Library
Anna Cimini Computer Resources
Carra Clisby Development and Alumni Relations
Douglas Cogger Computer Resources
Sean Conlon Registrar
Anne Creamer Career Services
Andrea Croteau Architecture
Sarah Dickinson Frances Loeb Library
Kerry Donahue Joint Center for Housing Studies
Barbara Elfman Advanced Studies Program
Stephen Ervin Computer Resources
Beth Falkof External Relations
Angela Flynn Joint Center for Housing Studies
Rena Fonseca Executive Education
Porscha Fontellio Human Resources
David Ford External Relations
Laura Forgea Human Resources
Jennifer Gala Executive Education
Heather Gallagher Executive Education
Erica George Landscape Architecture, UPD
Suneeta Gill Dean's Office
Keith Gnoza Student Services
Mark Goble Finance Office
Meryl Golden Academic and Student Services
Harold Gould Computer Resources
Norton Greenfeld Development and Alumni Relations
Arin Gregorian Academic Programs Business Office
Deborah Grohe Building Services
Kimberly Gulko Architecture
Gail Gustafson Admissions
Mark Hagen Computer Resources
Jennifer Halloran External Relations
Barry Harper Building Services
Cynthia Henshall Real Estate Academic Initiative
Christopher Herbert Joint Center for Housing Studies
Maggie Janik Computer Resources
Nancy Jennings Executive Education
Johanna Kasubowski Frances Loeb Library
Karen Kittredge Finance Office
Jeffrey Klug Career Discovery
Nissa Knight Development and Alumni Relations
Sarah Knight Finance Office

Ardys Kozbial Frances Loeb Library
Beth Kramer Development and Alumni Relations
Elizabeth La Jeunesse Joint Center for Housing Studies
Mary Lancaster Joint Center for Housing Studies
Ashley Lang Academic Services
Ameilia Latham Finance Office
B Kevin Lau Frances Loeb Library
Burton LeGeyt Fabrication Lab
Sharon Lembo Real Estate Academic Initiative
Irene Lew Joint Center for Housing Studies
Theresa Lund Dean's Office
Stephanie Marvel Development and Alumni Relations
Ellen Marya Joint Center for Housing Studies
Anne Mathew Academic and Student Services
Daniel McCue Joint Center for Housing Studies
Jennifer Molinsky Joint Center for Housing Studies
Margaret Moore De Chicojay Executive Education
Maria Moran Advanced Studies Program
Janina Mueller Frances Loeb Library
Maria Murphy Student Services
Gerilyn Nederhoff Admissions
Caroline Newton Landscape Architecture, UPD
Christine O'Brien Building Services
Trevor O'Brien Communications
Jacqueline Piracini Academic Services
Lisa Plosker Human Resources
Cecily Pollard Development and Alumni Relations
Benjamin Prosky Communications
Pilar Raynor Jordan Academic Programs Business Office
Julia Reiskind Frances Loeb Library
Carlos Reyes Student Services
Patricia Roberts Academic & Student Services
Rocio Sanchez-Moyano Joint Center for Housing Studies
Meghan Sandberg Harvard Design Magazine
Nicole Sander Landscape Architecture, UPD
Ronee Saroff Communications
Cary Saunders Frances Loeb Library
Jennifer Sigler Communications
Matthew Smith Computer Resources
Laura Snowdon Student Services
Melinda Starmer Faculty Planning
Shannon Stecher Exhibitions
Alexsandra Sternig Admissions
James Stockard Loeb Fellows
Jennifer Swartout Architecture
Aimee Taberner Academic Services
Kelly Teixeira Student Services
Julia Topalian Development and Alumni Relations
Jennifer Vallone Finance Office
Edna Van Saun Academic Services
Melissa Vaughn Publications
Rachel Vroman Fabrication Lab
John Watts Finance Office
Juliet Wendel Student Services
Ann Whiteside Frances Loeb Library
Sara Wilkinson Human Resources
Abbe Will Joint Center for Housing Studies
Janet Wysocki Executive Education
Sarah Young Loeb Fellows
Ines Zalduendo Frances Loeb Library
David Zimmerman-Stuart Exhibitions

Index

HARVARD UNIVERSITY
GRADUATE SCHOOL OF DESIGN

Drew Gilpin Faust President of Harvard University
Mohsen Mostafavi Dean of the Graduate School of Design
Iñaki Ábalos Chair of the Department of Architecture
Martin Bechthold Co-Director of the Doctor of
Design Program
Pierre Bélanger Co-Director of the Master in Design
Studies Program
Anita Berrizbeitia Director of the Master in Lansdcape
Architecture Program
Felipe Correa Director of the Master of Architecture
in Urban Design and the Master of Landscape Architecture
in Urban Design Programs
Ann Forsyth Director of the Master in Urban Planning
Program
K. Michael Hays Associate Dean for Academic Affairs
Erika Naginski Co-Director of the PhD Program in
Architecture, Landscape Architecture and Urban Planning
Rahul Mehrotra Chair of the Department of Urban
Planning and Design
Kiel Moe Co-Director of the Master in Design Studies
Program
Mark Mulligan Director of the Master in Architecture
Programs
Antoine Picon Co-Director of PhD in Architecture,
Landscape Architecture and Urban Planning and
DDes Programs.
Charles Waldheim Chair of the Department of
Landscape Architecture

Patricia Roberts Executive Dean
Beth Kramer Associate Dean for Development and
Alumni Relations
Benjamin Prosky Assistant Dean for Communications

PLATFORM 6 EDITORIAL & DESIGN TEAM

Rosetta Sarah Elkin - Faculty Editor

Simon Battisti MArch II 2014
McKenna Cole MLA I AP 2013
Carolyn Deuschle MLA I 2014
William DiBernardo MLA II 2013
Lauren Elachi MLA I 2013
Martin Pavlinić MLA I 2014

Melissa Vaughn, Director of Publications

ACTAR D TEAM

Ramon Prat
Núria Saban

PHOTOGRAPHY

Anita Kan
Christopher Myers

ADDITIONAL PHOTO CREDITS

Jerome Byron Hord
Maggie Janik
J. Arthur Liu
Connie Migliazzo
Yusuke Suzuki

IMPRINT

Published by Harvard University Graduate School
of Design and ActarD

Graphic Design, Platform Editorial Team

Production, ActarD Inc.

Printed in Grafos S.A.

GSD Platform 6 represents selected studios, seminars,
research, events, and exhibitions from the 2012-2013
academic year.

For additional information and a more comprehensive
selection of student work, please visit gsd.harvard.edu.

The Harvard Graduate School of Design is a leading center
for education, information, and technical expertise on
the built environment. Its Departments of Architecture,
Landscape Architecture, and Urban Planning and Design
offer masters and doctoral degree programs, and provide
the foundation for the school's Advanced Studies and
Excecutive Education programs.

ISBN: 978-1-940291-06-2

DISTRIBUTION

ActarD
New York
www.actar-d.com

151 Grand Street, 5th floor
New York, NY 10013, USA
T +1 212 966 2207
F +1 212 966 2214
salesnewyork@actar-d.com

SPECIAL THANKS

We would like to thank the following individuals, for
without their effors this publication would not have
been possible:

Mohsen Mostafavi, Benjamin Prosky, Patricia Roberts,
Dan Borelli, David Zimmerman-Stuart, Mark Hagen,
Matt Smith, Trevor O'Brien, and Elfie Lee.

A CIP catalogue record for this book is available
from the Library of Congress, Washington D.C., USA.